IMAGES
of America

CARY

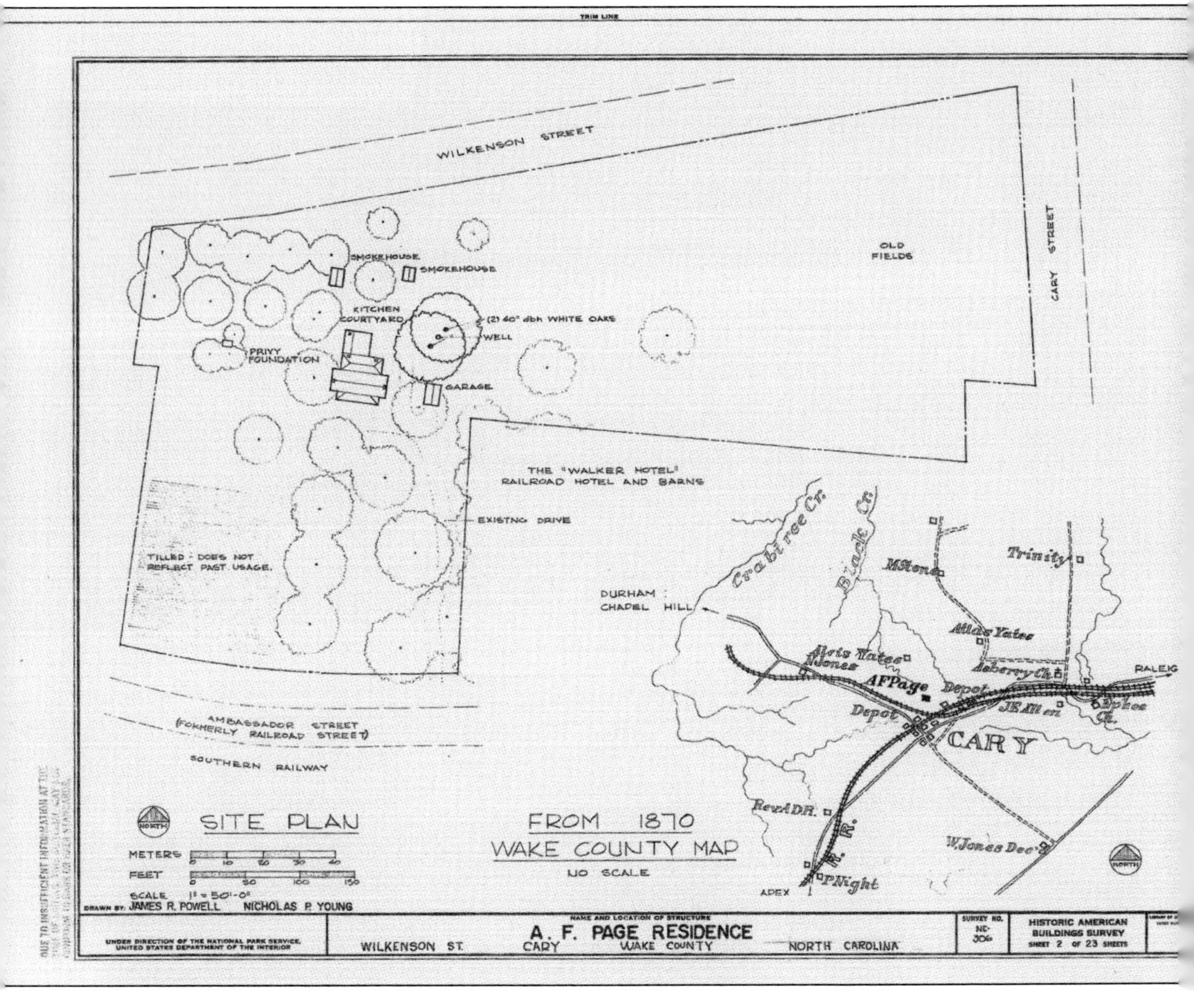

PAGE MAP. This blueprint was created in 1915 for Allison Francis "Frank" Page's hotel using an 1870 Wake County map. The land was part of the original royal grant to the Earl of Granville. Situated on a short ridge, in 1915, the hotel was the highest point for at least 5 miles in all directions. Its original middle section was built around 1782, when John Bradford owned the land. (Courtesy of Library of Congress, Prints and Photographs Division, HABS NC, 92-CARY, 1.)

ON THE COVER: 1950S FIREMAN'S DAY. The Cary Fire Department is getting ready for the parade to celebrate Cary's annual Fireman's Day fund-raiser. Pictured from left to right are Haywood Atkins in the truck, Billy Henderson, Tim Henderson, three unidentified, police chief Linville Midgette, and unidentified. (Courtesy of Stanley Lorren.)

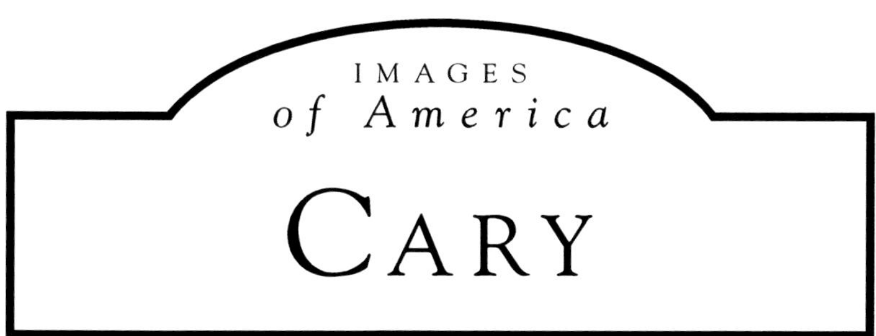

Sherry Monahan

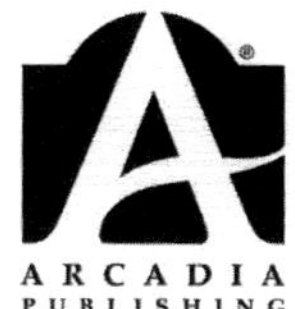

ISBN 978-0-7385-8695-3

Published by Arcadia Publishing
Charleston, South Carolina

Printed in the United States of America

Library of Congress Control Number: 2010931190

For all general information, please contact Arcadia Publishing:
Telephone 843-853-2070
Fax 843-853-0044
E-mail sales@arcadiapublishing.com
For customer service and orders:
Toll-Free 1-888-313-2665

Visit us on the Internet at www.arcadiapublishing.com

For my father-in-law, William Anthony Monahan

CONTENTS

ACKNOWLEDGMENTS

No book can ever be written alone. Authors depend on family and friends who kindly listen to our ups and downs and experts who assist us in various aspects of research. This book required me to reach out to strangers who I asked to let me into their lives—both past and present. This writing journey has shown me how generous, kind, and friendly people can be.

I have so many people to thank and a short space to do it in. These people shared their family stories and photographs, their knowledge of Cary's history, and their time. I cannot thank them enough. This list is alphabetical so I do not leave anyone out: Charlie Adams, Ralph and Daphne Ashworth, Lynn Banks, Koka Booth, Tom Byrd, Kris Carmichael, Kim Cumber, David and Jennifer Faircloth, Robert Heater, Carla and C. Y. Jordan, Sally Keisler, Stanley Lorren, Jim Matthews, Ada Dolla Pozza, Bill and Barbara Rogers, Maryann Rood, Peggy Van Scoyoc, and Robert Warner.

I also have to thank my husband, Larry, who listens, cooks dinner, brings me wine, and supports me as I pursue this crazy love of writing.

Last, I want to thank my acquisitions editor, Lindsay Carter at Arcadia. Lindsay makes me laugh, lets me pretend that I am her favorite author, and provides amazing support. I am thankful for everything she does.

INTRODUCTION

Even before Cary got its name, people lived in and visited the area. A settlement known as Bradford's Ordinary began around 1750, centered around its namesake, a roadside tavern operated by planter John Bradford. Bradford's establishment was still shown on maps as late as 1808; it sat approximately where Cary Town Hall stands today.

In 1854, Allison Francis "Frank" Page and his wife, Catherine "Kate" Robateau-Page, bought 300 acres in what is now Cary. Page also established a post office on March 25, 1856, and became the first postmaster of Cary, but before that, the village was known as Page's Station. Page named his development after Samuel Fenton Cary, a prohibitionist leader from Ohio whom he admired. Page established the town as a dry municipality where the sale of whiskey was forbidden within 2 miles of town limits. It would take almost 100 years before alcohol consumption within the city limits was made legal.

In addition to being postmaster and sawmill owner, Frank Page built a hotel about the same time the North Carolina Railroad reached Cary. Some speculated that the railroad and hotel were the true reasons that spurred Page's arrival and investment in the area. The enterprising Page built his hotel in 1868 and then leased it to Mrs. A. J. Clegg, who operated it as a hotel to accommodate railroad passengers.

When Frank Page laid out the town of Cary in the late 1860s, it was one square mile in size, and there was no doubt as to where the town was. Anyone living more than one-half mile out of town was thought to be living in the country. Today, that single square mile has exploded to 55 square miles, and while the original square mile is still the heart of Cary, the community has spread out around it in all directions.

Various professions and organizations emerged as people began to migrate to this new, prospering town. According to Branson's 1869 Business Directory, C. F. Dowd was the first and only doctor practicing in Cary. The good doctor also competed with Frank Page in the sawmill business, as did three other companies. In addition to the sawmills and Frank Page's hotel, there was one country merchant—Frank's younger brother, James R. Page—and three ministers.

In 1869, Cary opened a private boarding school in a wood-frame building located where Cary Elementary stands today. Frank Page ensured that there was a prominent spot for a school when he first laid out the town. According to Branson's Business Directory, Polly Adams was associated with the school, likely as the teacher or headmistress.

Cary was finally incorporated on April 3, 1871, several years after the Seaboard and North Carolina Railroads formed a junction in Cary. Not surprisingly, Frank Page became the town's first mayor. Due to a clerical error that was later amended, the charter read, "to incorporate the town of Carey in Wake County." Even as late as 1884, some business directories, signs, and even railroad maps perpetuated the misspelling. The town had fewer than 150 citizens when it was incorporated; nine years later, when the 1880 census was taken, Cary's population had grown to 316 people.

In 1884, Page sold his hotel to Jacob R. "Jake" Walker and his wife, Helen Nancy Walker, who renamed it the Walker Hotel and continued to offer rooms and meals to railroad passengers and Cary residents until 1916. While they both owned the hotel, Jake continued to farm and work for the railroad while Helen ran the hotel.

Cary's population was growing. By 1890, the number of general stores had grown to five, Dr. Samuel P. Waldo had opened a pharmacy, and local Masons had established Cary Lodge No. 198 and met on the Thursday evening before the second Saturday each month.

In June 1900, when the census was taken, Cary's downtown residents numbered 333, which had not grown much from the late 1800s. A few residents worked for the railroad; some were farmers; many were employed as day laborers, and some worked at the lumber mill. Cary's U.S. postmaster was a 33-year-old woman named Lucy Peavis; her older brother Lewis worked for her as a clerk. The town had just one fireman, one policeman, one telephone lineman, and one restaurant but boasted four blacksmiths, two wheelwrights, five general stores, four preachers, two teachers, and a physician named James Templeton. Ernest Waldo, Samuel Waldo's oldest son, was now the town's pharmacist.

In 1900, Cary's academy offered two five-month terms. In 1907, the private academy was converted into a public school when Cary became home to North Carolina's first public high school. Cary had already established a reputation for excellence in education, and it was now attracting boarding students from across North Carolina and various eastern states. To add to the town's growing list of establishments, the Bank of Cary was chartered in 1909.

Cary held its own in the early 1900s because of its farming and sawmills, corn mills, and flour mills, which employed a large number of residents. In 1915, Cary got its first telephone service, and its main roads were paved in the 1920s. When the population grew by over 60 percent, Cary needed additional services, and retail businesses quickly sprang up along the downtown streets. Chatham Street was a paved two-lane road also known as US 1 and US 64. Cedar Street was called Railroad Street in those days, and it served as the main road from Raleigh to Hillsborough. In the mid-1920s, Cary constructed its water and sewer systems, and deep wells became the town's primary sources of water for over 40 years.

As was the case with most towns, Cary suffered the effects of the Great Depression. The Bank of Cary failed in June 1931; by October 1932, the town government was bankrupt due to poor management and bookkeeping. However, a couple years later, the Durham Life Insurance Company purchased 138 acres on East Chatham Street, erected a radio transmission tower, and developed the remainder into the Urban Terrace subdivision. The federal government's Resettlement Administration began purchasing worn-out farmland along Crabtree Creek to develop into a park. The park was later named William B. Umstead State Park after the conservationist governor. The late 1930s also saw the development of two research farms near Cary, one run by North Carolina State University and the other by the North Carolina State Board of Health.

Cary was fortunate in 1947, when the Taylor Biscuit Company opened its bakery in town. It became Cary's largest employer and remained as such for over 30 years. The company is now known as Austin Quality Foods.

Founded in January 1959 by a committee of government, university, and business leaders as a model for research, innovation, and economic development, the Triangle Park (RTP) brought new jobs and numerous new residents to the area. Cary became a favorite relocation spot for new transplants to the area, and soon the town's population was exploding. Each year afterward, Cary's boundaries stretched towards RTP.

It was only natural that Cary grew and extended its borders past its original one square mile to accommodate its many new residents. Even Cary High School had trouble keeping up with the influx of new residents; in 1960, it was relocated to its current spot on Walnut Street.

Today Cary is a thriving community with eateries, shops, and businesses both in and around its original one square mile.

One

The Town's Founder and the School

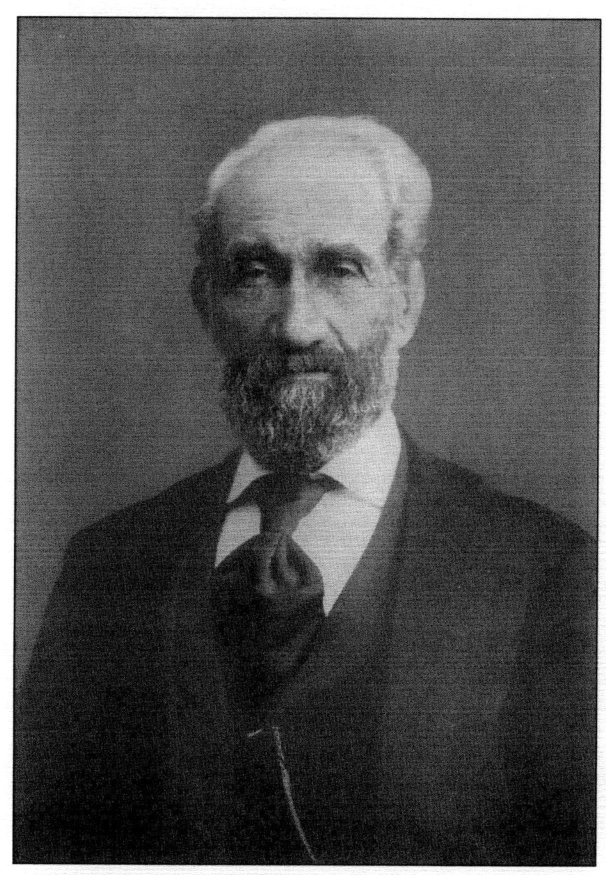

Allison Francis "Frank" Page. He not only founded Cary, he also established the town of Aberdeen. He built hotels and other buildings in Raleigh and developed the area around Pinehurst in Moore County. Page was a member of the Cary Masonic Lodge, and in May 1858, he was made a Master Mason. (Photograph from *The Life and Letters of Walter Hines Page*.)

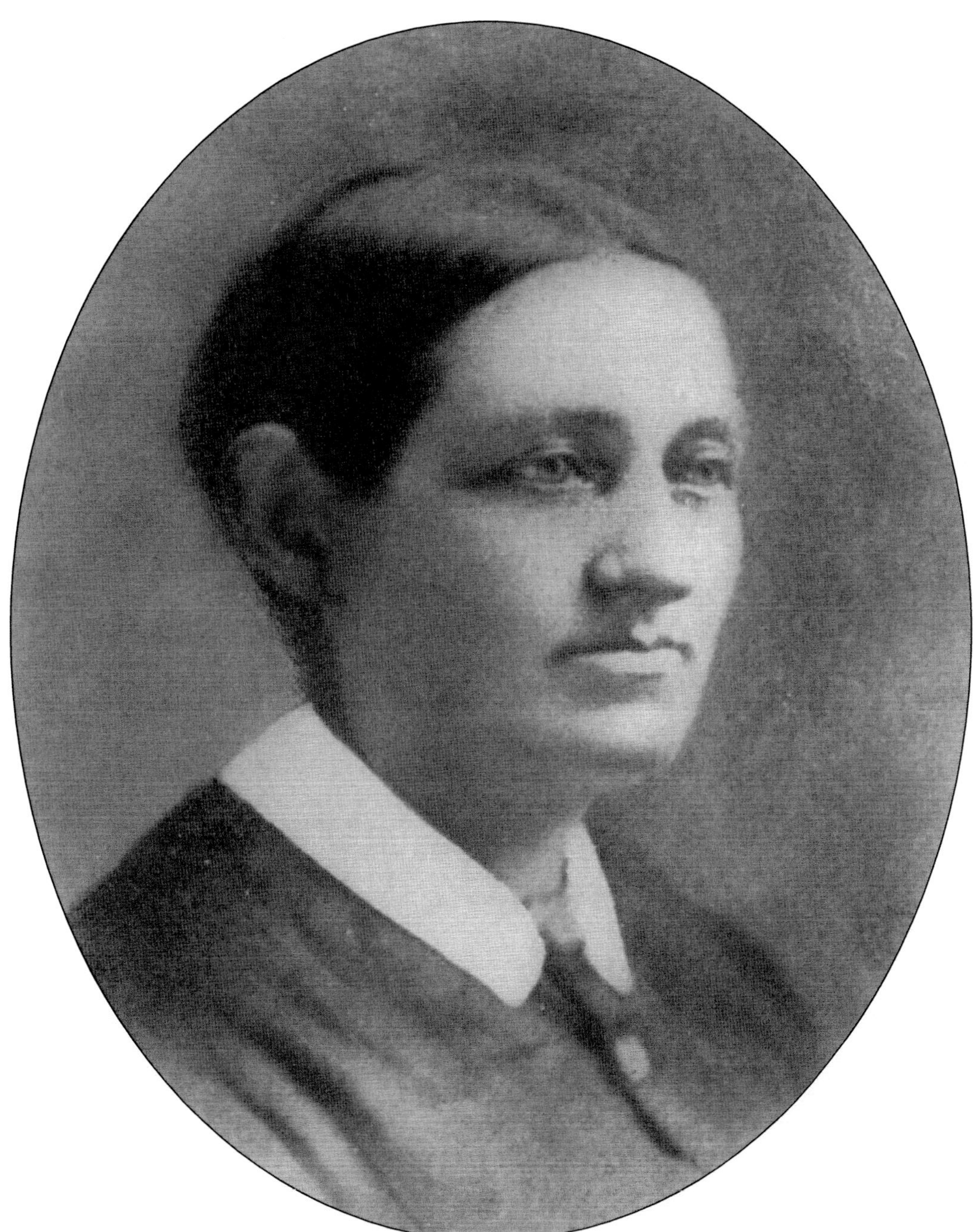

Catherine "Kate" Robateau-Page. Kate was the daughter of French Huguenot John Samuel Robateau and Esther Barclay-Robateau. Kate married Frank Page in Fayetteville, her hometown, on July 5, 1849. She was known for her Quaker-like ways and dressed in plain clothing with no frills or ruffles. She also wore her brown hair flat upon her head. She did not allow card playing, dancing, drinking, or any other frivolity in her home. She was seldom seen without a book or knitting in her hand. She liked to read books by authors like Charles Dickens and Sir Walter Scott. Seemingly in contrast to her stoic lifestyle, she enjoyed going for walks in the woods and fishing with her children. (Photograph from *The Life and Letters of Walter Hines Page*.)

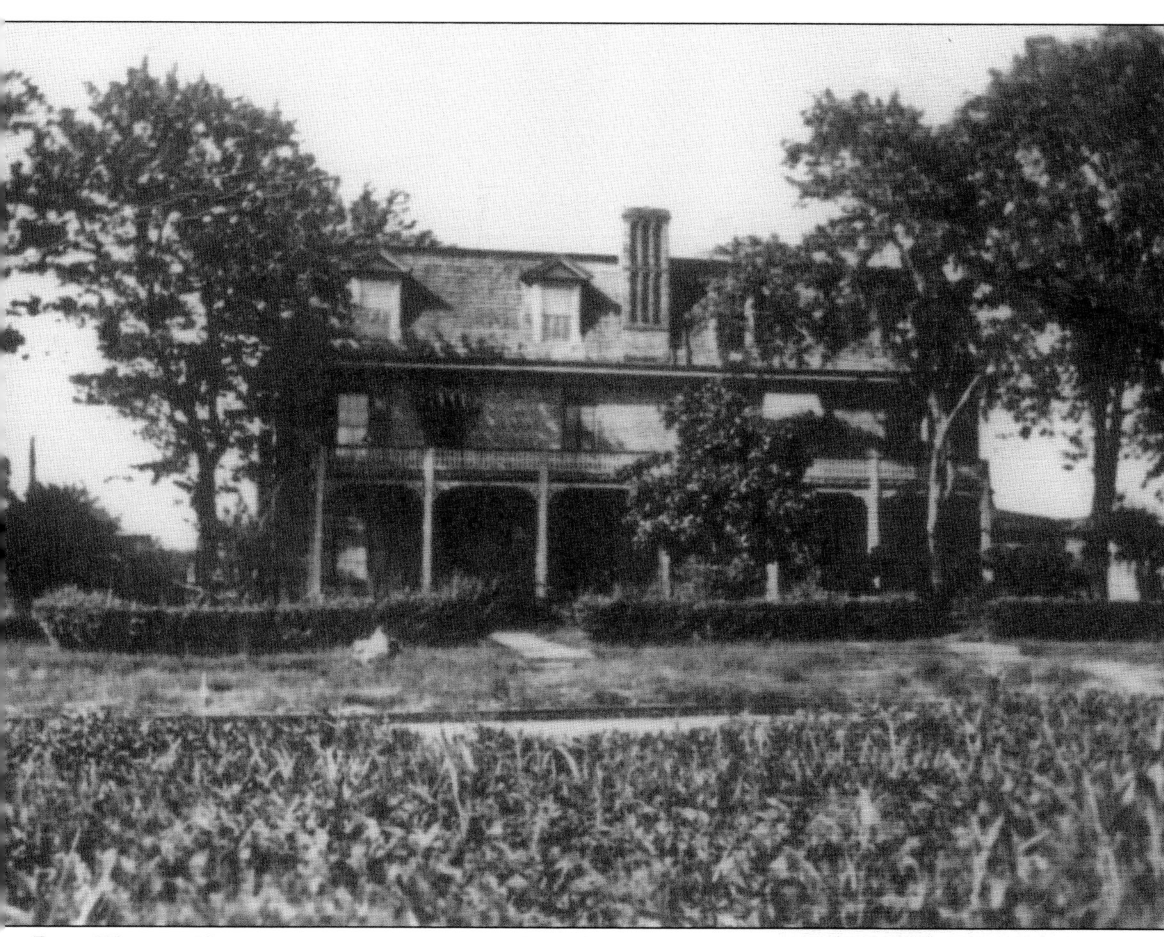

Page-Walker Hotel. In 1868, Francis Page built his hotel on a slight hill directly across from the railroad and then leased it to Mrs. A. J. Clegg. In 1884, Page sold it to Jacob R. "Jake" and Helen Nancy Walker, and they kept it until 1916. In 1922, the building was passed on to Helen Nancy Walker's grandchildren, who rented rooms to teachers and students associated with Cary High School. R. J. Coburn bought it for a private residence in 1926, and in 1941, it became the property of John F. Williams, a maintenance man for the Durham City School District. Williams owned a traveling summer entertainment business, and early town residents remember painted wagons and grazing ponies on the property. Robert Strother purchased the hotel in 1971 for his home, but he vacated the building in 1980. It passed to different owners over the years until the Town of Cary purchased it in 1985. It has been carefully restored to its original hotel configuration and operates as the Page-Walker Arts and History Center. (Courtesy of the Page-Walker Arts and History Center.)

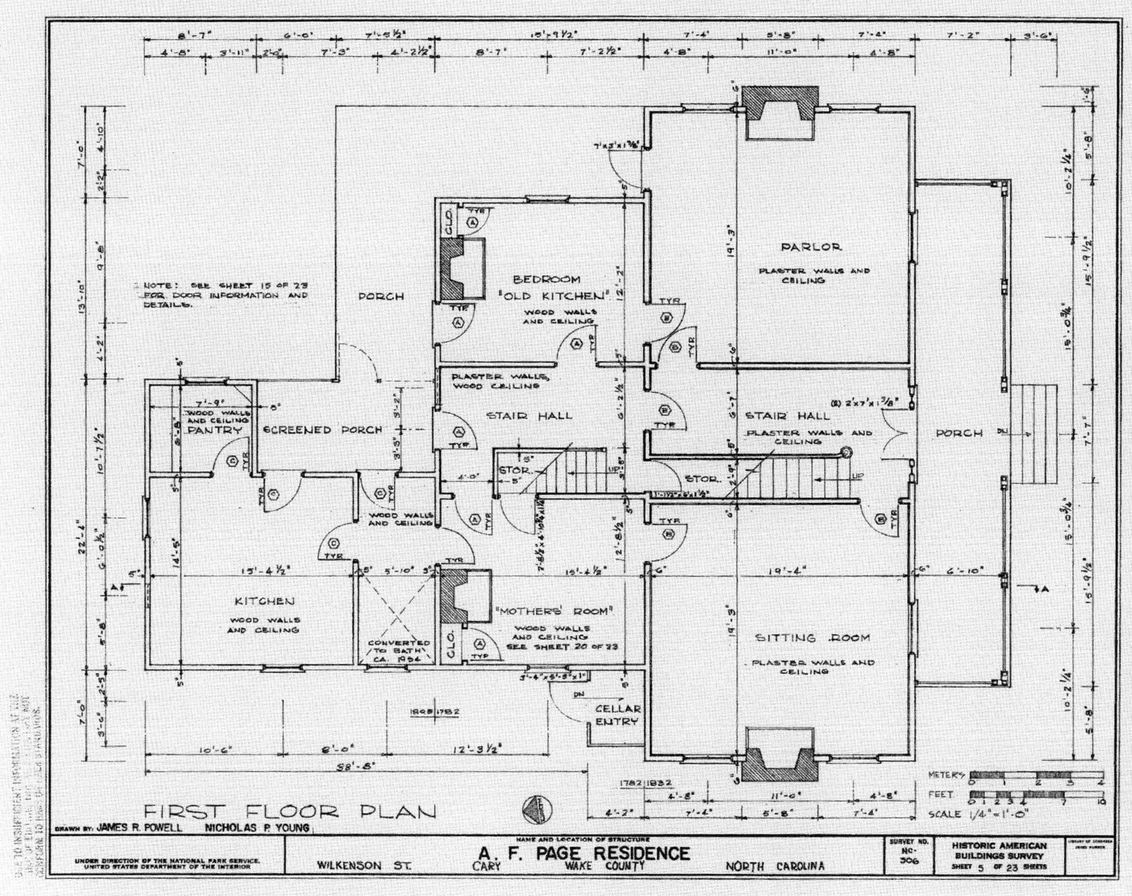

Allison "Frank" Page House, First Floor. These blueprints were made in 1916 to capture this historic structure, which burned down in 1970. Part of the original structure was Bradford's Ordinary, built around 1790. A couple of additions were made after Page bought the house in 1854. His first son, Walter Hines Page, was born there in 1855. (Courtesy of the Library of Congress.)

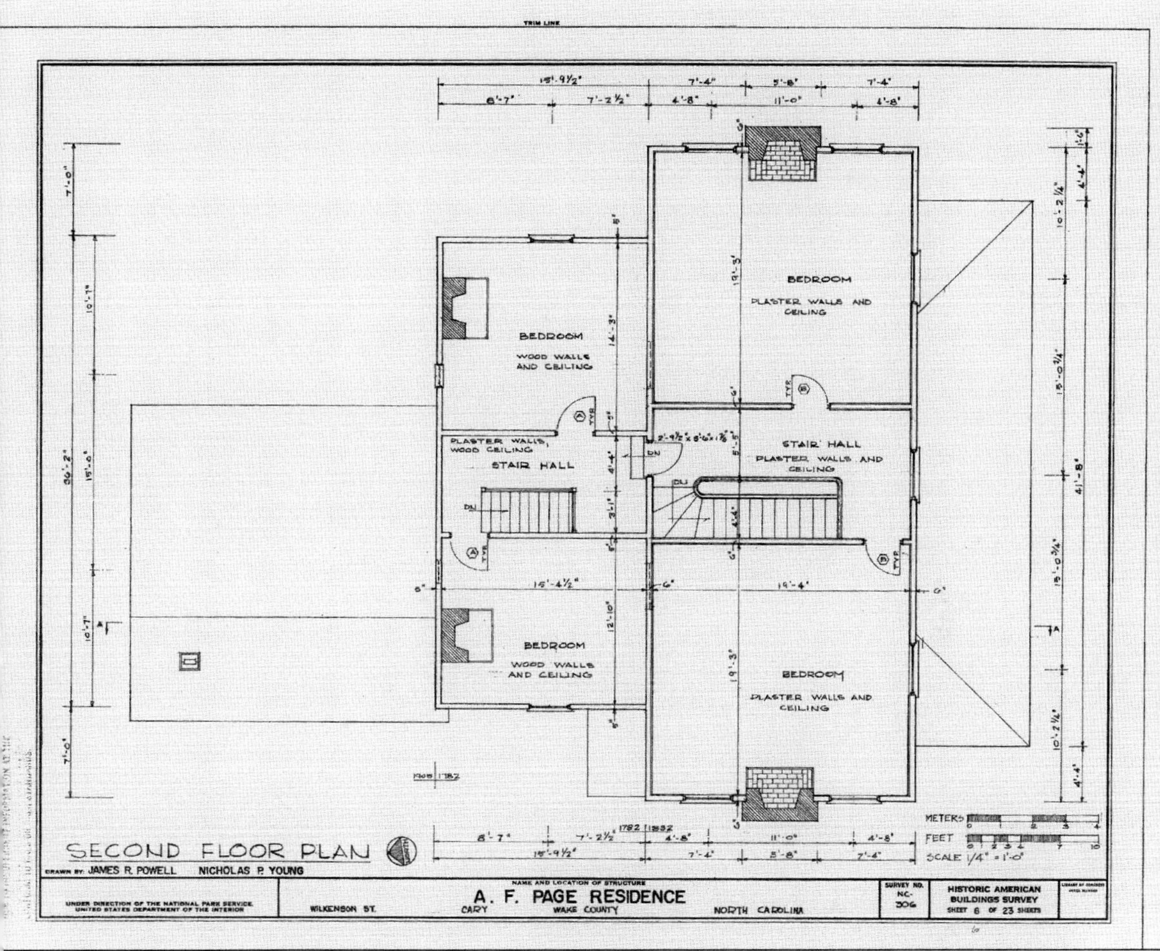

Allison "Frank" Page House, Second Floor. Walter Hines Page is probably Cary's most famous resident. He was an editor, publisher, social reformer, and like his father, a proponent of public education. He was ambassador to Great Britain during World War I, and Great Britain honored him with a tablet in Westminster Abbey in 1923. (Courtesy of the Library of Congress.)

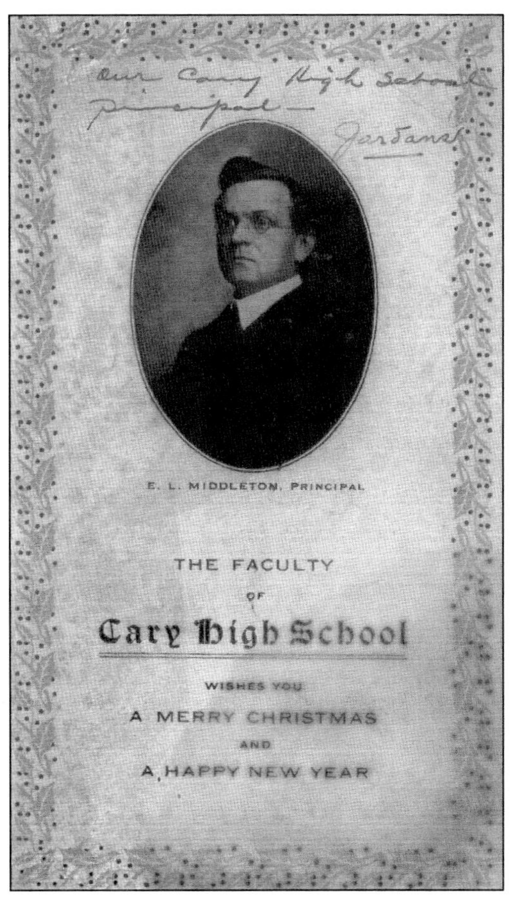

Christmas Card. In 1905, Cary High School's 39-year-old principal and teacher E. Lee Middleton and his faculty issued Christmas cards to students and their families. The senior class consisted of 18 students: Laurie Adams, Maude Broughton, S. I. Darden, Joe Franklin, Floyd Howard, T. J. Harrington Jr., Esther Ivey, Craige Jones, J. R. King, Norma Lynn, A. N. Scott, L. L. Tilley, Posie Tilley, W. P. Thompson, A. J. Templeton, Mary Woodward, L. E. Winston, and Lydia Yates. Esther Ivey was the vice president of the Browning Literary Society. She recalled, "We went on horse and buggy to Raleigh . . . I went to private school . . . on Chatham Street." She then went to Cary High School, where she graduated in 1906. (Both, courtesy of C. Y. Jordan.)

Faculty

E. L. Middleton, Principal

O. J. Jones	Stella Pasmore
C. A. Sigmon	Alice F. Best

Officers of Clay Literary Society

J. C. Jones	President
J. R. King	Vice-President
T. J. Harrington	Secretary
J. M. Adams	Censor
L. L. Tilley	Critic

Officers of Browning Literary Society

Lydia Yates	President
Esther Ivey	Vice-President
Elsie Scott	Secretary
Lina Stephenson	Supervisor
Ada Middleton	Treasurer

Senior Class, 1905

Laurie Adams,	Norma Lynn
Maude Broughton	A. N. Scott
S. I. Darden	L. L. Tilley
Joe Franklin	Posie Tilley
Floyd Howard	W. P. Thompson
T. J. Harrington, Jr.	A. J. Templeton
Esther Ivey	Mary Woodward
Craige Jones	L. E. Winston
J. R. King	Lydia Yates

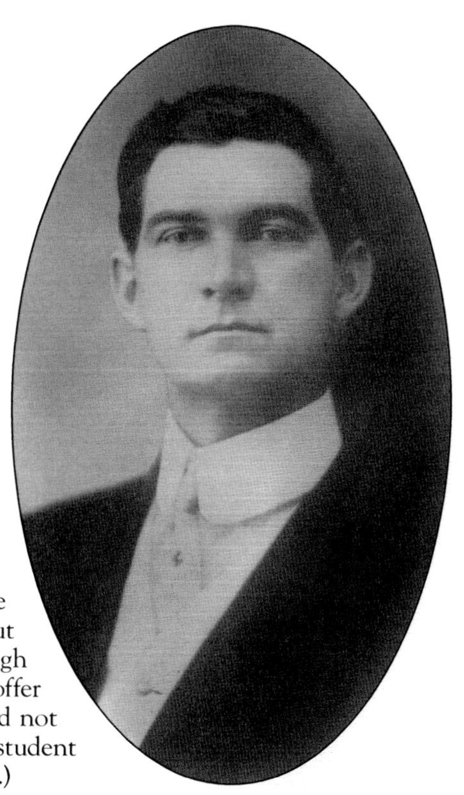

MARCUS BAXTER DRY AND 1915 CARY HIGH SCHOOL YEARBOOK. Marcus Baxter Dry was born October 21, 1871, in Union County. He studied at Wake Forest College and Columbia University. He served as an under-principal in 1898 and was Cary High School's principal from 1908 to 1942. In 1915, he was elected to the board of directors of the Cary Bank. He served as principal and teacher during his tenure at Cary High School, and Dry Avenue is named after him. Under the direction of Principal Dry, the Cary High School put out its first yearbook in 1915. By that year, Cary High School was one of the few high schools in the state to offer vocational agriculture and home economics. Dry did not believe in giving anyone a score of 100, so the best a student could get was a 98. (Both, courtesy of Charlie Adams.)

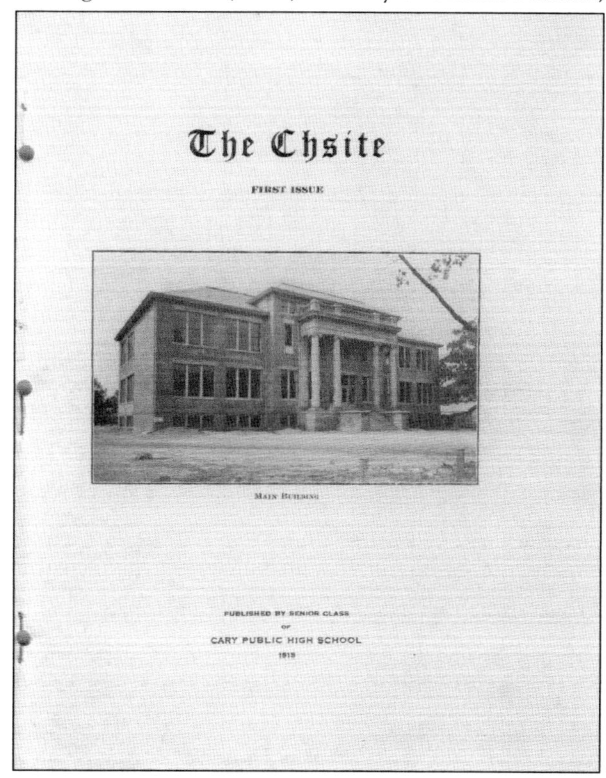

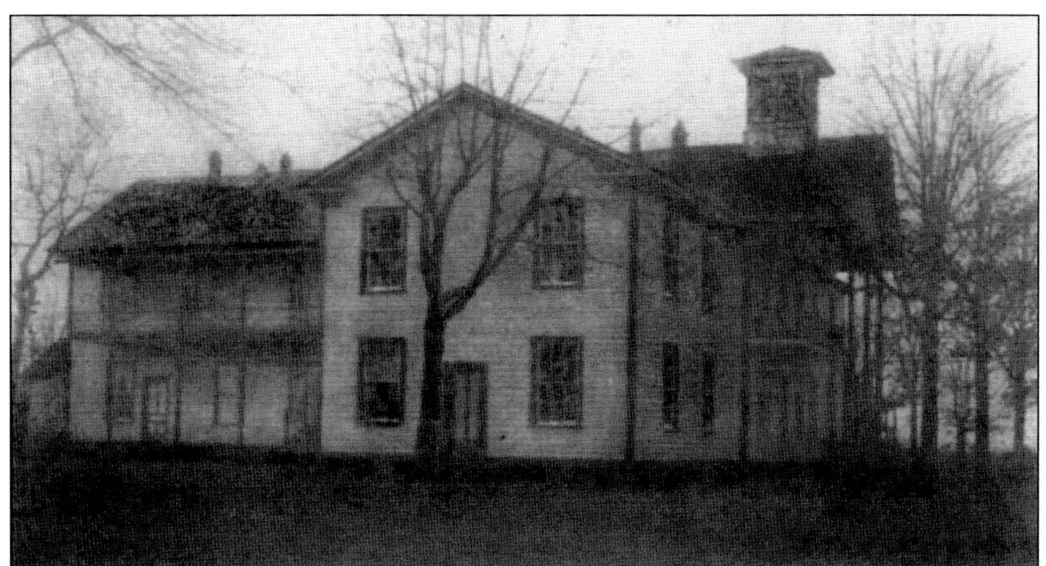

PRE-BRICK CARY HIGH SCHOOL. This postcard was printed to allow students to send correspondence while boarding at the school. (Courtesy of C. Y. Jordan.)

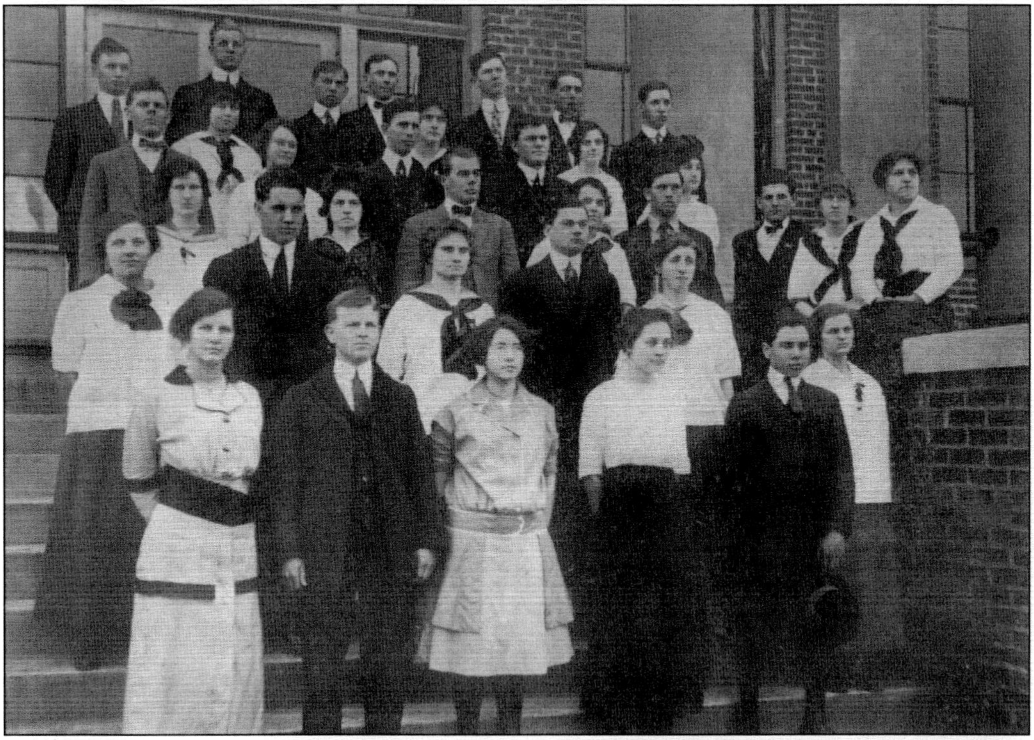

CARY HIGH SCHOOL 1915 JUNIOR CLASS. The junior class wrote this poem for the yearbook: "Seniors, now you all must leave us, But we hate to see you go, For your parting long will grieve us, As our tear-stained eyes do show.—Look! thy falter; how they peeve us—We don't need them here, oh no! Ah, the dignified have parted, From our dear old high school gate, Join the chorus we had started, 'Raising yells that will elate, We are now the merry-hearted—Soon our name will be great.' " (Courtesy of C. Y. Jordan.)

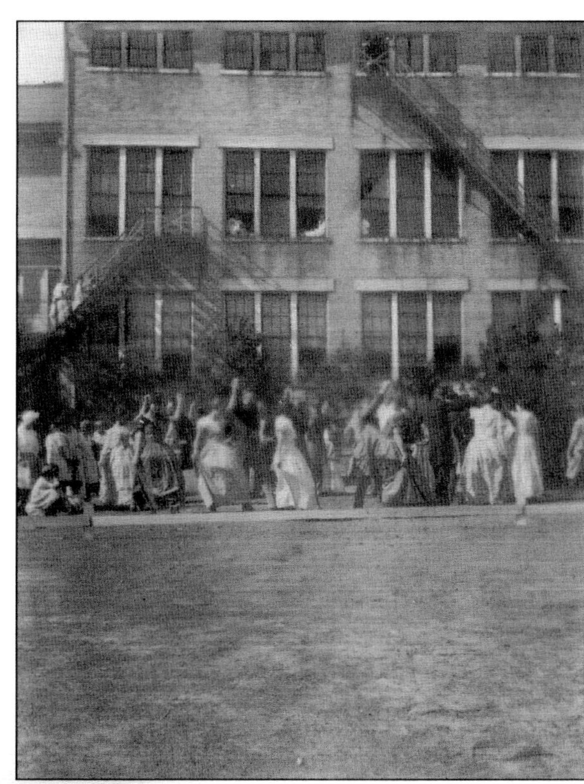

Cary High School Minuet Dance. In 1923, Cary High School performed a minuet, an 18th-century dance. (Both, courtesy of Mary Ann Rood.)

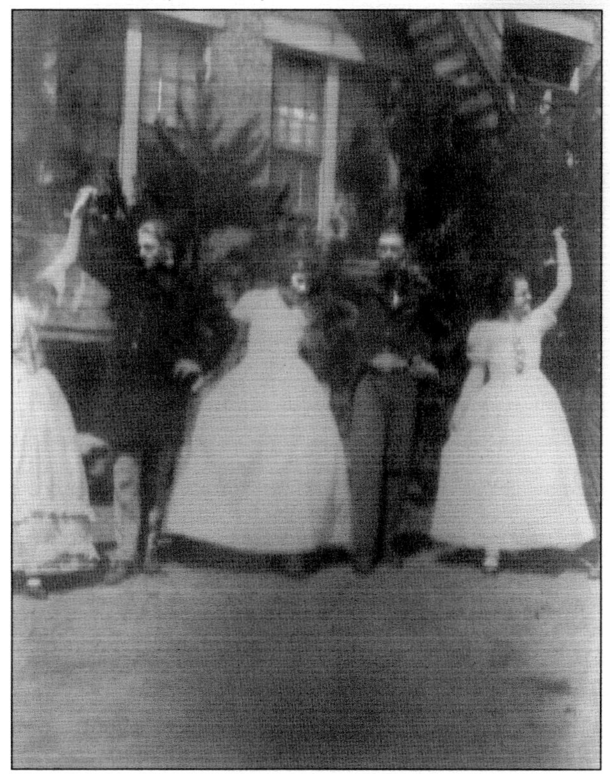

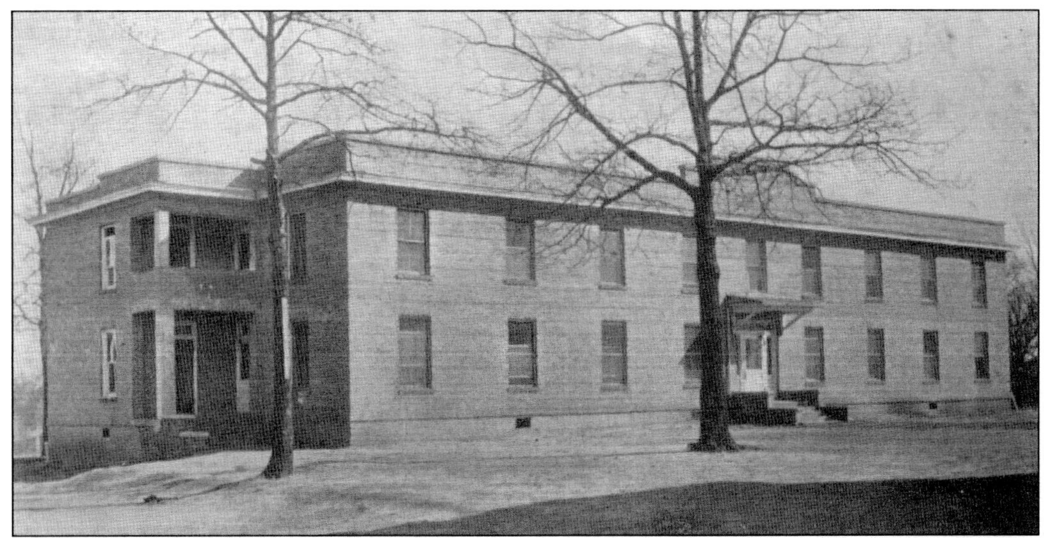

Cary High School Boys Dormitory. This dormitory was built around the same time that the wooden school building was replaced. Until then students roomed upstairs above the classrooms. (Courtesy of Charlie Adams.)

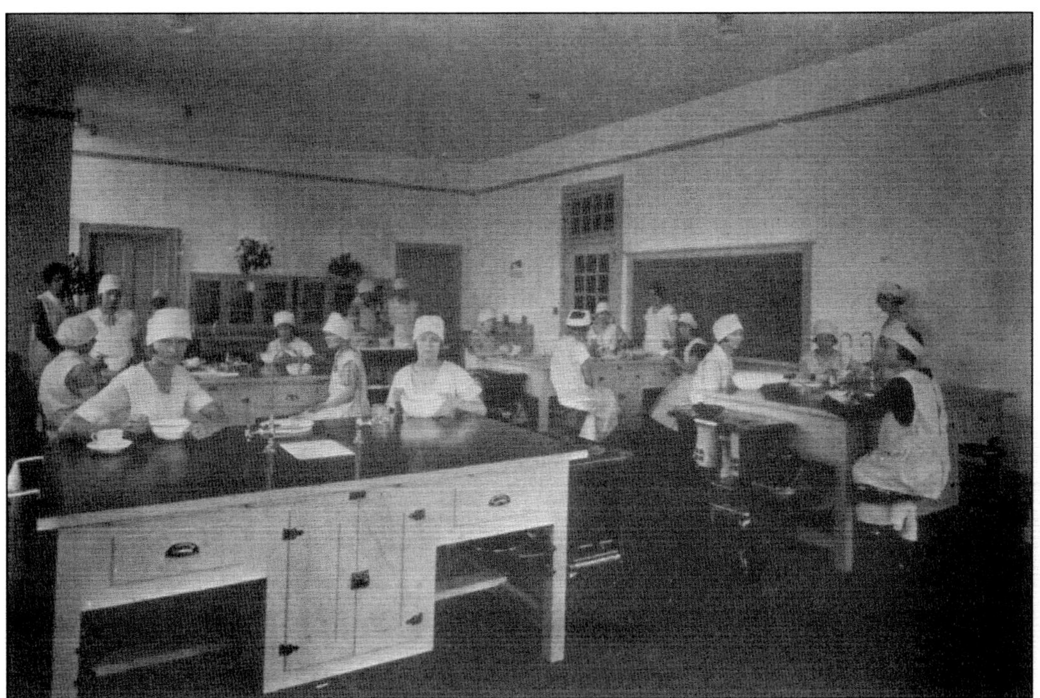

Cary High School 1925 Cooking Lab. The school's two-year-long home economics course was designed for eighth- and ninth-graders. This first year was devoted to food, textiles, and clothing. The second year was dietetics, textiles and clothing, home nursing, house planning, and interior decoration. Classes were taught by Mary York, who had received a bachelor's degree in science at the North Carolina College for Women. (Courtesy of Charlie Adams.)

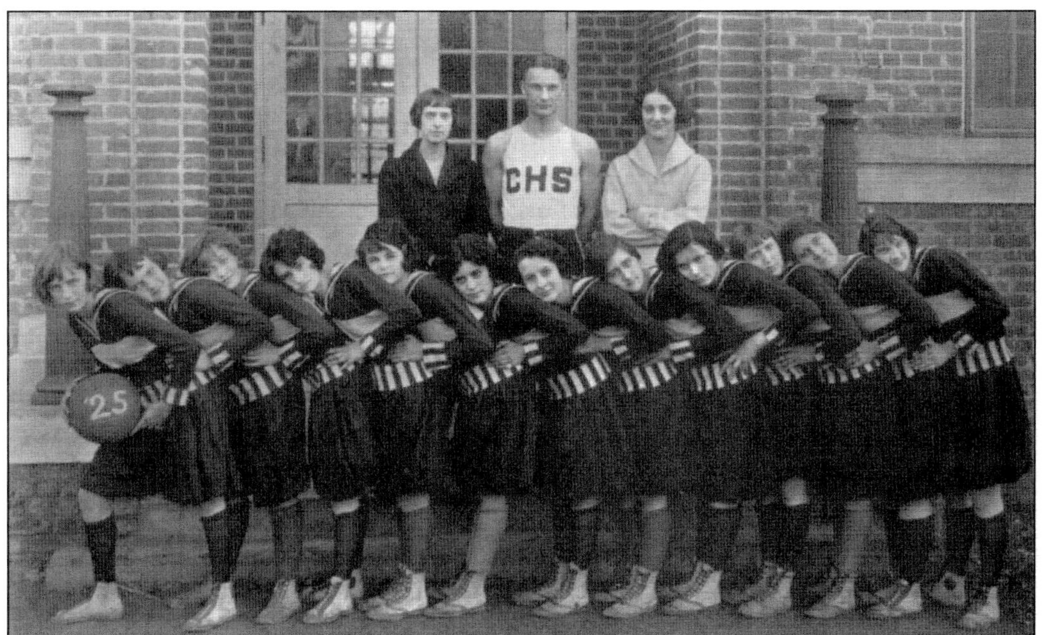

Cary High School 1925 Women's Basketball Team. Shown here from left to right are (first row) Olga Poplin, Annie Hayes, Hallie Dry, Ruby Duke, Evelyn Sherwin, Hazel Branton, Mabel Hunt, ? Jones, Vivian Shaw, Elizabeth Sorrell, captain Rosa Pleasants, and Rose Crocker; (second row) team manager ? Jones, Vallin Estes, and Coach Ellis. (Courtesy of Charlie Adams.)

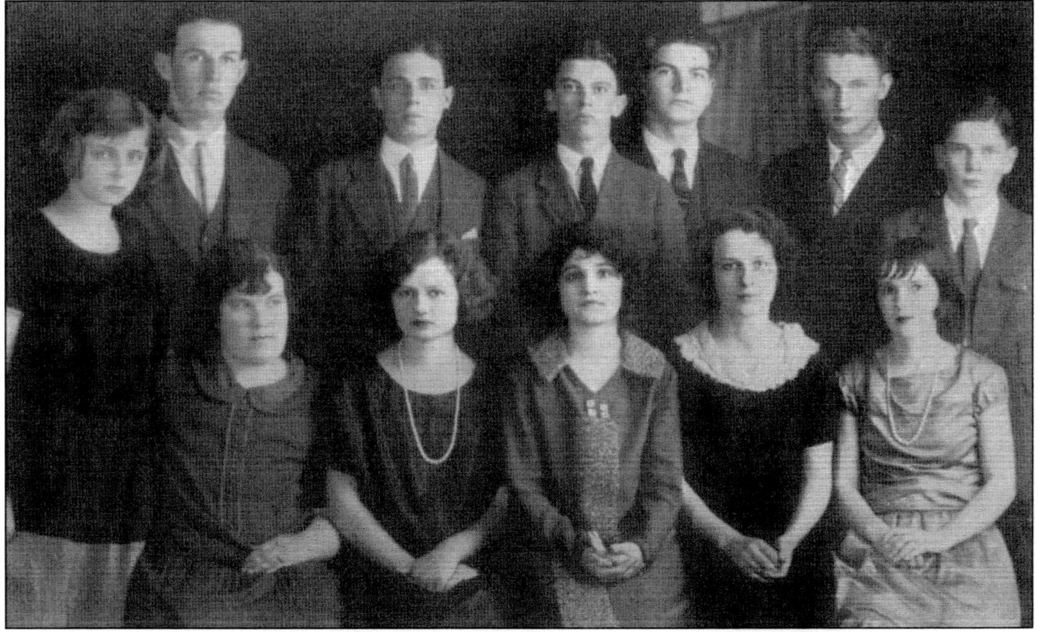

Cary High School 1925 Commencement Debaters. The commencement debaters for 1925 chose this as their query: "Resolved, that North Carolina's primary election law should be repealed." Participants in the debate included Clyde Franklin, Olga Poplin, Ina Atkins, Nell Waldo, Grace Hunt, Clellie Jones, John Lee Hester, Wallace Shearon, William Harris, James Bashaw, Willie Dry, and Vallin Estes. (Courtesy of Charlie Adams.)

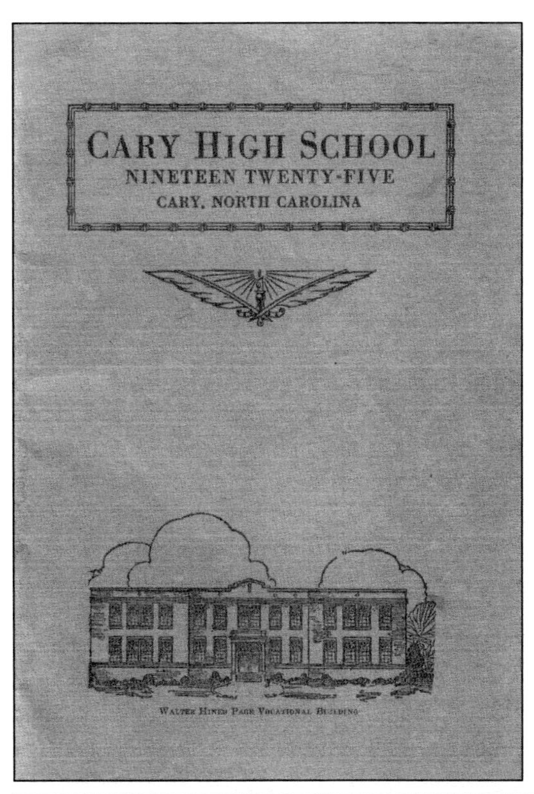

1925 CARY HIGH SCHOOL. The cover of the 1925 CHS yearbook, shown here, features a sketch of the Walter Hines Page Vocational Center. The fall term began August 31, 1925, and the spring semester ended on April 23, 1926. The school committee included chairman Dr. J. M. Templeton, secretary M. T. Jones, D. A. Morgan, E. J. Byrum, and A. H. Pleasants. Former principal Marcus Dry was promoted to superintendent but continued to teach geometry. J. H. Roller was the academic principal, while E. N. Meekins was the principal for the farm life department. The women had their own principal, Rena King; Irma Ellis was the elementary school teacher. (Courtesy of Charlie Adams.)

SCHOOL COMMITTEE

DR. J. M. TEMPLETON, *Chairman*
M. T. JONES, *Secretary*
D. A. MORGAN
E. J. BYRUM
A. H. PLEASANTS

CALENDAR 1925-1926

Fall Term opens.......................August 31, 1925
Fall Term closes...................December 23, 1925
Spring Term opens.................January 4, 1926
Spring Term closes.....................April 23, 1926

HOLIDAYS

Fair Week—Thursday, October 15.
Thanksgiving—Thursday and Friday, November 26 and 27.

DEBATES

Clay-Calhoun for Faculty Cup—December 7.
Lowell-Irving—January 21.

OFFICERS AND INSTRUCTORS

M. B. DRY, *Superintendent*
J. H. ROLLER, *Principal Academic Department*
MISS RENA KING, *Lady Principal*
E. N. MEEKINS, *Principal Farm Life Department*
MISS IRMA ELLIS, *Principal Elementary School*

HIGH SCHOOL DEPARTMENT

M. B. DRY, A.M.
(Wake Forest College)
Geometry

J. H. ROLLER
(University of Tennessee)
Science

B. B. DALTON, A.B.
(State University)
English and Athletics

MRS. J. W. DANIEL, A.B.
(LaGrange College)
History and Typewriting

MISS CLAIRE NICHOLS, A.B.
(Duke University)
French and Latin

MISS JULIA PASMORE, A.B.
(N. C. College for Women)
(State University, A.B.)
Mathematics and Latin

E. N. MEEKINS, B.S.
(N. C. State College)
Agriculture

L. E. RAPER, B.S.
(N. C. State College)
Agriculture

MISS MARY E. YORK, B.S.
(N. C. College for Women)
Home Economics

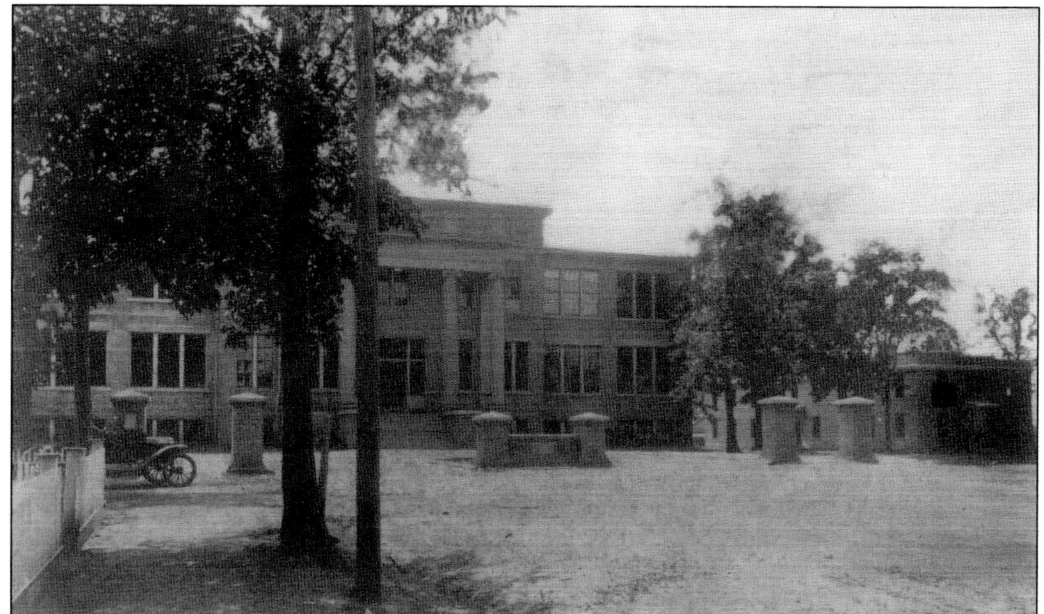

Cary High School Girl's Dormitory. This *c.* 1935 photograph shows the girls dormitory. In 1938, the old school was torn down and replaced with a new building that cost $132,000. Gov. Clyde Hoey, who came out for the dedication on March 2, 1940, called Cary "a beacon of hope and inspiration to other communities of the state." (Courtesy of Charlie Adams.)

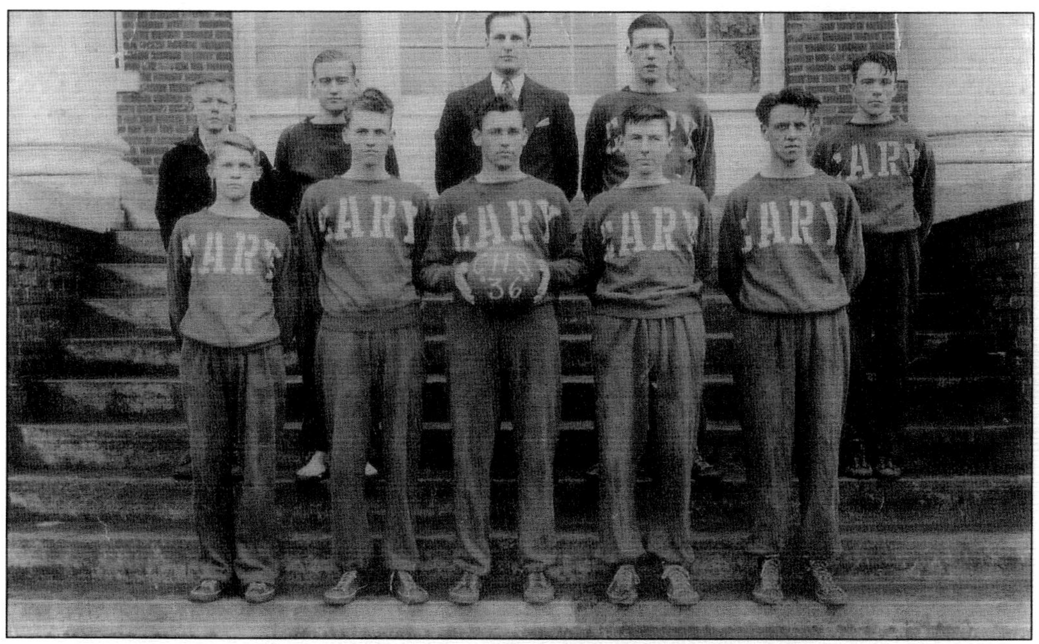

1936 Cary High School Men's Basketball Team. Shown here from left to right are (first row) Green Stanfield, Bruce Branton, Dabney Craddock, Nick Pleasants, and Van Newman; (second row) Perry Sloan, Ed Beal, Coach ?, Thoo "Preacher" Hurley, and Stanley Milner. (Courtesy of Charlie Adams.)

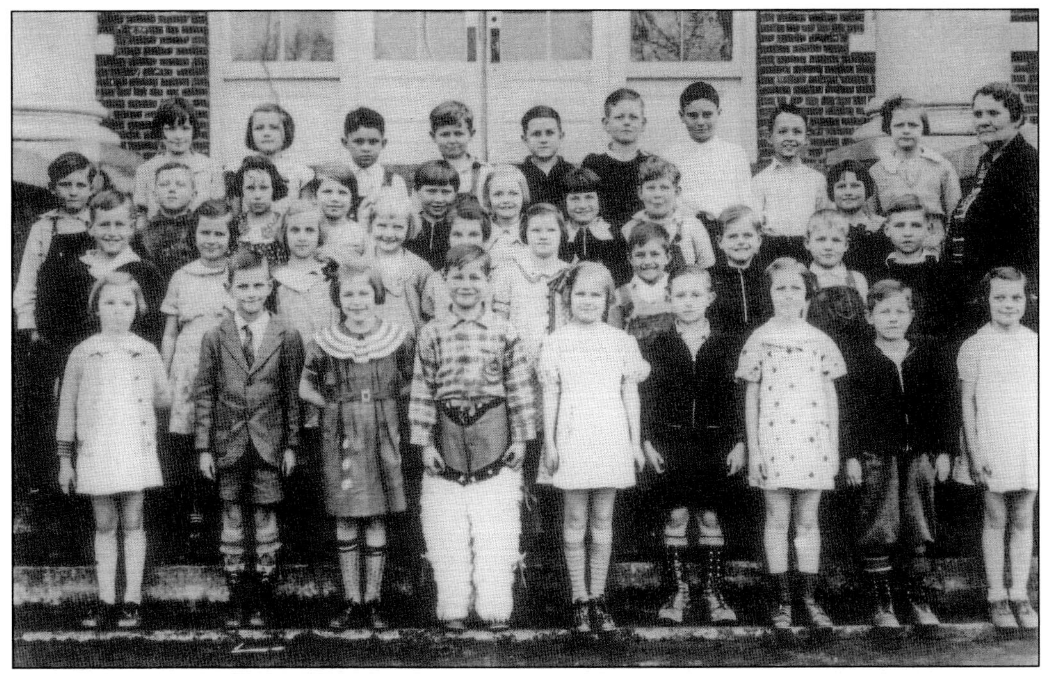

Second- and Third-Grade Classes. The second-grade class photograph (above) was taken about 1934; the third-grade class photograph was taken about 1935. Miss Massey was the second grade teacher. C. Y. Jordan attended both of these classes, but he recalls how he struggled with his fifth-grade class. It was 1938, and the town was demolishing the old high school. Jordan recalls, "It interfered considerably with my education because I could watch the wrecking ball knock that old building down. . . . That was a whole lot more interesting that listening to the teacher." (Both, courtesy of C. Y. Jordan.)

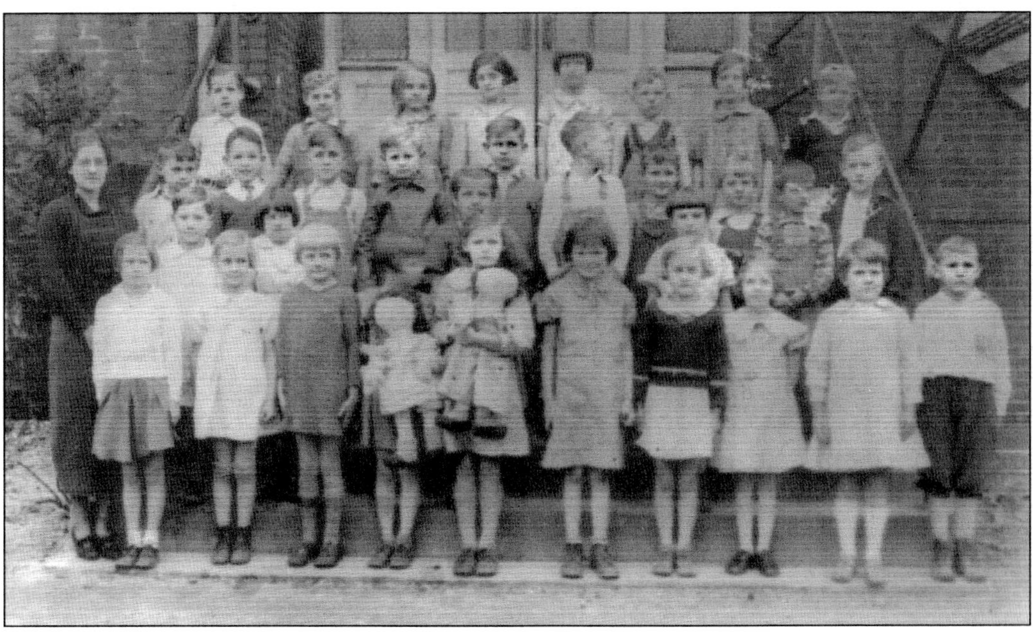

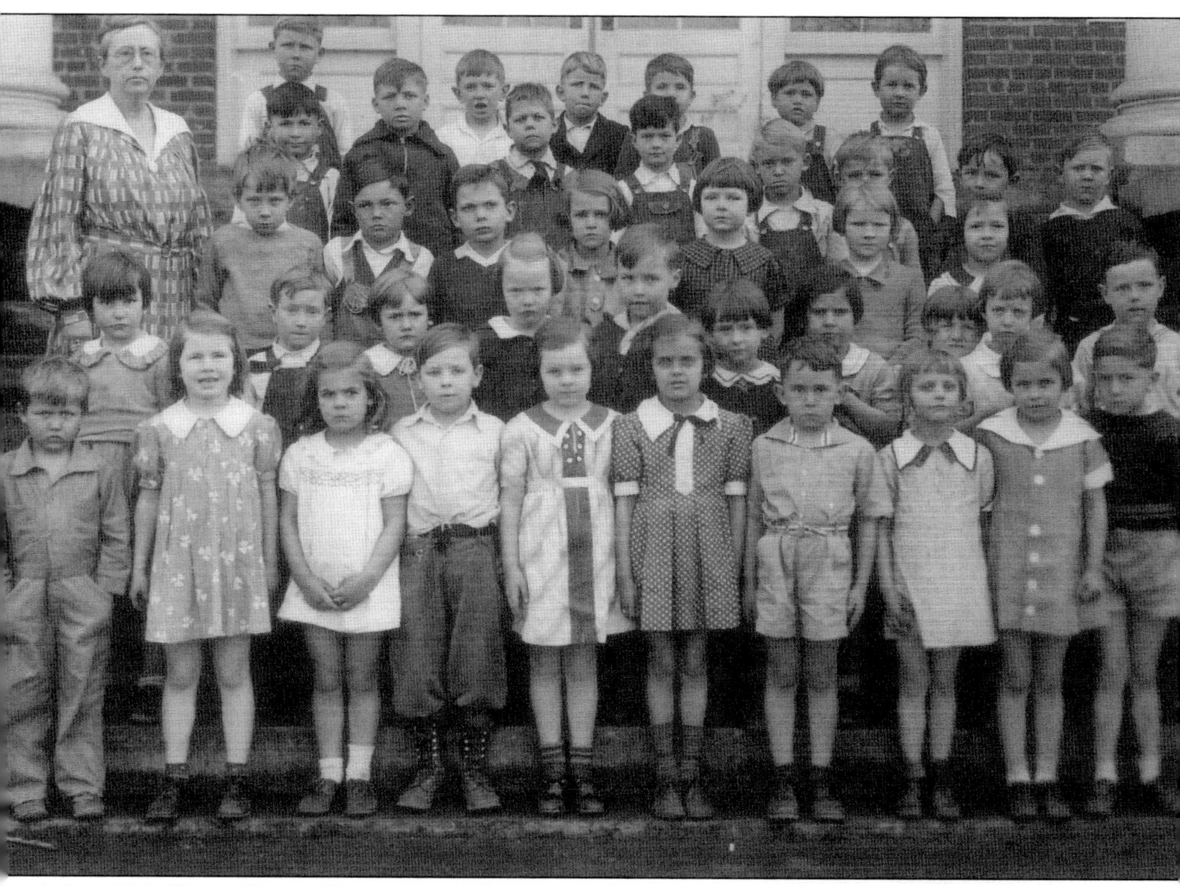

MID-1930S FIRST-GRADE CLASS. Irma Ellis was a well-respected teacher in Cary for many years. In 1910, Irma was a high school teacher and lived with her mother, Maggie Ida Jordan Ellis, and grandfather Henry B. Jordan. (Courtesy of C. Y. Jordan.)

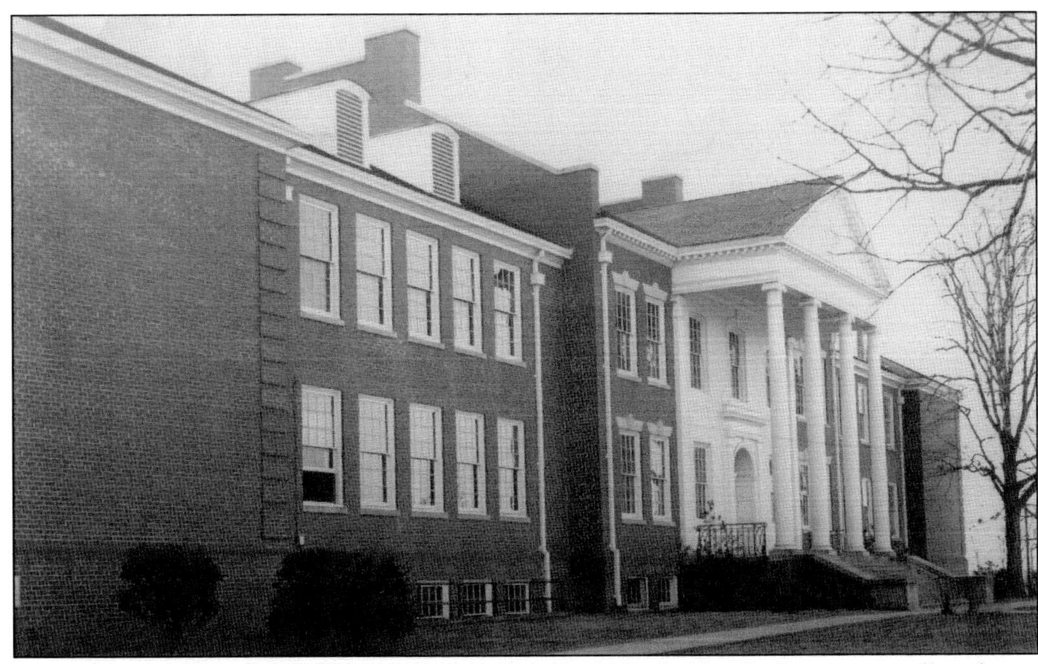

Cary High School, 1950s. These pictures show Cary's high school when it was still a whites-only school. In 1893, a log school building formerly used by for white students was given to black students and renamed the Cary Colored School. In the 1920s, the one-room school was expanded, and a second teacher was added, making it a two-room school with outside privies and a wood-burning stove for heat. Both black and white students would walk up Academy Street going to their schools. In the 1960s, Cary's schools were desegregated. (Above, courtesy of Charlie Adams; below, courtesy of Jim Matthews.)

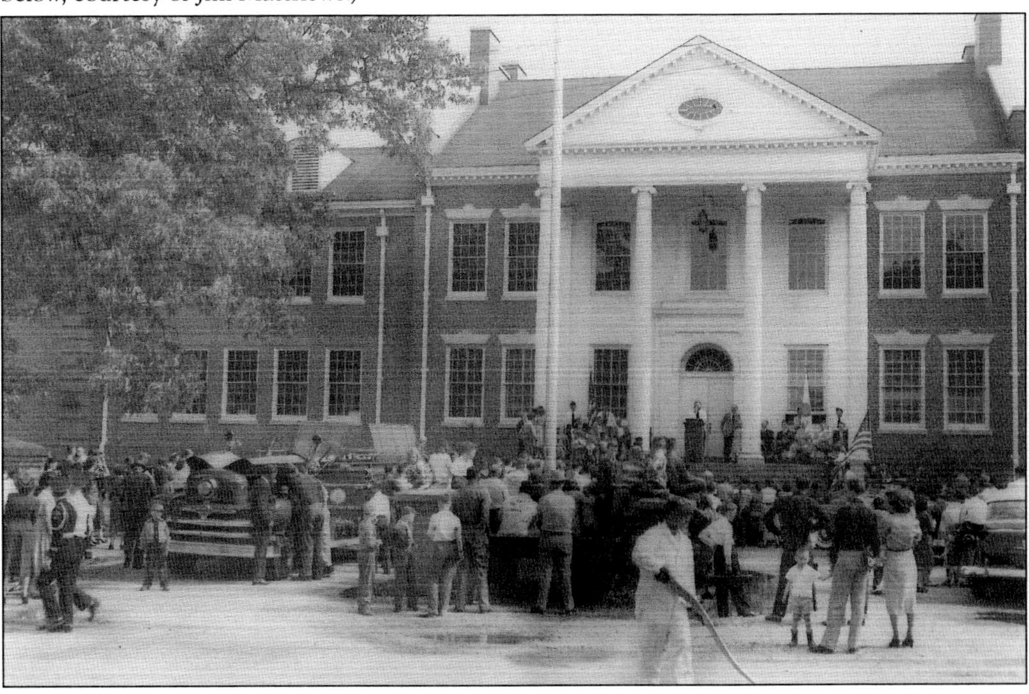

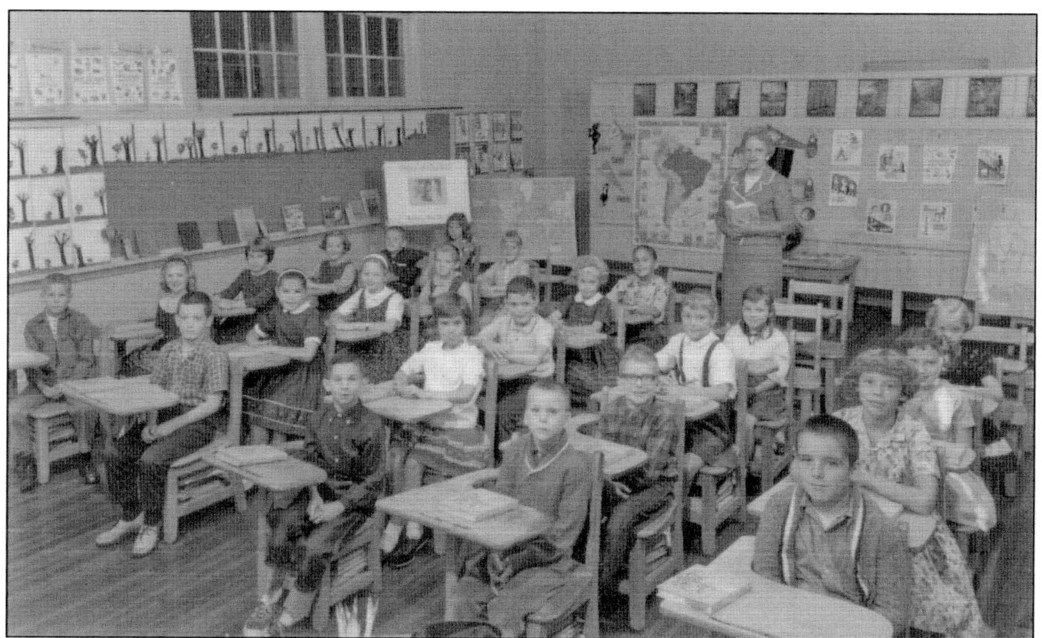

ETHEL ADAMS'S THIRD-GRADE CLASSES. In 1924, Ethel Copeland Adams graduated from Cary High School, where she had studied teacher training. Her senior class quote was "There's just one in the world for me," referring to her future husband. She became a sixth-grade teacher at Cary High School in 1926. She went on to teach the second and third grades as well. Students remembered her as a disciplinarian who tried to be fair and caring. She was often referred to as "Old Lady Adams." An alumna recalled once asking the teacher if she could use the bathroom. "I don't know if you can," Adams replied, "but you may." (Courtesy of Charlie Adams.)

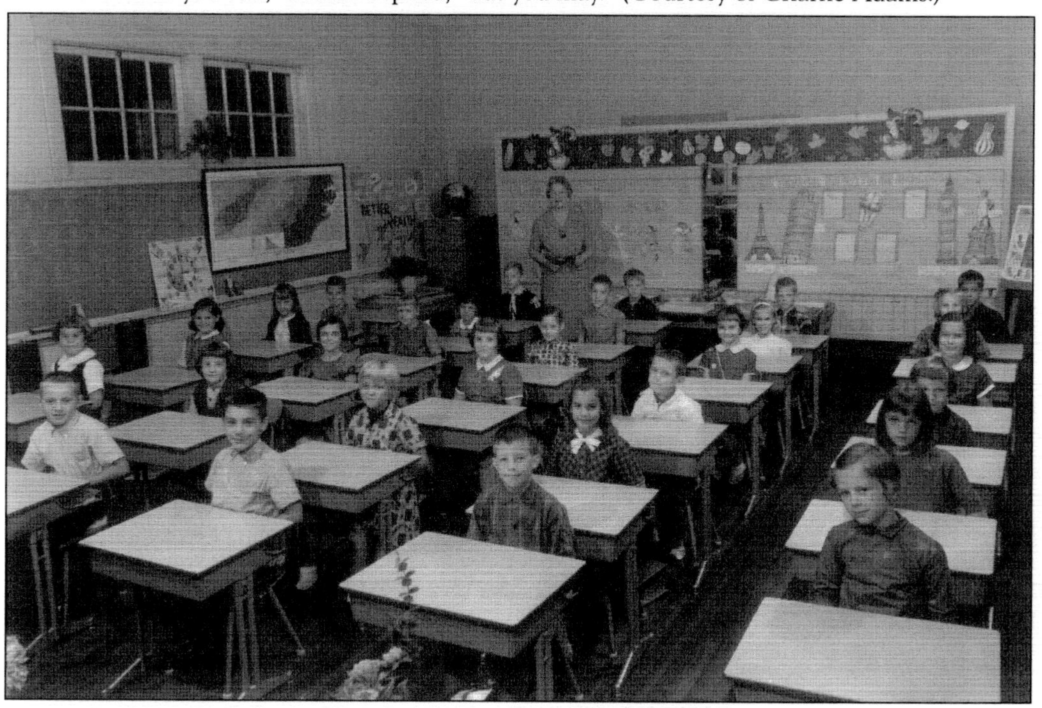

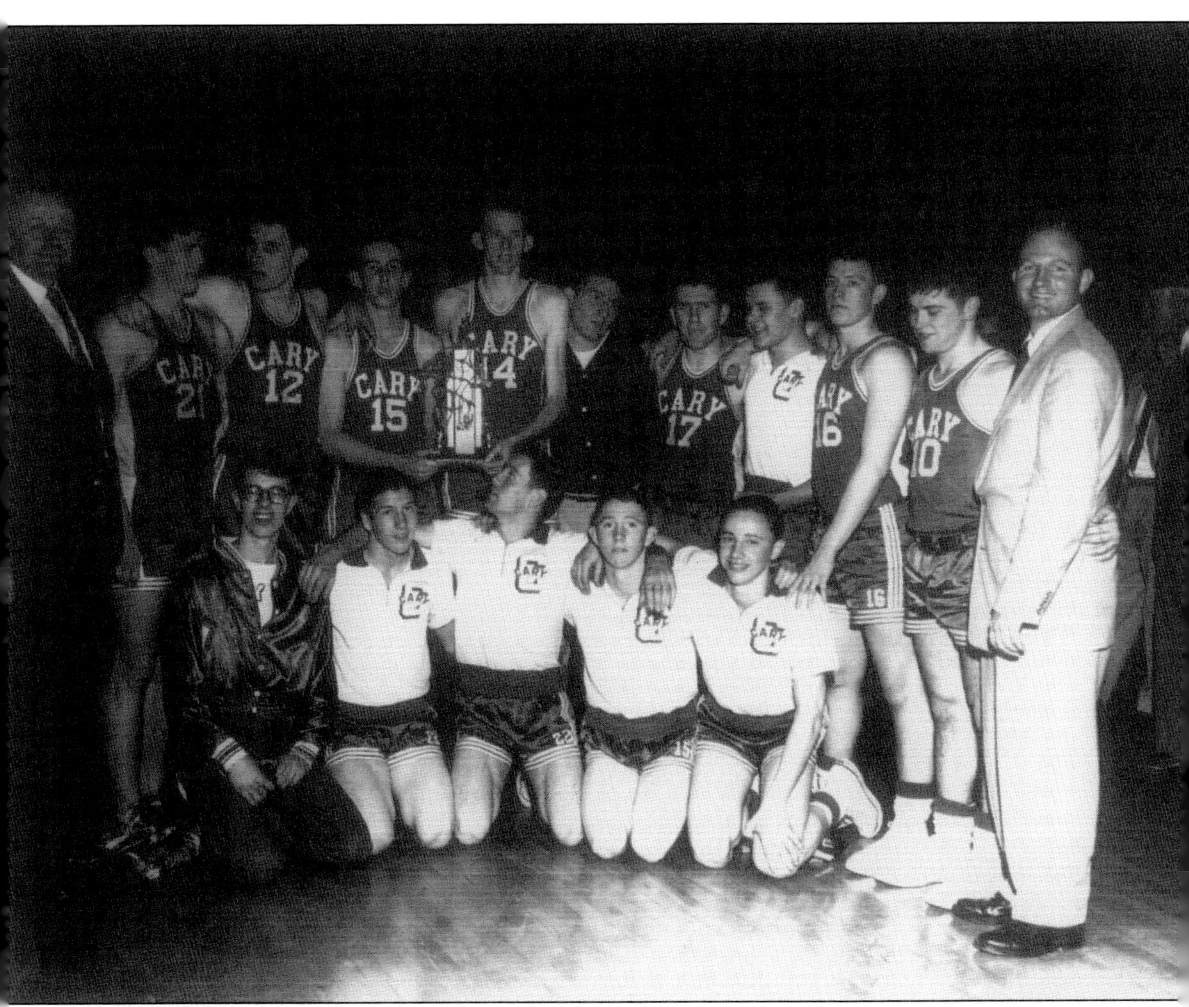

1954 Basketball Team. In 1954, the Cary White Imps took the Class-A state championship. From left to right, the team included (kneeling) manager Jimmie Womble, Charles Maidon, Harold Smith, Johnny Maidon, and Jerry Green; (standing) principal Paul W. Cooper, Bill Mooneyham, C. W. Jones, Charlie Adams, Guy Mendenhall, manager Archie Beal, Donnie Taylor, Paul Cooper, Joe Dickerson, Ben Strother, and coach Simon Terrell. Mendenhall and Adams were named to the All-Tournament Team. (Courtesy of Charlie Adams.)

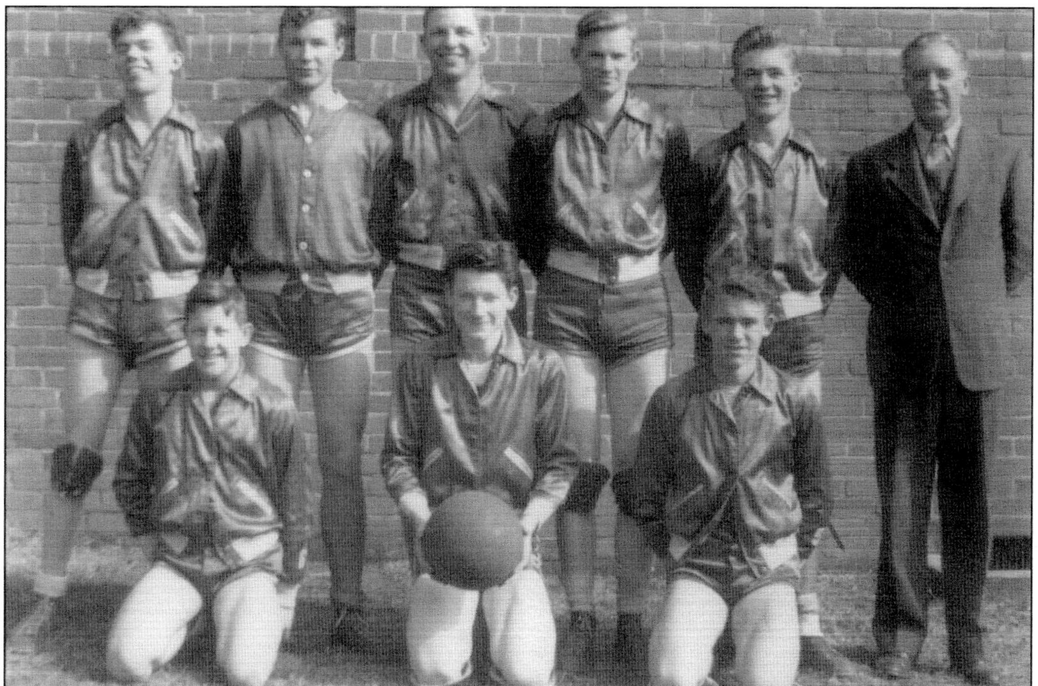

1940s Cary High School Men's Basketball Team. Seen here from left to right are (first row) David Stanfield, Jimmy Newton, and Peter Fralich; (second row) Billy Smith, Herbert Young, Francis Dellinger, Thomas Haddock, Horace "Fuzzy" Thomas, and manager/principal Marcus Dry. (Courtesy of C. Y. Jordan.)

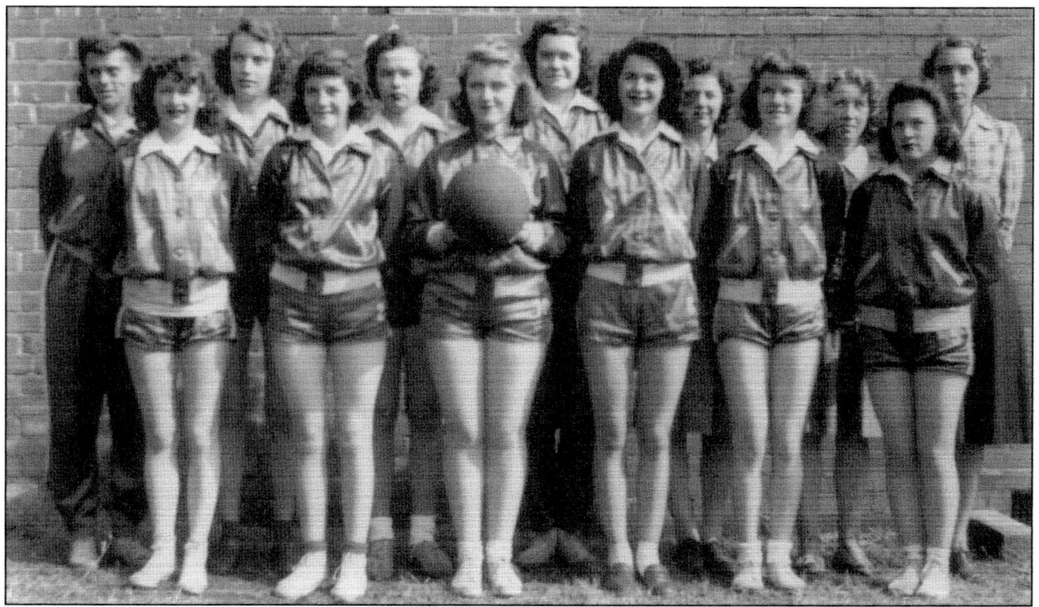

1940s Cary High School Women's Basketball Team. From left to right are (first row) unidentified, Irene Sox, Jean Bowing, unidentified, Patricia Sanderford, and Dorothy Murray; (second row) Peggy Phillips, unidentified, Dollie Morris-Jordan, Peggy ?, two unidentified, and an unidentified teacher. (Courtesy of C. Y. Jordan.)

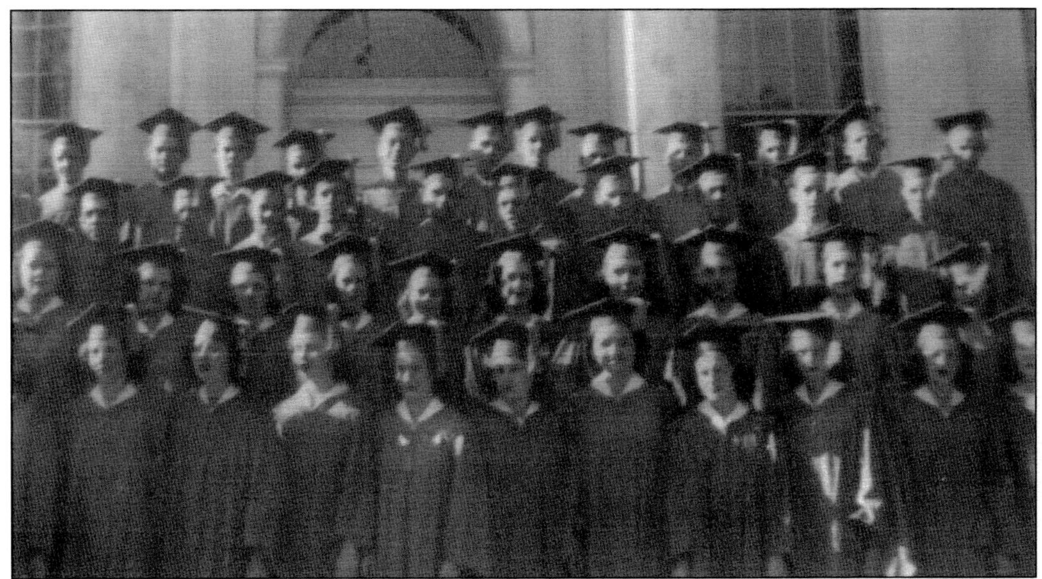

1944 Cary High School Graduating Class. Students from Cary, Morrisville, and Sorrell's Grove community attended Cary schools from first grade through graduation. CHS was called a "consolidated high school" because starting with high school, students from outlying areas would ride the bus to Cary to attend class. These students came from areas as far-flung as Swift Creek and the Mount Vernon Goodwin School near the fairgrounds. A number of buses brought the students each day. Most students came from families that had lived in the area for many years. The class of 1944 was the last class to graduate after 11 (not 12) years of schooling. (Courtesy of C. Y. Jordan.)

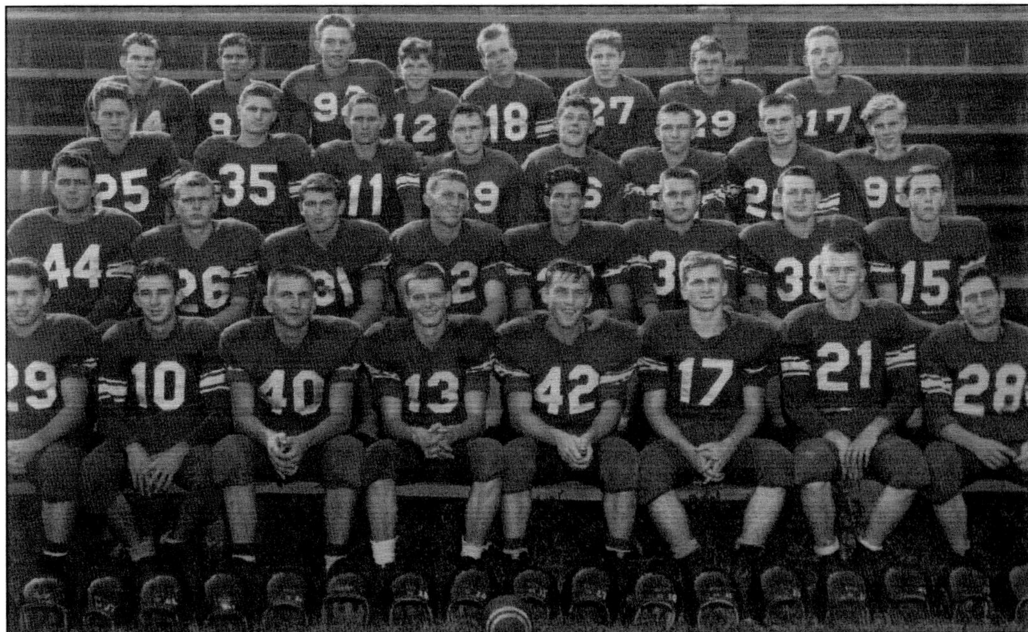

1952 Cary High School Football. From 1952 to 1954, Simon Terrell was the all-sports coach and athletic director at Cary High School. His two football teams had stellar records. (Courtesy of Charlie Adams.)

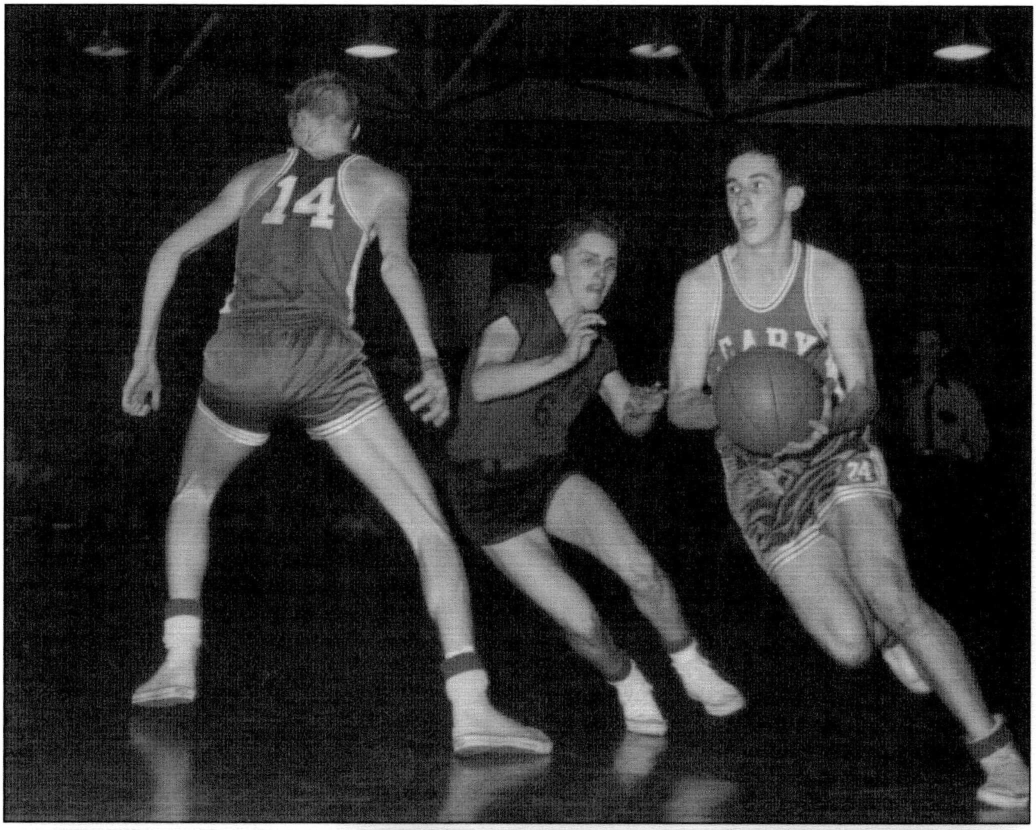

1954 Cary Basketball Team. In 1954, Cary's high school basketball team won the Class-A state championship. On March 24, 1954, the White Imps played the King High School Eagles in a suffocatingly small gym in Aberdeen. They capped their 30-1 season by beating King 63 to 54. More than 1,600 people watched the exciting game. Pictured here from left to right are 6-foot-5-inch King player Guy Mendenhall and 6-footer Charlie Adams. Adams and Mendenhall were the top scorers in the game. Adams was also the regular-season scoring star for Cary. (Both, courtesy of Charlie Adams.)

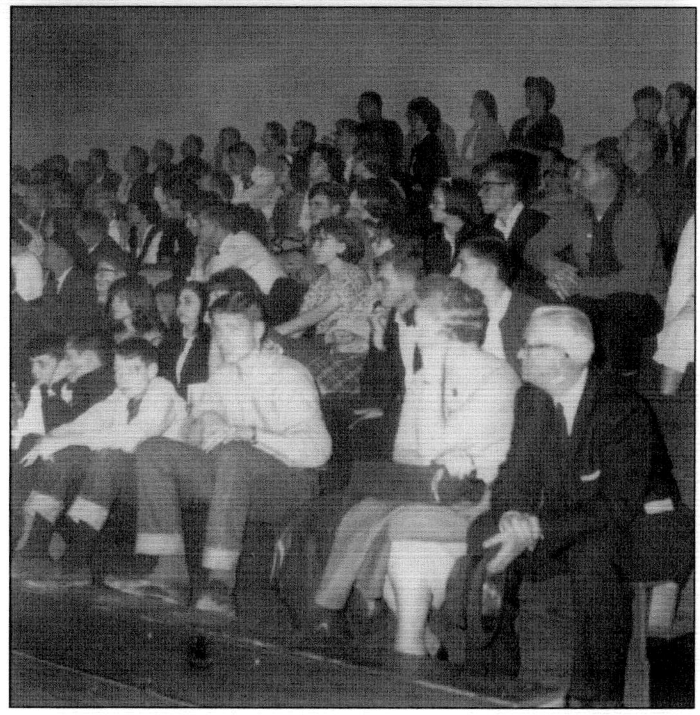

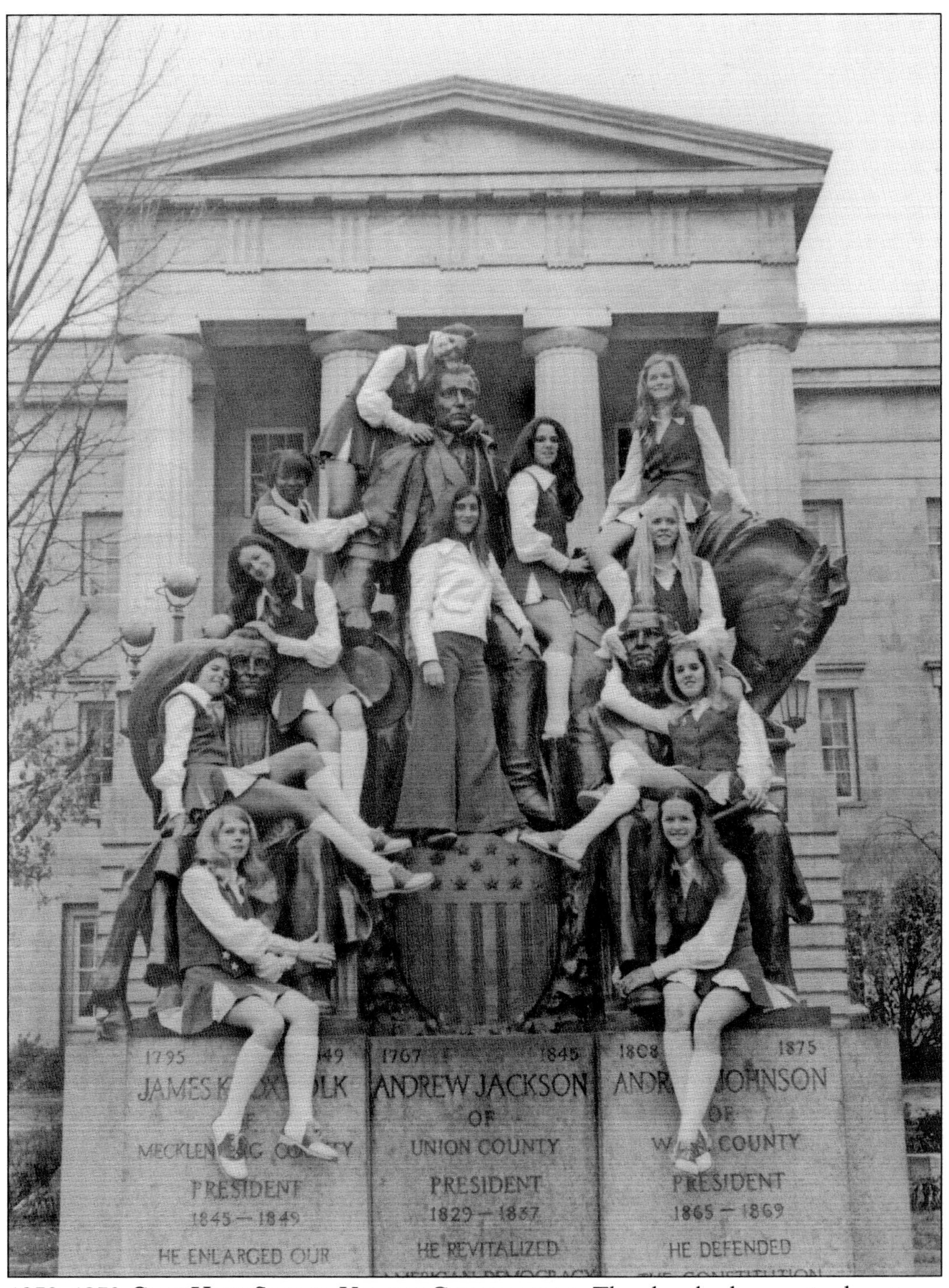

1972–1973 CARY HIGH SCHOOL VARSITY CHEERLEADERS. The cheerleaders are in downtown Raleigh and have decided to have a little fun. Pictured from left to right are (first row) head cheerleader Sue Holder and co-head Carla Jordan; (second row) Peggy Clark and Pam Wilson; (third row) Mary Davison, manager Ann Curtis, and June Durham; (fourth row) Gloria Williams, Pam Thomas, Sandra Lowry, and Sandy Burns. (Courtesy of C. Y. Jordan and Carla Michaels.)

Two

One Square Mile and More

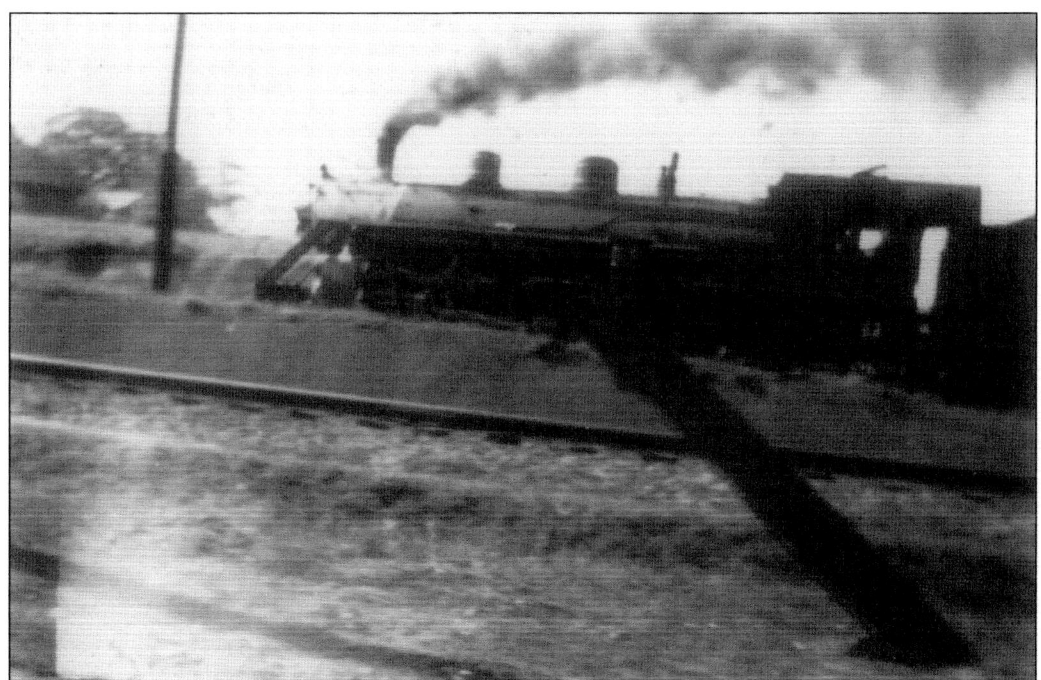

Southern Railroad. In the early 1900s, trains passed through town about every hour in the afternoon; the Seaboard and Southern raced to Cary, and the town's younger residents rushed down to the station to see the trains come in. Elva Templeton remembered, "If the Southern came in first, we met it, but if we'd hear the Seaboard coming, we'd run to the Seaboard." (Courtesy of C. Y. Jordan.)

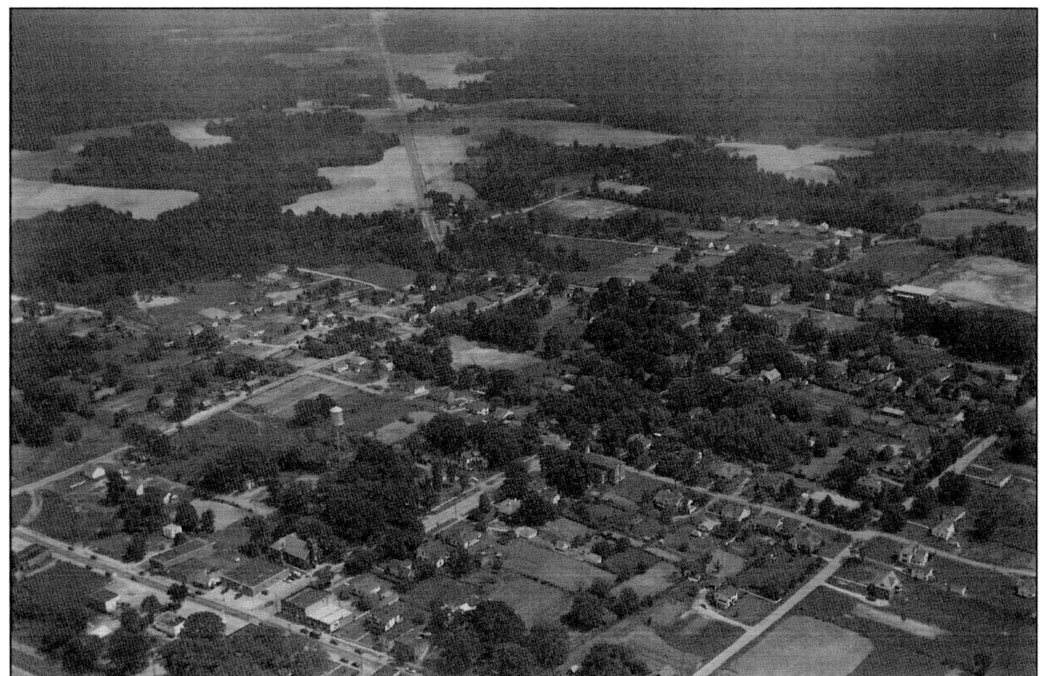

C. 1950 Aerial View of Cary. On May 9, 1933, radio station WPTF was granted permission to raise its power from 1,000 to 5,000 watts during daylight hours and to move its transmitter locally to Cary. Two new 370-foot Ideco towers were installed to support the station's antenna. Starting on June 10, 1933, WPTF transmitted from its new site on East Chatham Street in Cary, about 7 miles west of Raleigh. (Courtesy of Stanley Lorren.)

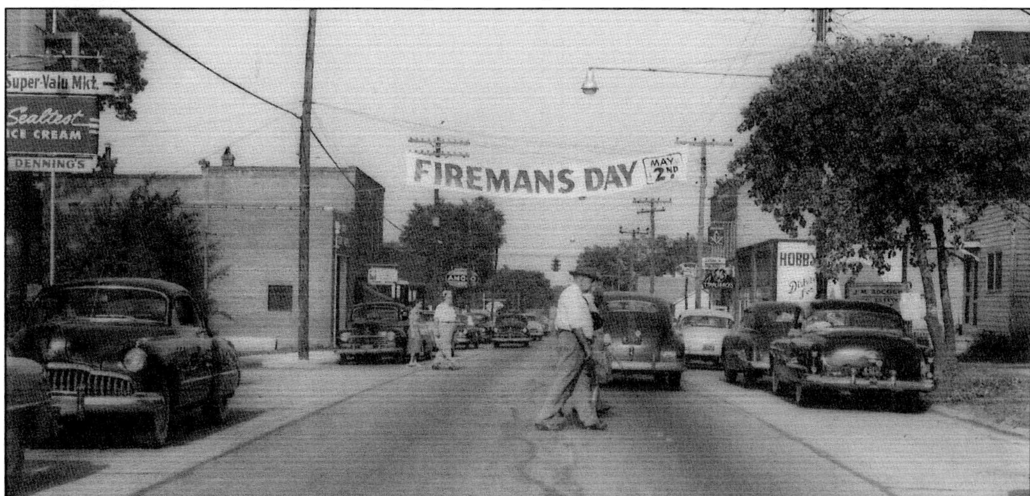

East Chatham Street. This view looks east down Chatham Street. It was taken in late April or early May, just prior to the first-ever annual Fireman's Day parade on May 2, 1953. This was the same year that the Cary Fire Department received its new Seagrave pumper, which was displayed on Fireman's Day. The 202-horsepower, 12-cylinder Seagrave pumped out 750 gallons per minute and included a 500-gallon water tank. It cost the town $15,000. Representing the Seagrave Company of South Carolina, Tom Stewart presented the truck to mayor H. Waldo Rood. (Courtesy of Stanley Lorren.)

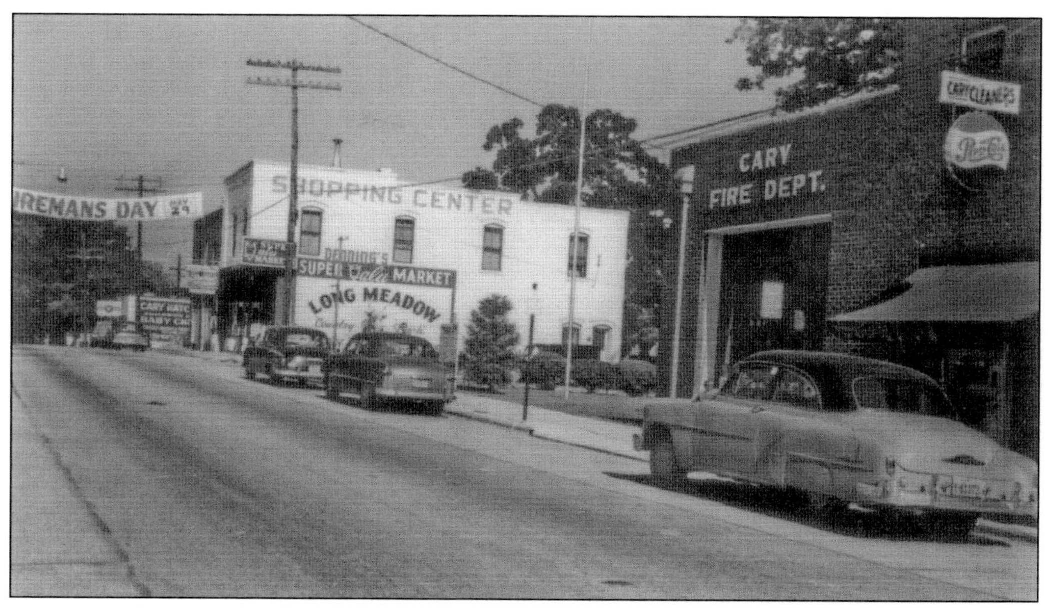

West Chatham Street. These two photographs also show Cary on May 29, 1953. They both look westward down Chatham Street, but at different angles. Note the fire station on the right and Denning's supermarket down a little further. The lower photograph also shows Watson's Florist and Cary Cleaners. They were taken prior to the first Fireman's Day parade. (Both, courtesy of Stanley Lorren.)

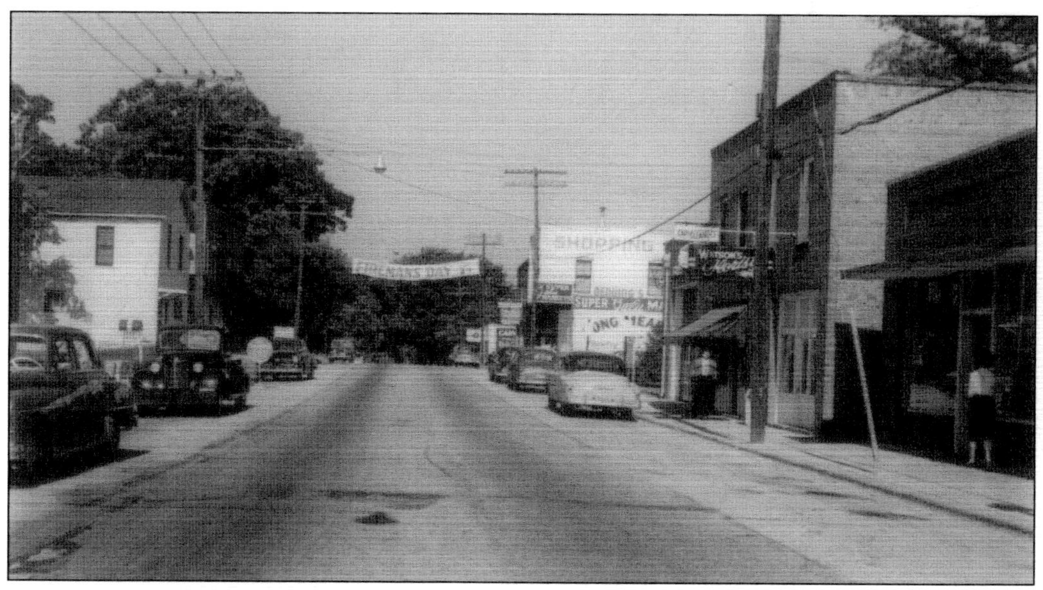

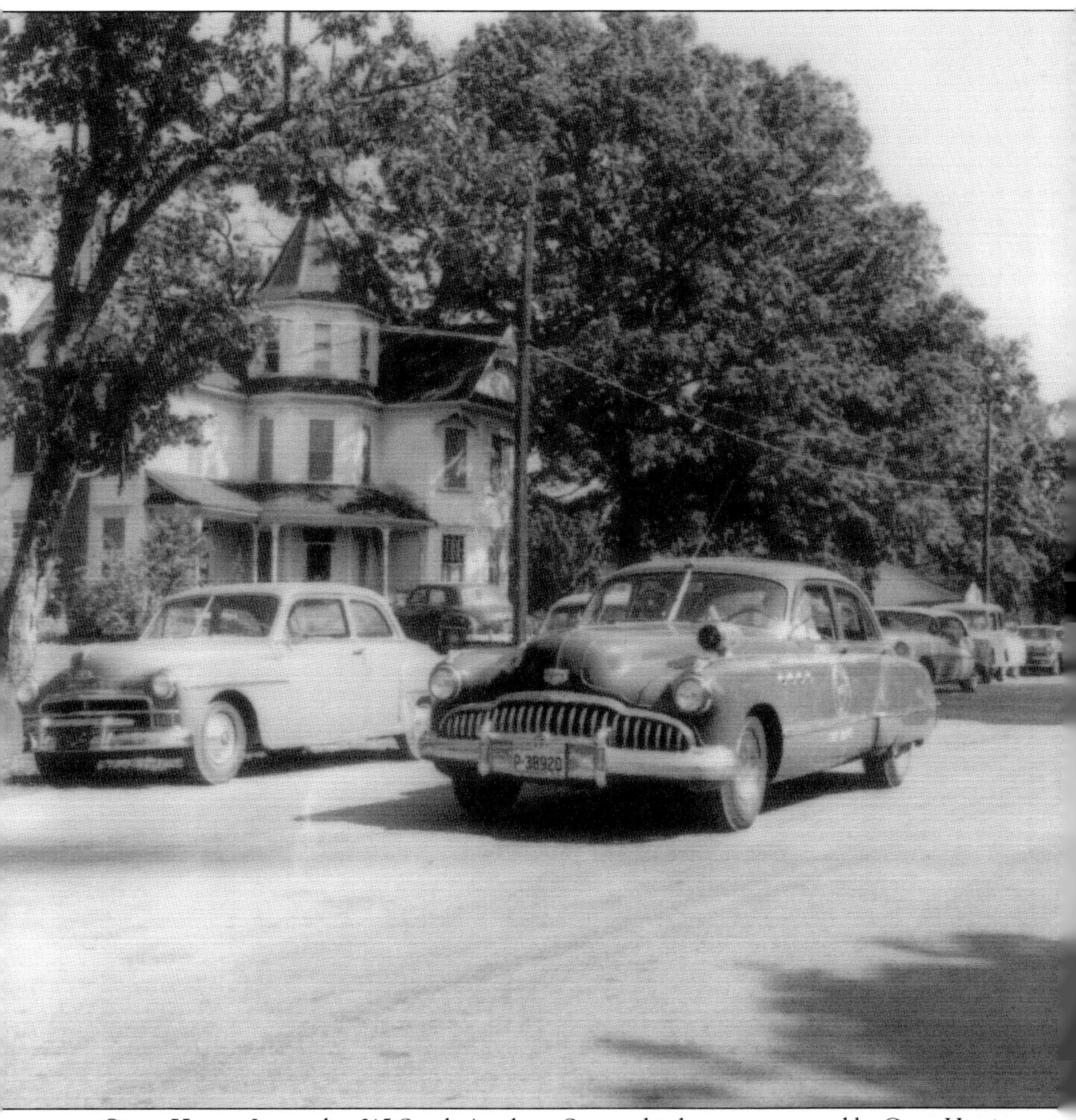

Guess House. Located at 215 South Academy Street, this house was owned by Capt. Harrison P. Guess, master of Cary Masonic Lodge No. 198 from 1888 to 1898. The house is of Queen Anne–style architecture but was expanded over the years to reflect the architectural styles of the time. It was adapted from an I-house in the Greek Revival style to a Queen Anne structure in the mid- to late 19th century. (Courtesy of Stanley Lorren.)

CARY, N. C.

For numbers not listed or to report telephone out of order dial "Operator."

For Instructions on "How to Use the Dial Telephone" see page following Raleigh listings.

Adams Drug Co 2351
Adams H R r 2371
Ashburn M C Mrs r 2661

Baum H B r 2102
Baxter W F Mrs r 2501
Beddingfield C L r 2692
Bennett W H r 2122
Branch Douglas M Rev r 2372
Branton's Grocerteria 2281
Braswell C O r 2291
Breeze Alice Mrs r 2101

Cary Hatcheries ofc 2602
Cary High School 2512
Cary Town of
 Town Hall 2141
 Chief of Police's Res 2171
 Clerk's Res 2392
Coggin J K r 2482
Craddock G E r 2721
Crosby J J r 2541

Davis Burton I r 2681
Dawkins Lacy L r 2261
Dry M B r 2121
Dudley Claude H r 2191
Dunham R S r 2341

Edwards H M r 2573

Fourle L J r 2621
Fox Charles G r 2791

Gray Chester O r 2582

Hart Miles I r 2711
Hawkins J S r 2162
Heater C R r 2574
Heater R O r 2641
Hedrick H George r 2701
Hobby J G r 2592
Hobby's Cash Grocery 2321
Holleman C W r 2551
House Herbert W r W Park dr 2232
Hunter J P Dr ofc 2492
Hunter J P Dr r 2461

Jewell W L contr 2741
Jones M T r 2521
Jones Pauline Mrs r 2181
Jones Wiley P r 2401

Jordan Ida F Mrs r 2271
Jordan's Esso Service Station 2451

Lane J R r 2601
Leavitt A E r 2461
Lee S R Jr r 2151

Martin W R r 2162
Matthews J C Jr r 2572
Maynard J T r 2611
McGeary John K r 2781
Meekins E N r 2591
Mitchell Lily E Miss r 2161
Murdock W B r 2492

Newman S B r 2581

Perry R L r 2192
Philips J F r 2331
Phillips Mary Belle Mrs r 2531
Phillips W C r 2732
Police Headquarters ofc 2171

Rogers Pansy Miss r 2612
Rogers W L Grocery Store 2301

Sipe B W r 2762
Smith B M r 2561
Smith C A r 2671
Smith S F r 2772
Sorrell N S bldg mtrl 2631
Southern Bell Tel & Tel Co Inc
 For all business transactions including inquiries concerning accounts, applications for and changes in service etc
 dial Operator and ask for 9011
Sox J L r 2761
Sprinkle H L Service Station 2471
Stanfield Lewis S 2502
Sturdivant L E r 2571

Town of Cary .... (See Cary Town of)
Turner George S r 2362

WPTF Radio Station 2251
Waddell H H r 2632
Waldo Joe Mrs r 2771
Wilkinson T F Jr r 2241
Williams R B r 2651
Womble D J r 2112
Wood Annie D Mrs r 2292

Yarborough Frank R Dr phys 2231

1939

PHONE

1939 CARY PHONE BOOK. This single page shows the entire list of Cary residences and businesses with phones in 1939. Cary's downtown population in 1940 was about 1,100 people, but there are a total of 83 entries in the phone book. Prior to residents having phones in their own homes, they visited the drugstore in town to make their calls. Cary resident Robert Heater recalls referring to the operator as "Central;" callers would pick up the phone and say, "Central? Get me [such and such a number]." Two single older women ran the switchboard. They lived in a house on Academy Street where the library now stands. (Courtesy of Ralph Ashworth.)

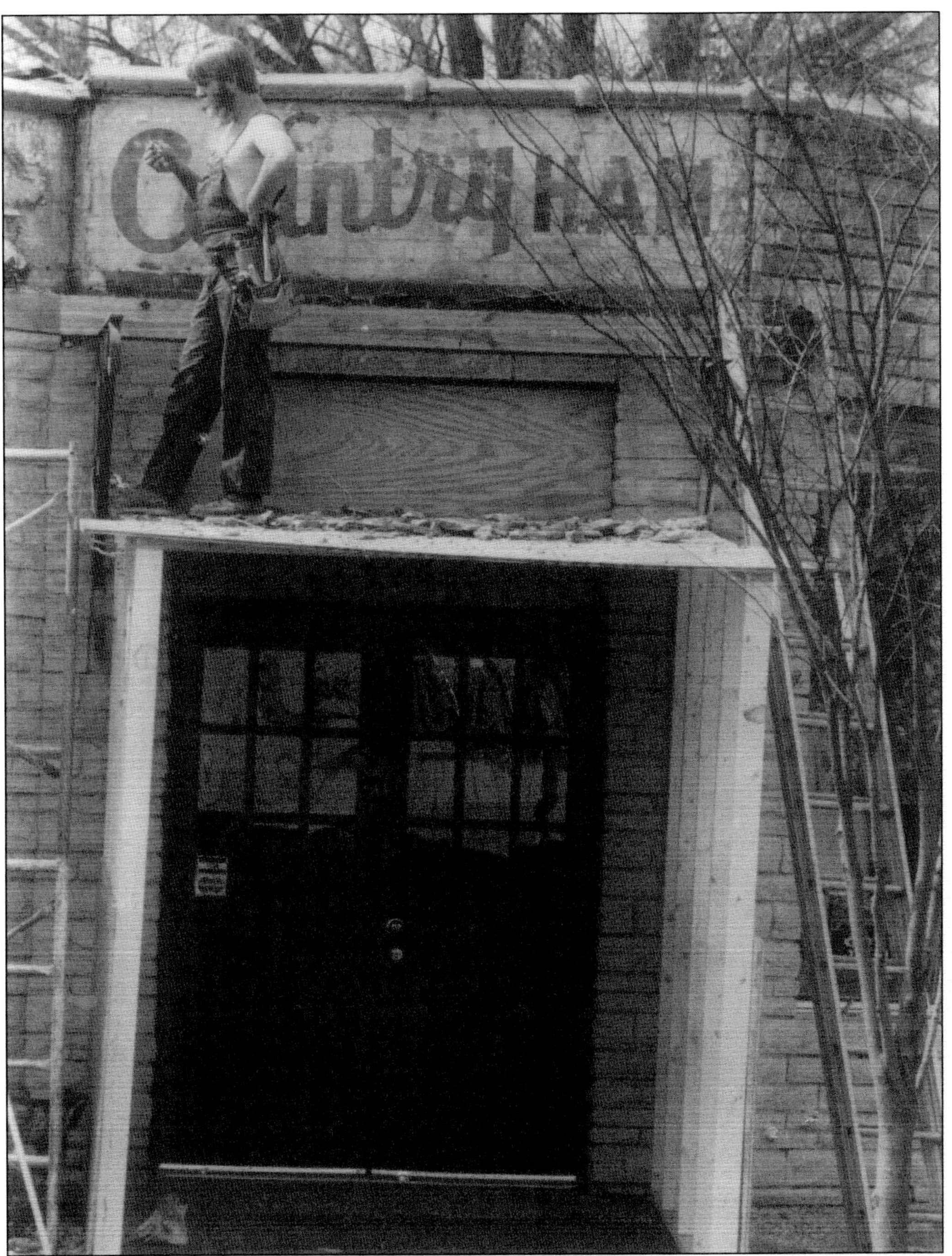

Rogers Restaurant. In September 1953, William Lemuel Rogers opened the first Rogers Restaurant in what is now Johnson's Jewelers. In 1961, he moved to the location that is now the café across the street from the existing Rogers Motel. He renovated the building and installed terrazzo floors and new walls. One dining room accommodated up to 60 people and was often used by civic clubs as a meeting space. Prior to opening a restaurant, William ran a grocery shop in town. (Courtesy of Bill Rogers.)

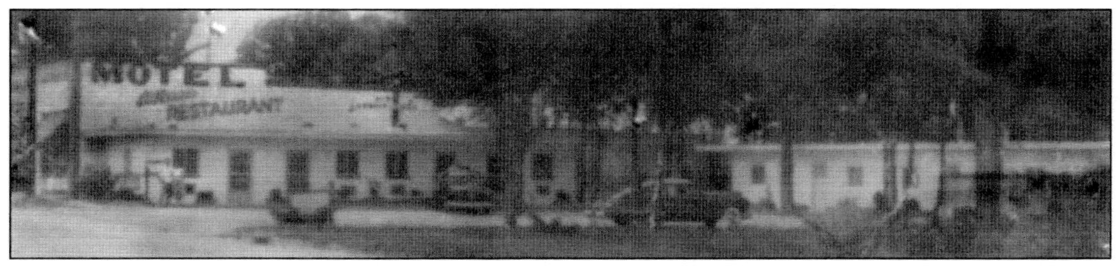

Rogers Motel and Restaurant. In 1961, Rogers purchased a larger property at 149 East Chatham Street where Rogers Motel stands today. There were seven rooms and one apartment. The rooms rented for $5 per night (single) and $7 per night (double occupancy) when he bought the property. Bill's son and daughter-in-law bought the property in 1966. They added six more rooms and still offer weekly rentals. The full-service, sit-down restaurant offered a variety of dishes. They served a traditional country breakfast with sausage and country ham biscuits for 15¢. They also offered a variety of items for lunch for $1, and dinner included sandwiches, barbecue, hamburger steaks, seafood, steaks, prime rib, soups, salads, chowders, home-cooked vegetables, and homemade desserts. The restaurant closed in 1991. (Both, courtesy of Bill Rogers.)

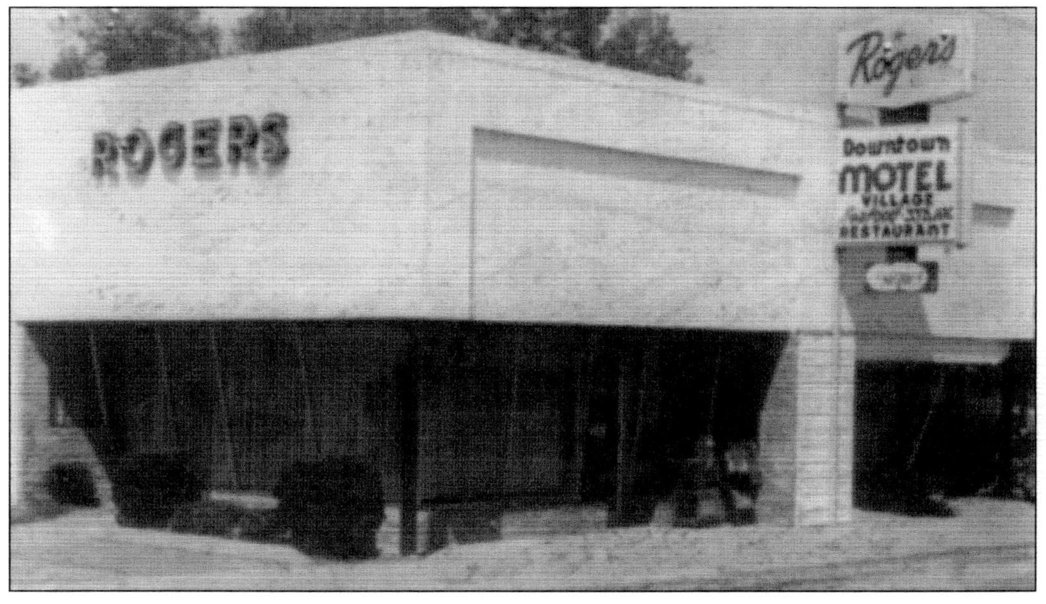

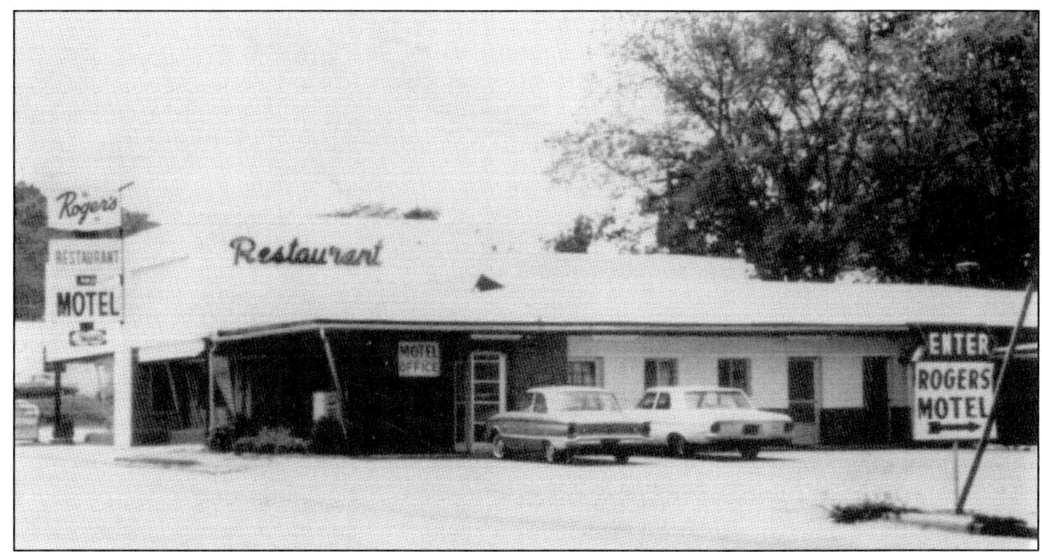

ROGERS MOTEL AND RESTAURANT, 1960S. Rogers Restaurant was one of only two restaurants in town. It was very popular with local builders, especially when Cary started to boom. People like Buck Jordan, Jeff Sugg, and Clint Williams were breakfast regulars at Rogers, which served traditional blue-plate specials later in the day but also operated as a steak house. The Cary Rotary Club also met here. (Courtesy of Bill Rogers.)

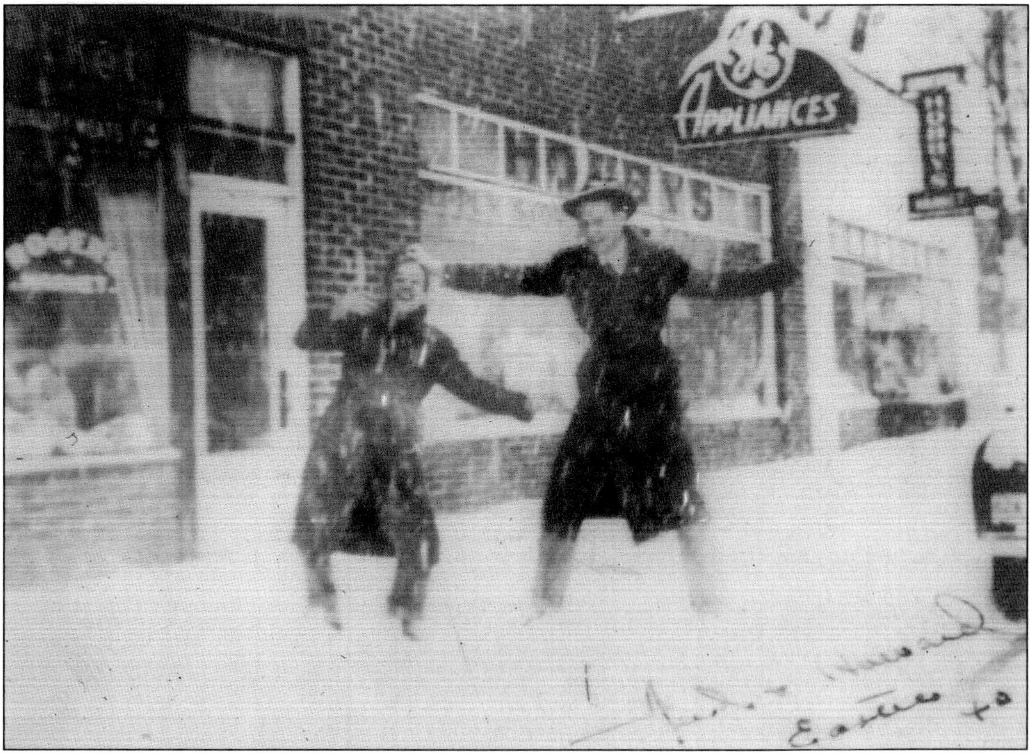

FUN IN A CARY SNOWSTORM. The tall man, Howard Franklin, and his friend Fred are having a blast in a rare Cary snowstorm in front of Hobby's Supply Store. Hobby's was in business from as early as 1950 until 1964. (Courtesy of the North Carolina Office of Archives and History.)

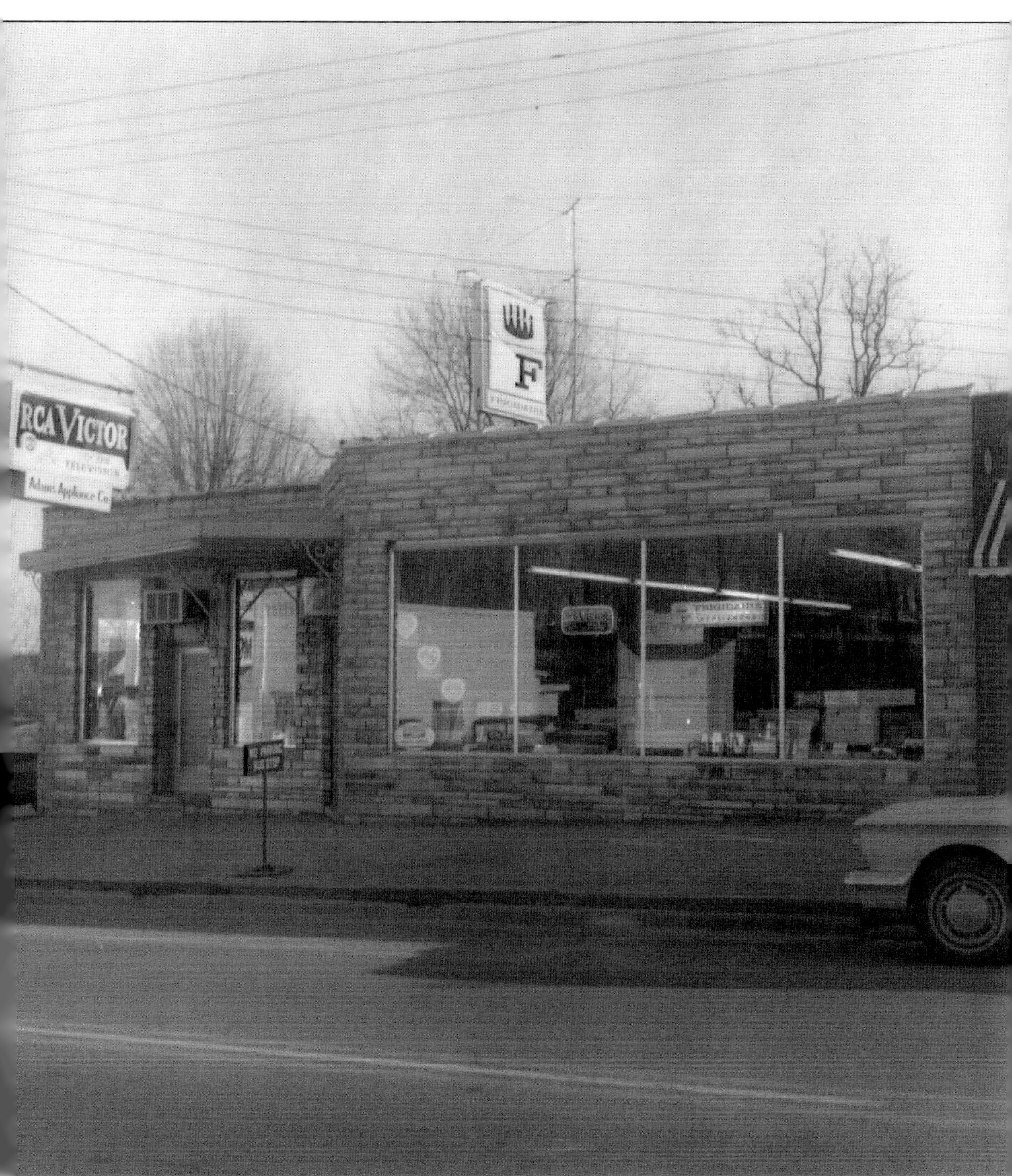

Adams Appliance Store. Henry Adams opened his appliance store in 1954, after he sold his pharmacy to Ralph Ashworth. He had planned to turn the pharmacy business over to his only son, but when Charlie decided he did not want to go into the family business, his father sold it. Henry sold RCA and Frigidaire appliances to Cary residents. Adams Appliance Store was also a spot where local residents paid their phone and light bills. Henry was very active in the community, and he worked at his store until his death in 1968. (Courtesy of Charlie Adams.)

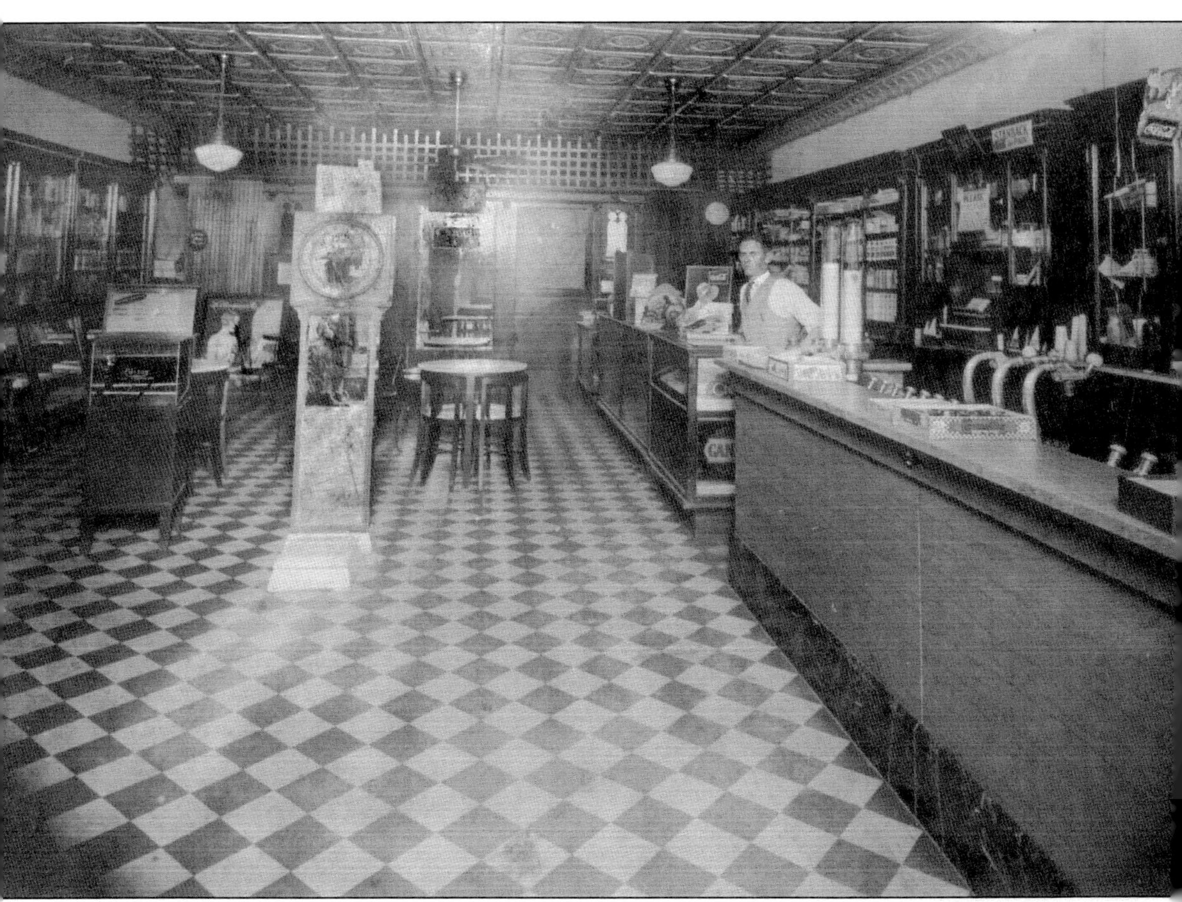

ADAMS REXALL DRUG STORE. Henry Adams worked as a drug salesman in his own store in 1930, and in 1931, the cornerstone for his store at the intersection of Academy and Chatham Streets was laid. Cary resident Bob Heater recalls, "He was a quiet person. Not real outgoing. But when he did speak, he spoke strongly, if you know what I mean. My earliest memories as a child are of [the days] when the drugstore was just the town meeting place. It was open until about 9:00 o'clock at night, and the men would sit around and talk." Henry sold his drugstore in 1957, and it is known today as Ashworth's Drugs. (Courtesy of Charlie Adams.)

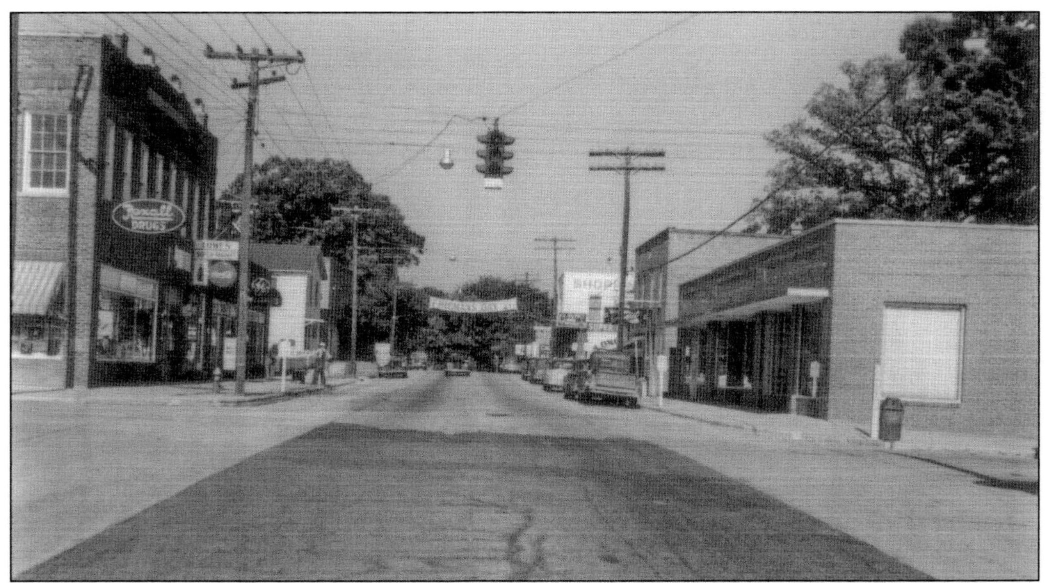

WEST CHATHAM STREET AND ASHWORTH'S DRUGS. These 1950s photographs show Ashworth's Drugs. The above photograph looks westward down Chatham Street, and the lower photograph shows the drugstore looking up Academy Street toward the high school. The lower photograph also shows the building before its renovation. In April 1957, Ralph walked into Adams's Rexall Drug store and asked owner Henry Adams if anyone in town was selling a pharmacy. Henry had just learned that his son Charlie did not want the business, so Henry made Ralph an offer. In the early days, Ashworth's alternated staying open on Sundays between 2:00 p.m. and 6:00 p.m. with Mitchell's Pharmacy down the street. (Above, courtesy of Stanley Lorren; below, courtesy of Ralph Ashworth.)

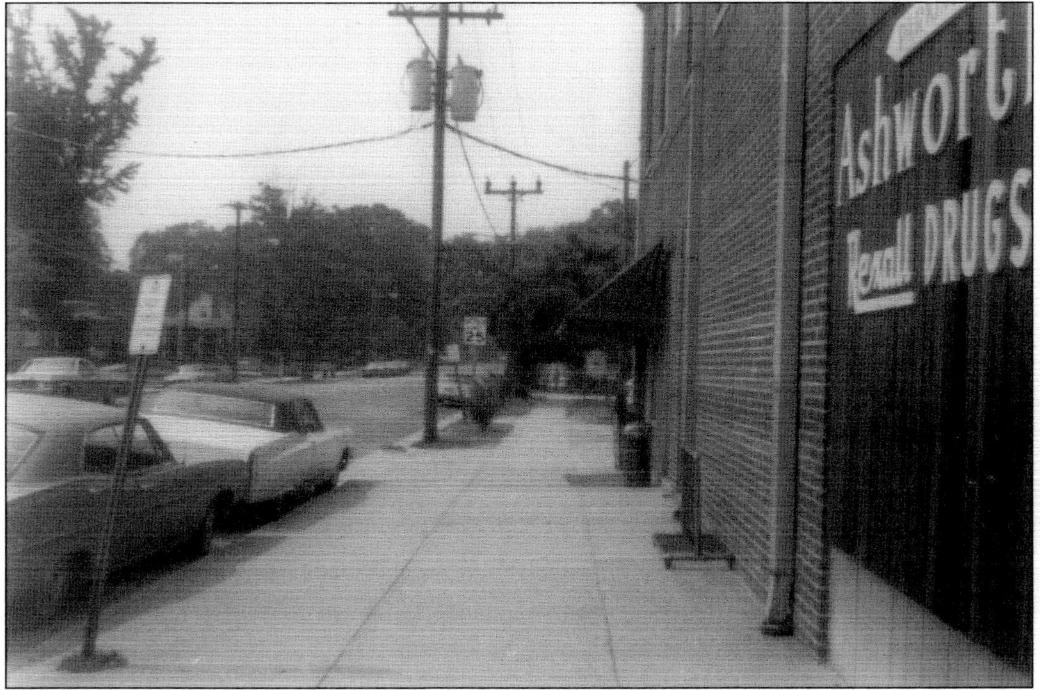

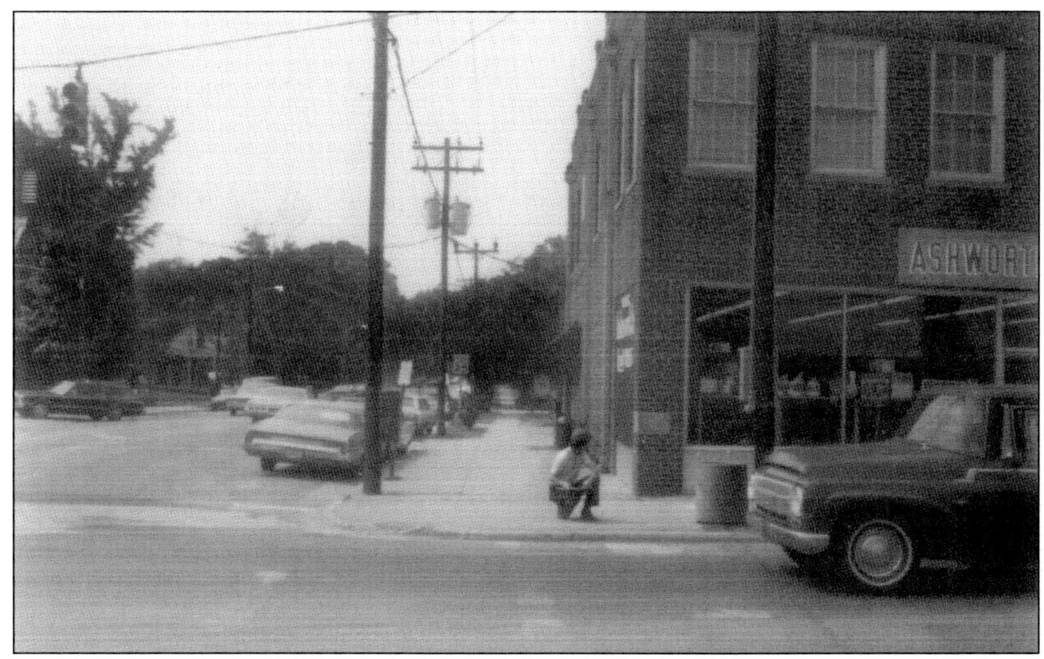

Ashworth's Drugs. Like Adams's before it, Ashworth's Drugs quickly became the central meeting place in town. It was half its current size, and it was expanded in 1960. The soda counter was on the opposite wall from where it is today. Around 1970, Ralph bought the building next door and renovated. (Courtesy of Ralph Ashworth.)

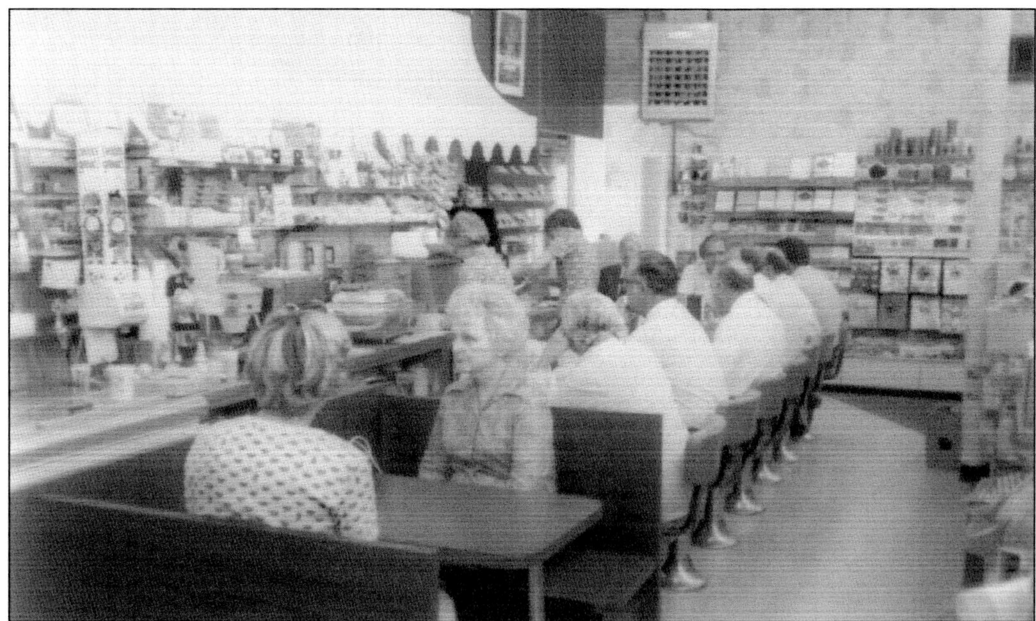

Ashworth's Drugs Lunch Counter. The lunch counter and soda fountain have been a staple at this corner drugstore since before it was Ashworth's. Edna Cyrus was also a staple. She worked the lunch counter from 1959 to 1982. When she first started, she only planned to stay for two years, but that turned into 23. She served chicken salad, Jesse Jones hot dogs, and chili to students and local residents. (Courtesy of Ralph Ashworth.)

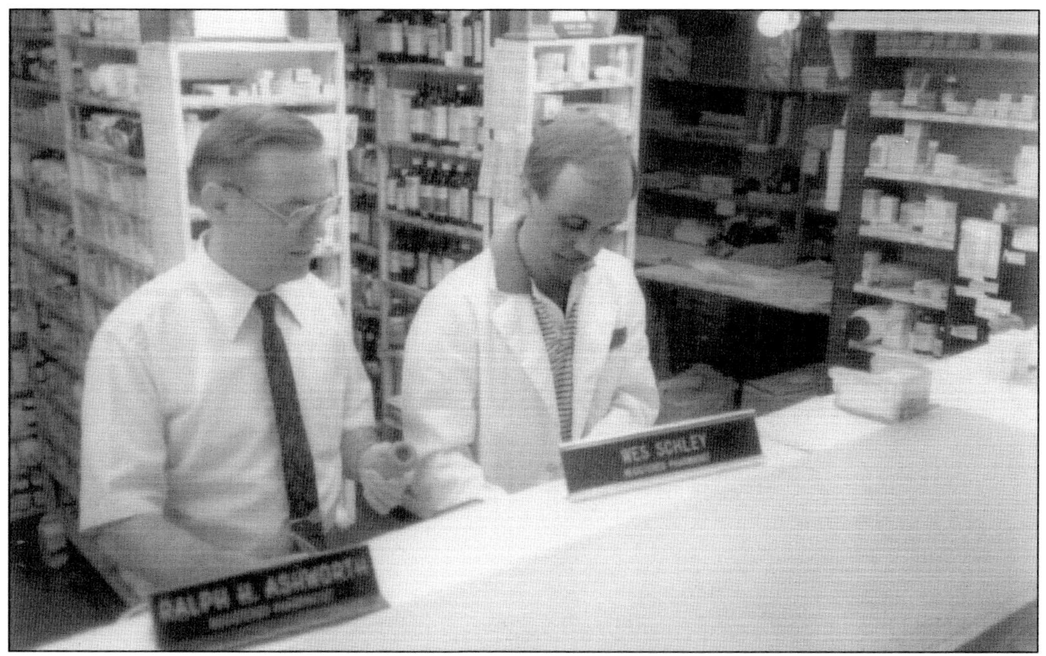

PHARMACIST RALPH ASHWORTH. A native of Fuquay-Varina, Ralph Ashworth studied at UNC-Chapel Hill, where he finished pharmacy school in 1955. In 1957, Ashworth's received the Rexall Drug Company award for outstanding achievement in sales improvement. Pictured here are Ralph Ashworth (left) and Wes Schley. (Courtesy of Ralph Ashworth.)

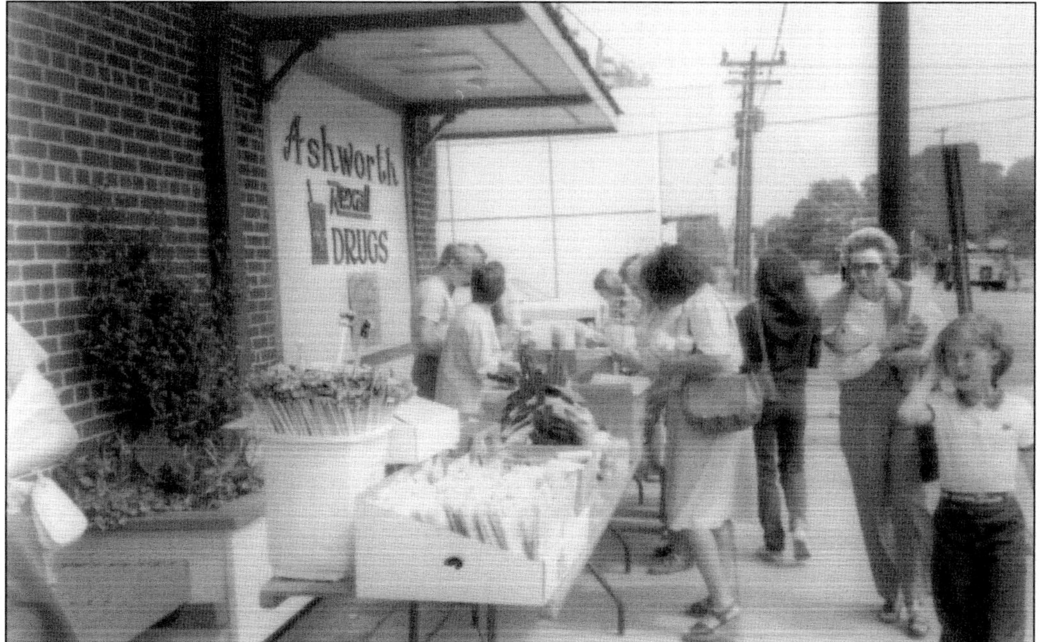

ASHWORTH DRUGS SIDEWALK SALE. In the 1960s, Ashworth's used to have sidewalk sales to attract customers. Inside, Ashworth's continued the Adams tradition of serving Jesse Jones pork hot dogs, homemade chicken salad, pimento cheese, ice cream soda, root beer floats, and freshly squeezed orangeade and lemonade. (Courtesy of Ralph Ashworth.)

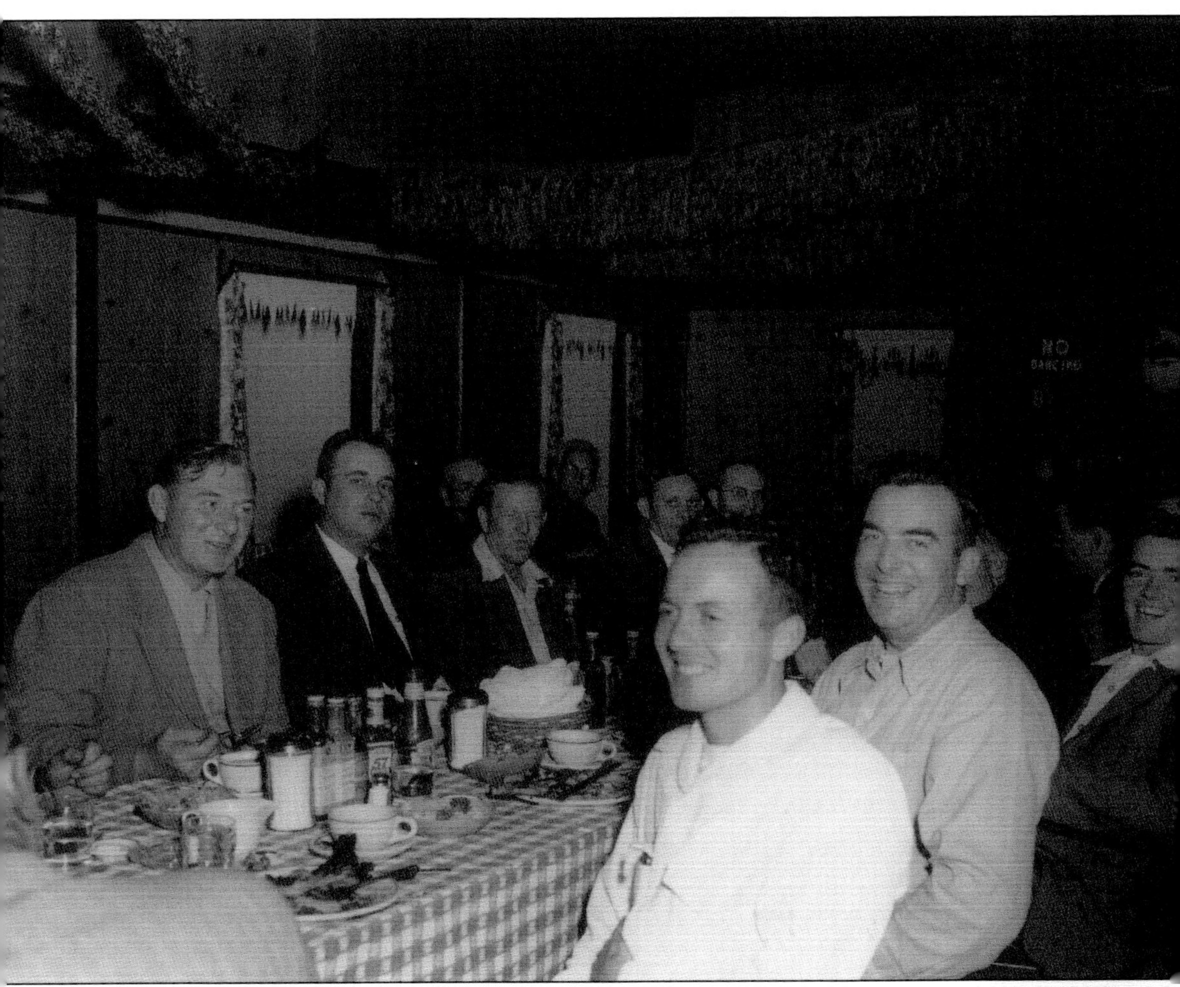

PROESCHERS RESTAURANT. The Heater Well Company held their 1952 company Christmas party here. It was considered the best restaurant in Cary, and it was the only place in town (or nearby) where diners could order a lobster. Everett Case, who played basketball for North Carolina State University, ate dinner here after each game. Pictured from right to left are Percy McNeil (in front) and N. B. Daniels—the rest are unidentified. Like much of the South, Cary was fairly segregated; Russell Heater had to ask if black employees could dine at his table with their white coworkers, and the owner agreed. The restaurant went out of business in 1957. (Courtesy of Robert Heater.)

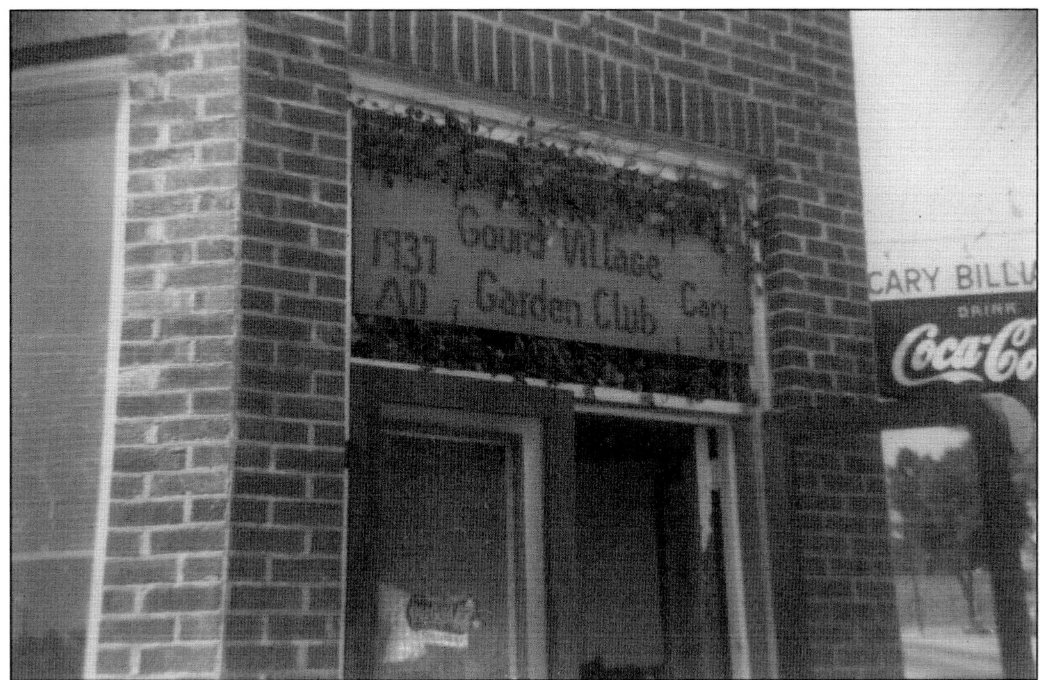

The Cary Gourd Village Garden Club. One year, Mary Wilkinson and a small group of friends and relatives planted one packet of seeds and waited to see what they would yield. In 1937, Cary became the gourd capital of the nation when Wilkinson began the Alpha Chapter of what is now the North Carolina Gourd Society. Charter members included Mary Wilkinson, Ann "Nannie" Maynard, Elizabeth Rood, Ann McLean, R. S. Dunham, T. F. Bower, and Mossa Eaton. (Courtesy of Mary Ann Rood.)

Cary Gourd Festival. Pictured here is Esther Ivey, who joined the club in 1938. She is displaying her loofah collection, including the hat she is wearing, a gourd sponge bonnet. She once served as president and told new members, "Our only membership requirement is that you plant a hill of gourds, but nobody says that seed has to come up." (Courtesy of Mary Ann Rood.)

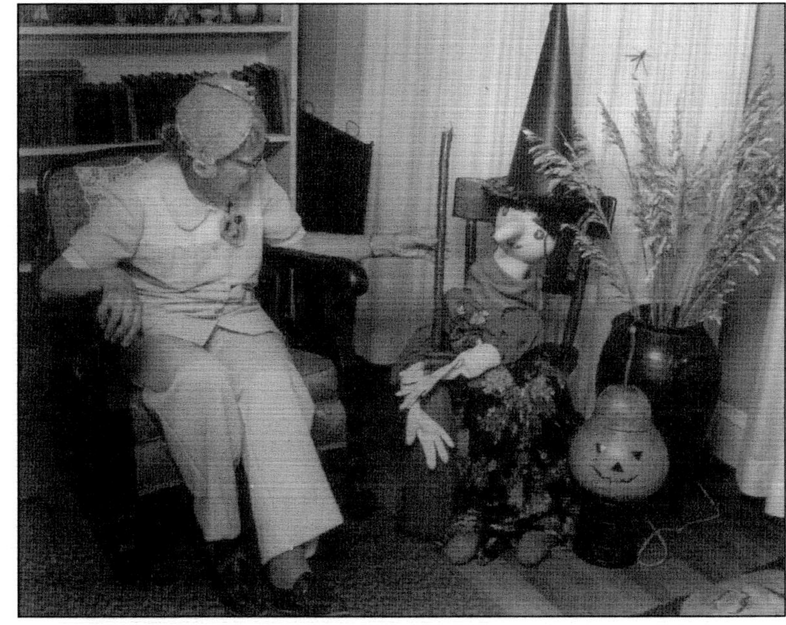

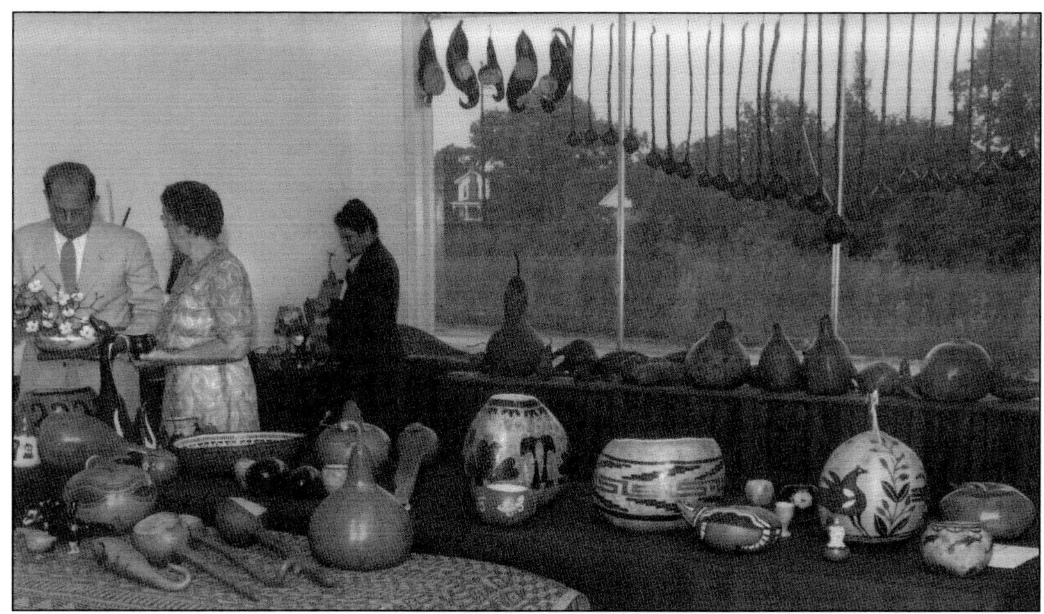

1940s–1950s Gourd Festival. Early festivals were held in the school cannery, dry cleaners, and a furniture store. Over the years, festivals have featured dolls, a gourmet gourd buffet, hard-working, practical gourds, Mother Goose gourds, and many others. Pictured from left to right are Frank Ivey, Miss Bailey, and Esther Ivey. (Courtesy of Mary Ann Rood.)

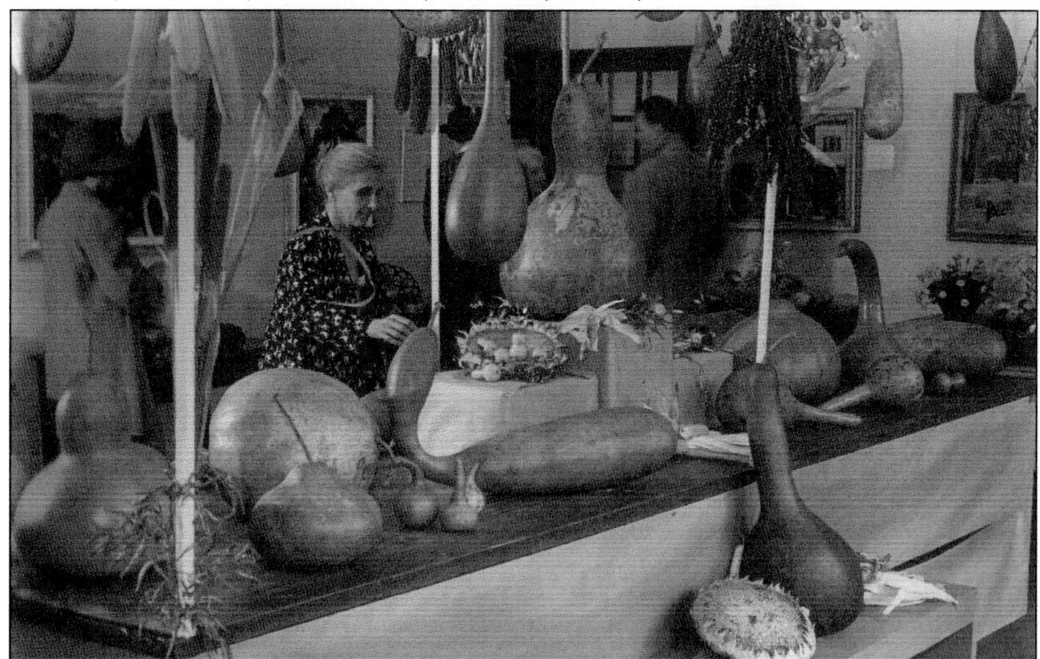

Mary Wilkinson at the Gourd Festival. The photograph was taken some time in the 1940s or 1950s. Gourds are grown as craft material, musical instruments, and working implements. The smallest can be the size of a marble, and the largest can be a 200-pound armful. Gourds have been a household necessity since the beginning of civilization. Many growers today use them as purple martin birdhouses, table decorations, and loofah sponges. (Courtesy of Mary Ann Rood.)

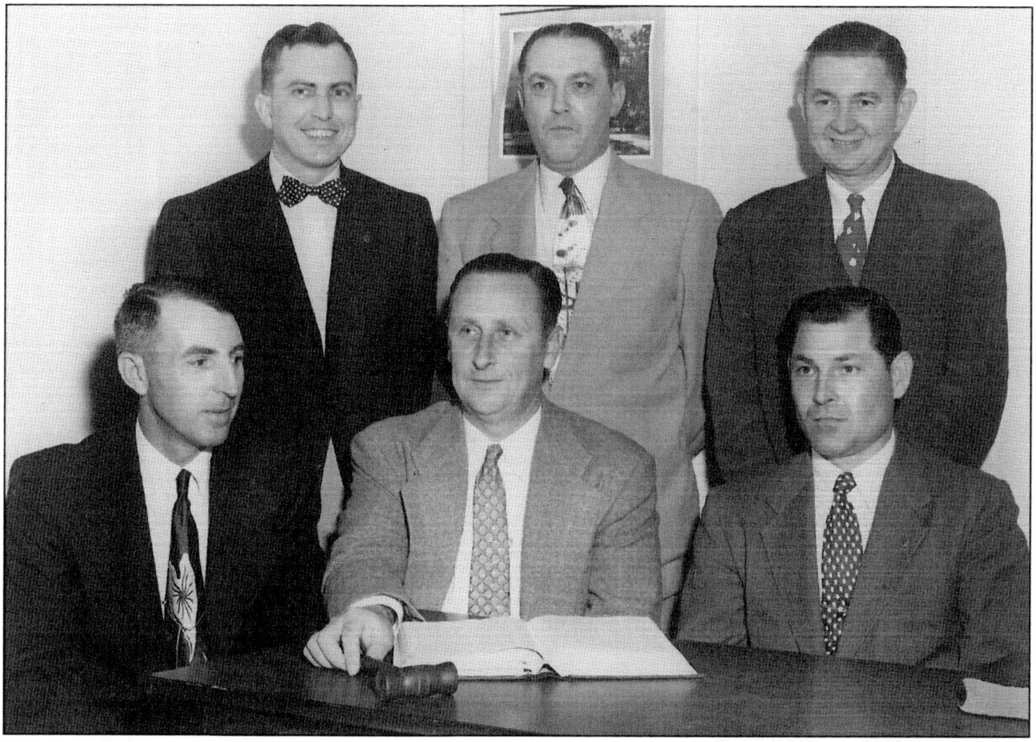

MAYOR H. WALDO ROOD. Cary's mayor from 1949 to 1961, H. Waldo Rood's friends and family called him Waldo. These photographs show the mayor conducting business. In addition to being mayor, Waldo also helped organize the Cary Rotary Club in 1964 and was also named treasurer. He also held the office of president from 1970 to 1971. Prior to being elected mayor, Waldo worked for WPTF as a radio engineer. He was also a master for the Masons of Cary Lodge No. 198. (Above, courtesy of Stanley Lorren; below, courtesy of Mary Ann Rood.)

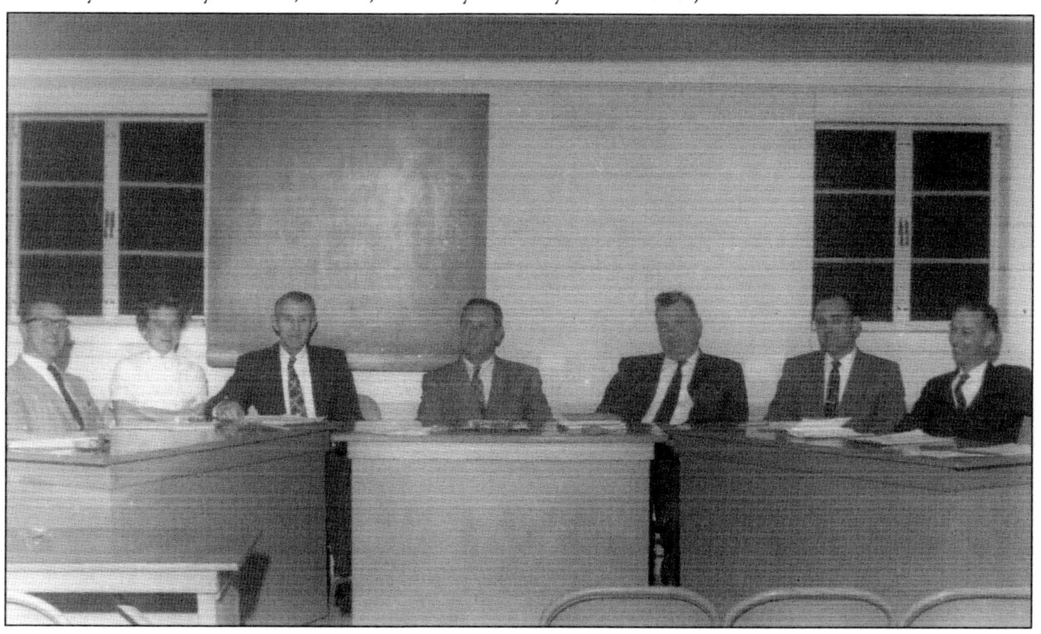

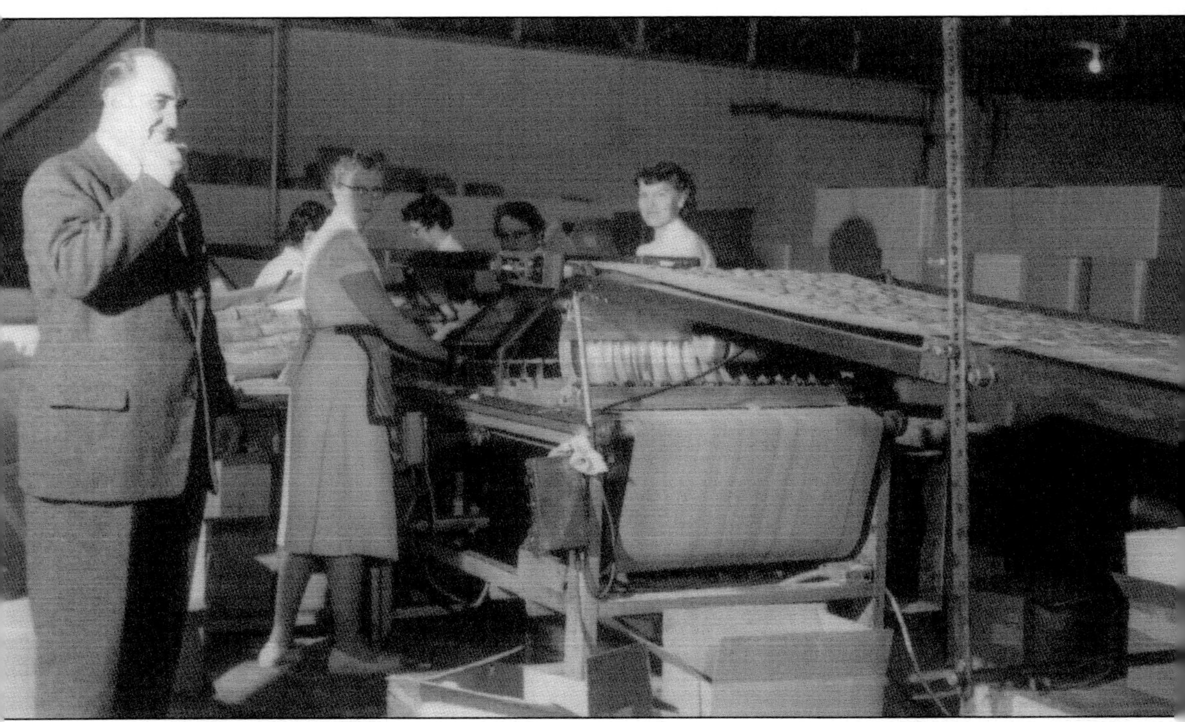

Taylor Biscuit Company. In 1947, Flay Morrison Taylor opened the Taylor Biscuit Company (now Austin Foods) on Chatham Street in Cary. It became the largest employer in town for almost 30 years, with as many as 150 people staffing the production lines and an additional 50 people employed in sales. They are known for their cheese and peanut butter crackers. Taylor appears to be sampling his own product in this photograph. (Courtesy of Stanley Lorren.)

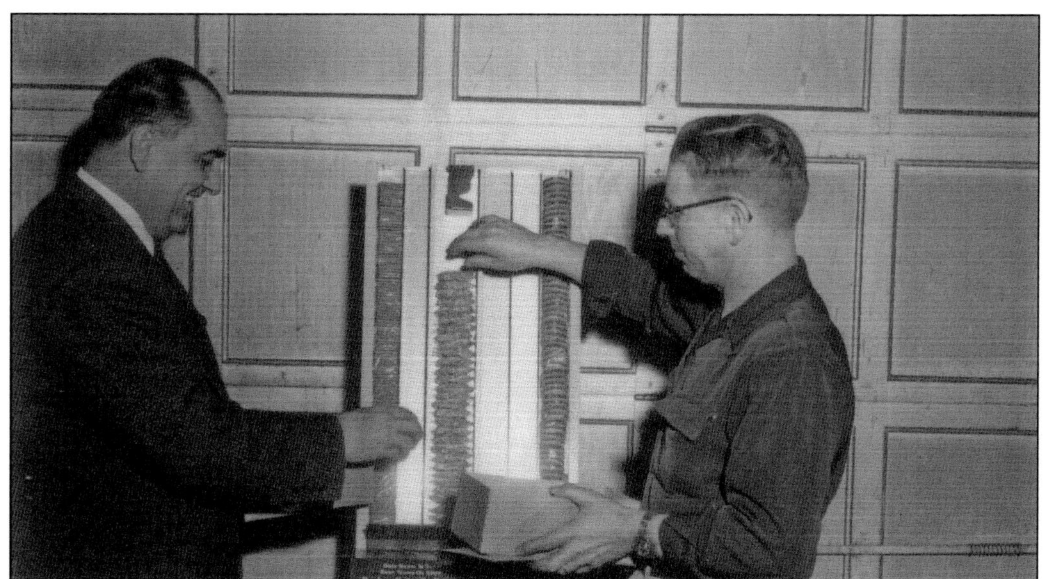

Taylor Biscuit Company Vending Machine. In 1958, Charles Fazekas patented a coin-operated vending machine to disburse the Taylor Biscuit Company's products. The vending machine operator, who is unidentified, gives owner Flay Taylor a demonstration of how the coin-operated machine works. (Courtesy of Stanley Lorren.)

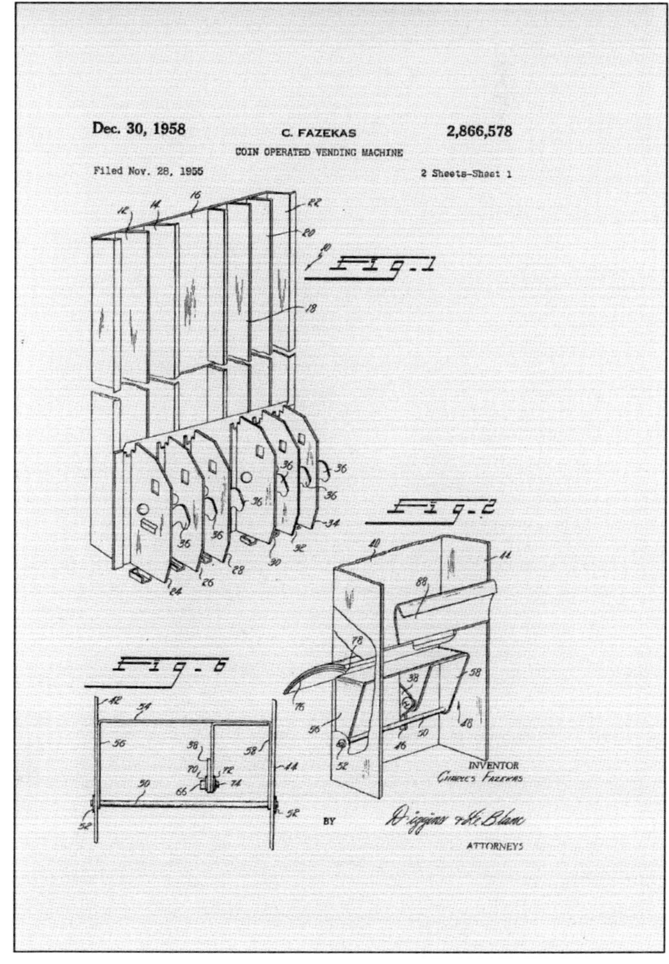

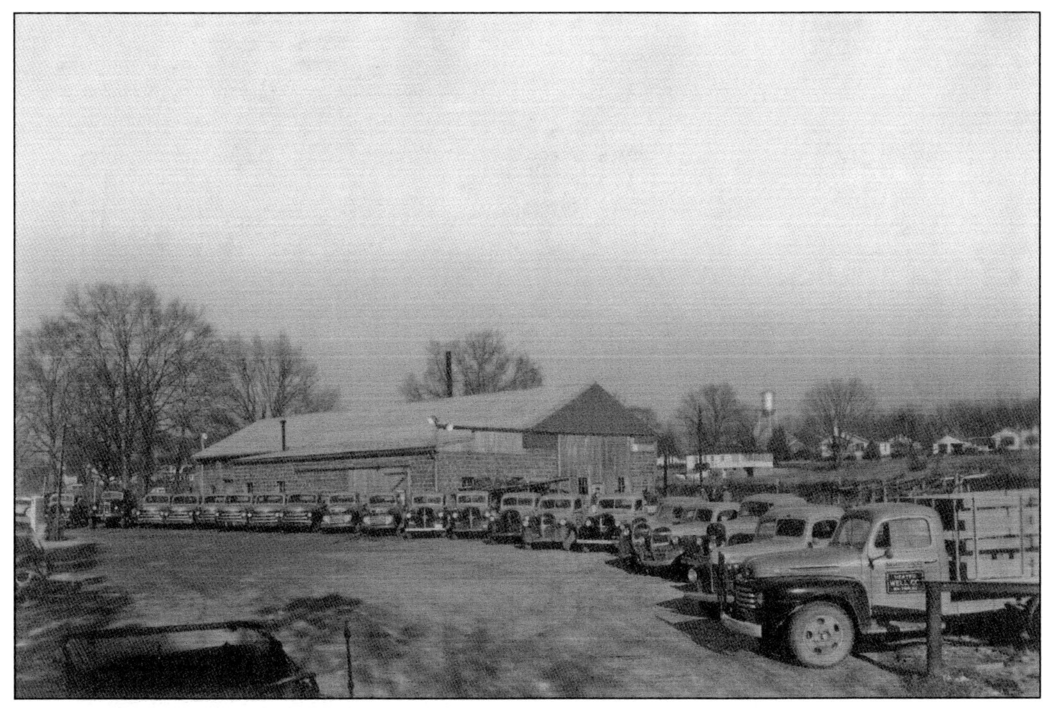

Heater Well Company, 1940s. Russell Heater's father was a well driller from West Virginia. In 1918, Russell served in World War I, and in 1920, he was a 24-year-old salesman living in Cary. Shortly after 1930, he opened Heater Well Company, and he was doing quite well in the 1940s. In 1945, Russell began developing Veteran Hills subdivision, with home sites intended for returning soldiers. In the 1950s, he developed Russell Hills. Due to this growth and increasing annexation, Cary's population more than doubled during the 1950s—from about 1,500 to 3,300 in 1960. Russell is on the left in the photograph below; longtime employee Herman Edwards is on the right. (Above, courtesy of Robert Heater; below, courtesy of Stanley Lorren.)

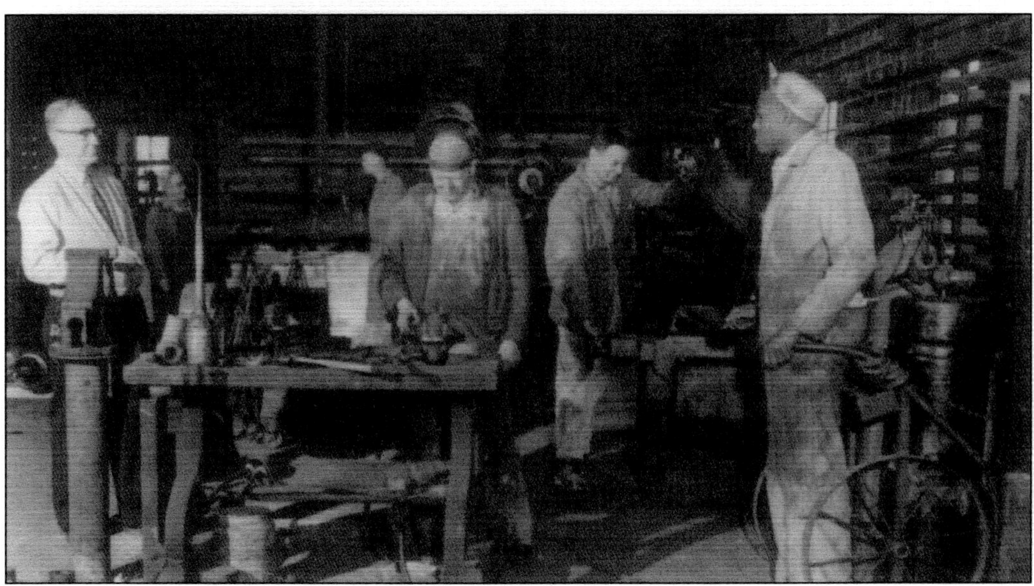

Three

Family Fun and Social Events

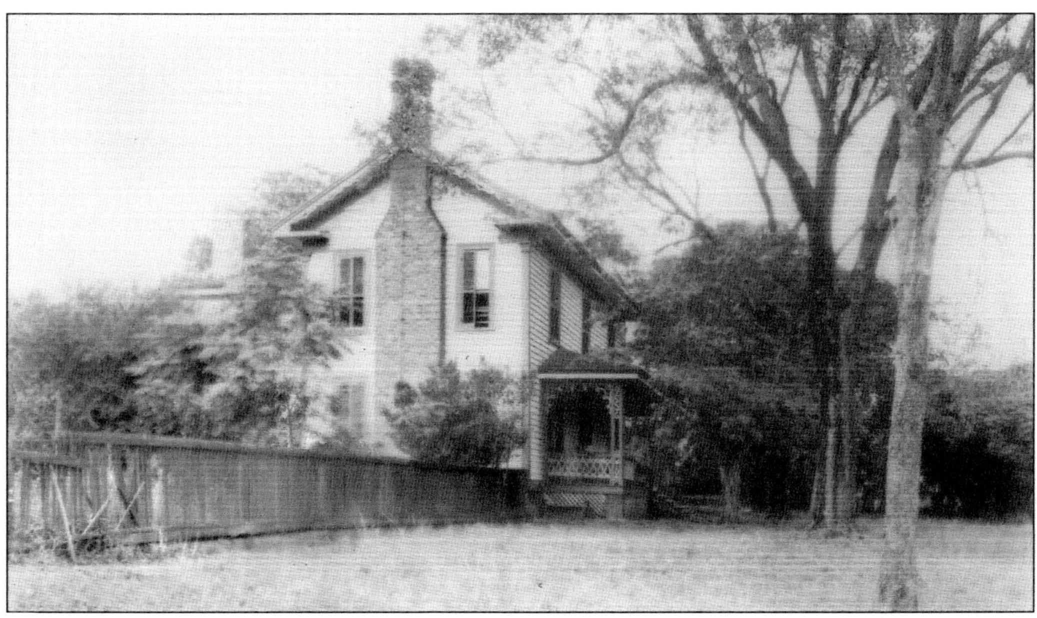

Walter Hines Page Birthplace. Walter Hines Page, the eldest son of Frank Page, was born and raised in this home, which was once the location of Bradford's Ordinary. Walter Hines Page was a journalist and diplomat. In 1871, he entered Trinity College in North Carolina—now Duke University. Two years later, he transferred to Randolph-Macon College in Ashland, Virginia. There he met Thomas Randolph Price, who aroused in Page a love of England and English literature. Page was a humorous and sociable man with many friends; these included Woodrow Wilson, whom he supported for the presidency. Wilson eventually repaid his friendship by offering Page the post of ambassador to Great Britain, which he gladly accepted in 1913. (Courtesy of the North Carolina Office of Archives and History.)

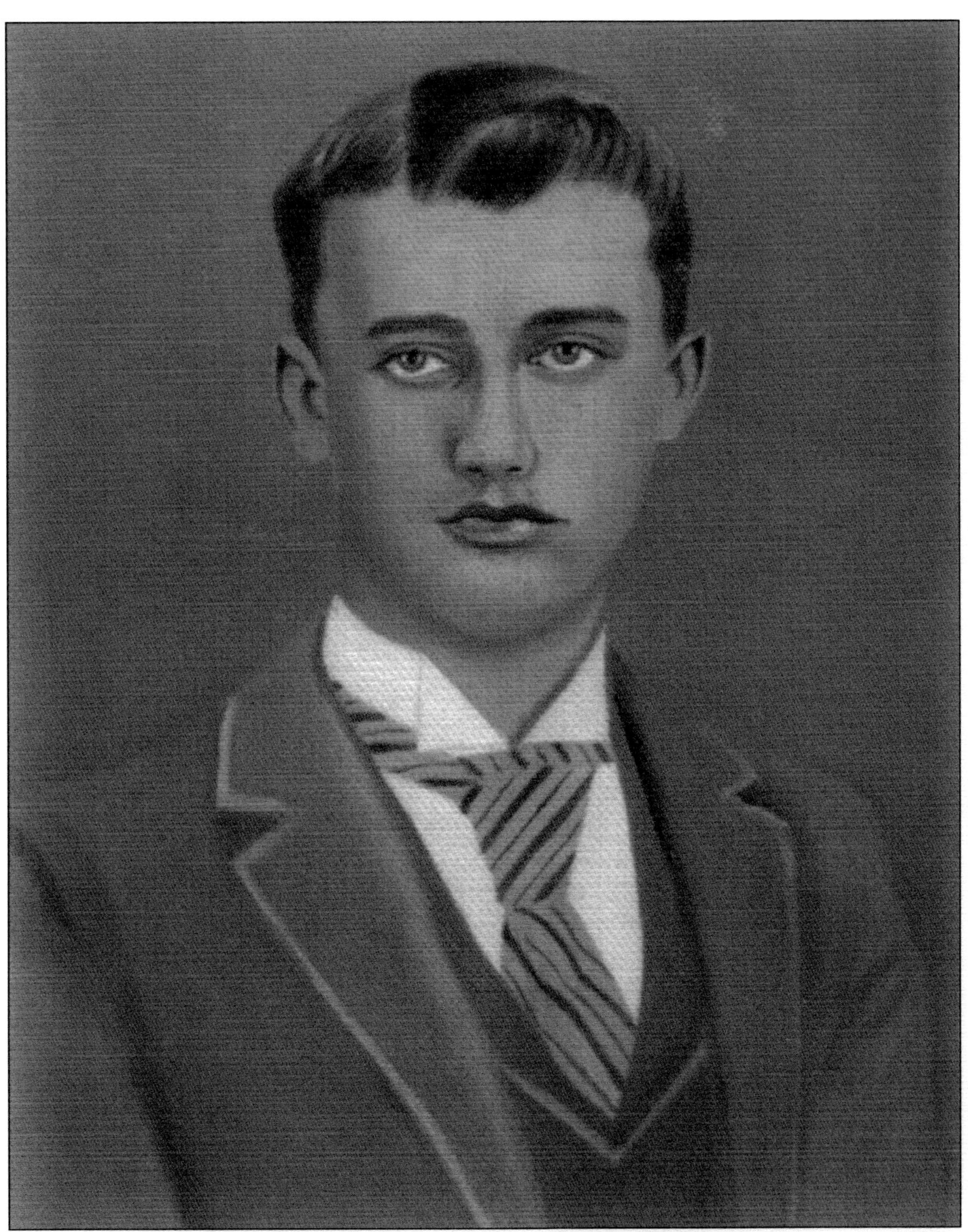

THOMAS FERDINAND WILKINSON. Thomas was born on October 19, 1868, in Amelia, Virginia, to C. P. and Virginia Caldwell Wilkinson. Thomas married a 22-year-old North Carolina woman named Mary Moye in 1898. In 1900, Thomas and Mary, along with their son, Thomas Jr., lived with Mary's parents, Alfred and Venia Moye, in Cary. According to the census, Thomas was working as a bookkeeper at a lumber mill. Wilkinson was a native Virginian, but in 1902, he became Cary's mayor. The 1920 Federal Census shows him as a superintendent at one of the lumber mills. By 1930, he owned his own garage in town. He was retired when he died in Cary at the age of 72. (Courtesy of Mary Ann Rood.)

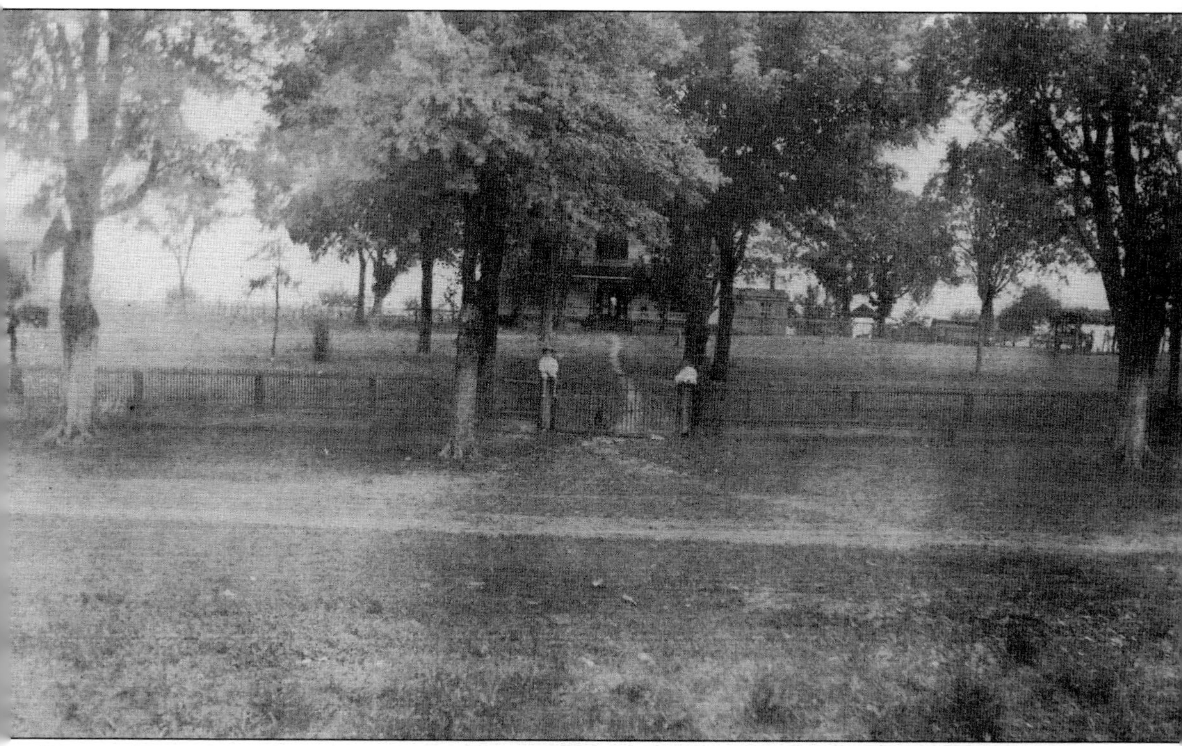

Thomas Ferdinand Wilkinson Home around 1910. Around 1906, Wilkinson remarried. In 1910, he was still listed as a bookkeeper in Cary, but he had purchased the old Frank Page residence. His second wife was 25-year-old Mary Sturgeon-Wilkinson, who was from Pennsylvania. Mary's sisters, Ann "Nannie," Elizabeth, and Amelia, lived with them on the farm. The little boy on the left is Thomas Ferdinand Wilkinson Jr., and the little girl is one of their two daughters, Ann or Elizabeth. (Courtesy of Mary Ann Rood.)

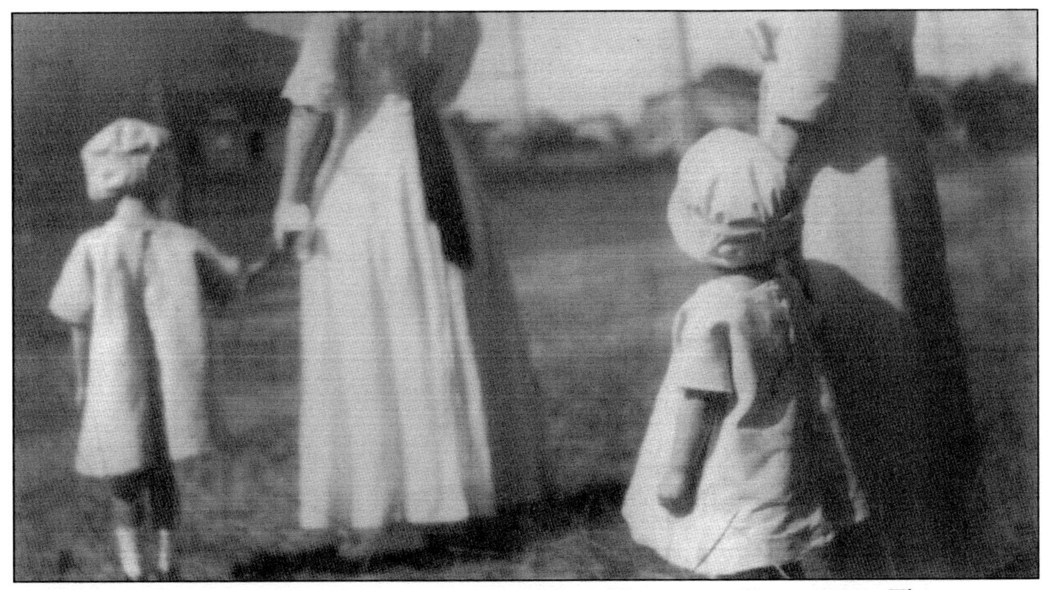

VICTORIAN GALS, 1910S. This photograph shows the Wilkinson girls with their aunt and mother in their Victorian whites. From left to right are Ann Wilkinson, Ann "Nannie" Sturgeon, Elizabeth Wilkinson, and Mary Wilkinson. (Courtesy of Mary Ann Rood.)

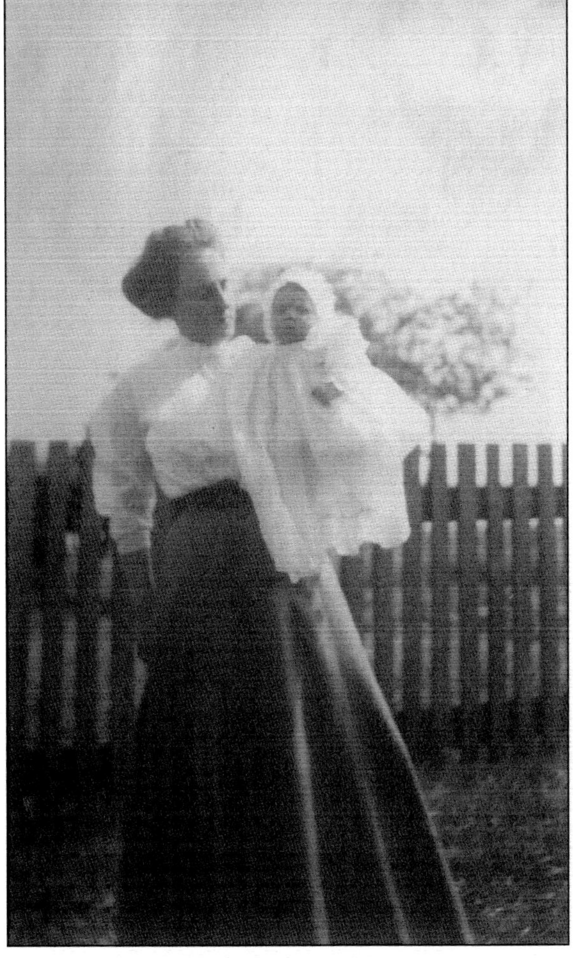

AUNT NANNIE AND ELIZABETH AROUND 1910. Elizabeth was just a baby when her aunt Nannie held her. Nannie was born in Pennsylvania on April 25, 1878, to Eugene and Ann Lee Young Sturgeon. Nannie married electrician Alfred C. Maynard on December 6, 1916, and was a registered nurse. She passed away on July 16, 1967, at the age of 89. (Courtesy of Mary Ann Rood.)

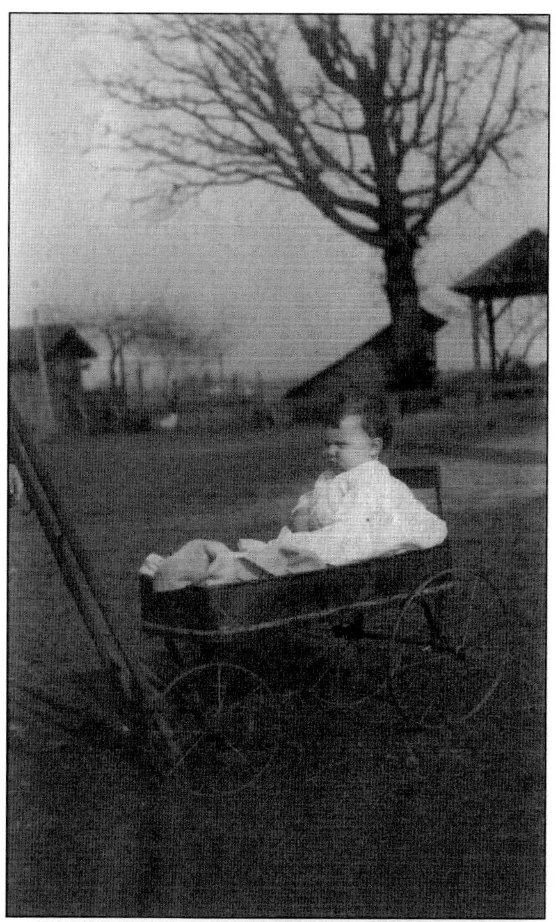

Baby Elizabeth Wilkinson, 1910s. Elizabeth was born on March 1, 1909, in Cary. She married Hood Waldo Rood, and she passed away at the age of 50 on October 17, 1959. (Courtesy of Mary Ann Rood.)

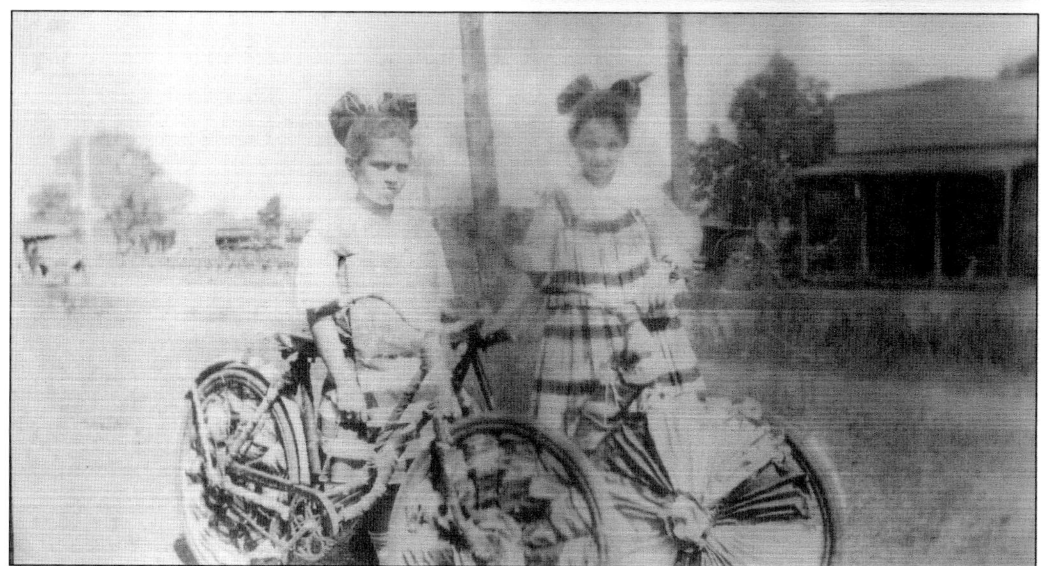

Cary Cyclists around 1919. Elizabeth (left) and Ann Wilkinson decorated their bicycles and rode in a Cary parade in their pretty dresses and bows. (Courtesy of Mary Ann Rood.)

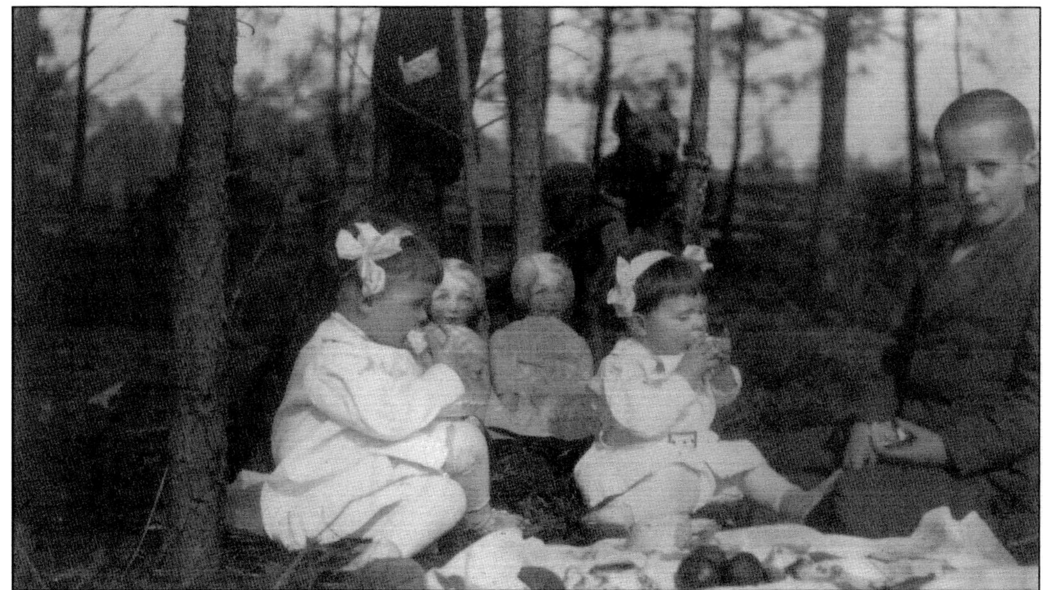

The Picnic, around 1912. The Wilkinson children enjoy a picnic. Pictured from left to right are Ann Wilkinson, dolls Peggy and Polly, Bill the dog, Elizabeth Wilkinson, and Thomas Ferdinand Wilkinson Jr. (Courtesy of Mary Ann Rood.)

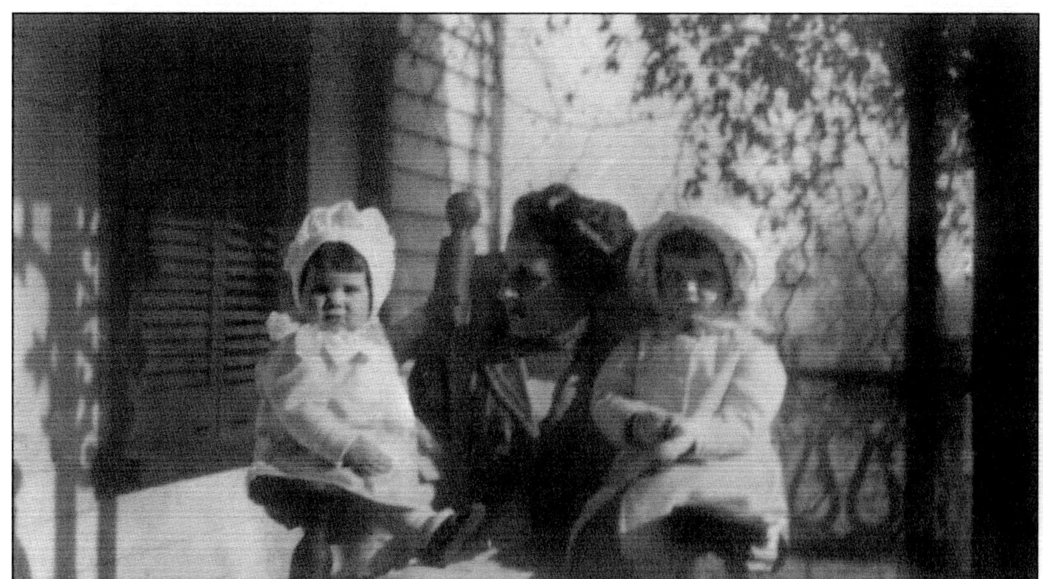

Nannie and the Girls, 1910s. Aunt Nannie Sturgeon lived at the Wilkinson home across from the railroad tracks and next to the Walker Hotel. She is spending time with her niece Ann, who is on her left, and her niece Elizabeth, who is on her right. (Courtesy of Mary Ann Rood.)

LUNCH ON THE PORCH, 1910S. Pictured here from left to right are Thomas Ferdinand Wilkinson Jr., Ann Wilkinson, and Elizabeth Wilkinson as they enjoy a meal on their front porch. (Courtesy of Mary Ann Rood.)

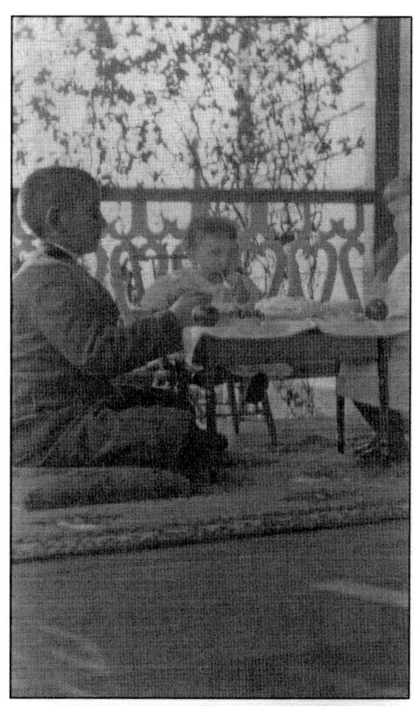

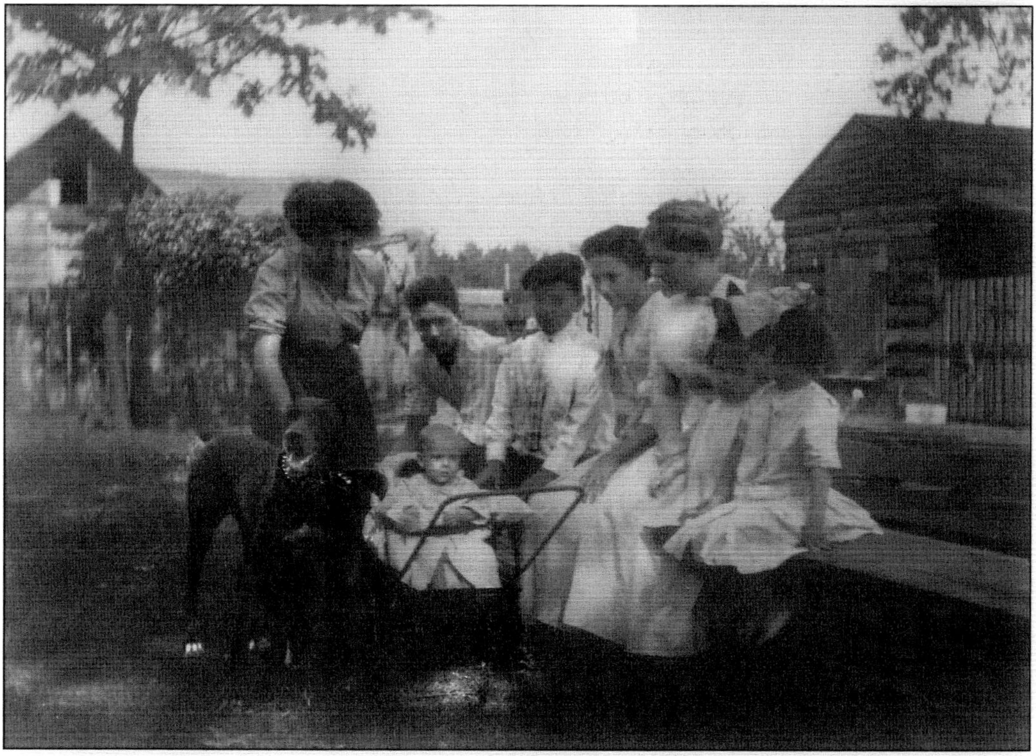

BILL THE DOG, 1910S. The Wilkinson family loved their dog Bill, and he was often photographed with them. This picture was taken behind the Wilkinson home. From left to right are Nannie Sturgeon, unidentified, Thomas Wilkinson Jr., two unidentified, Elizabeth Wilkinson, and Ann Wilkinson. (Courtesy of Mary Ann Rood.)

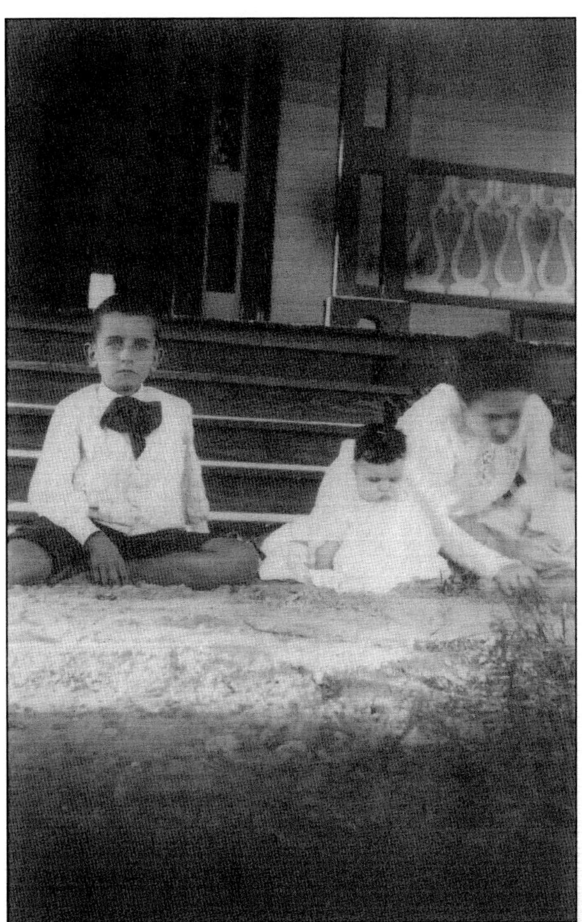

Playing in the Front Yard, 1910s. This photograph was taken in front of the Wilkinson home. It appears that Thomas Wilkinson Jr., baby Elizabeth, and Aunt Nannie Sturgeon are enjoying playing in the dirt. (Courtesy of Mary Ann Rood.)

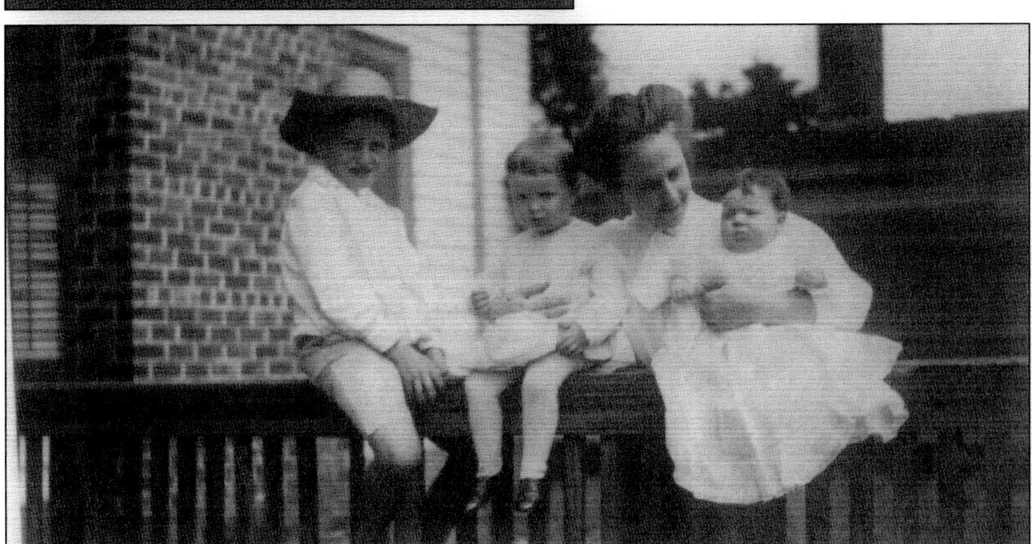

Just Hanging Around, 1910s. It is not know where this photograph was taken in Cary, but Thomas Wilkinson Jr., Ann Wilkinson, Nannie Sturgeon, and Elizabeth Wilkinson are enjoying themselves. (Courtesy of Mary Ann Rood.)

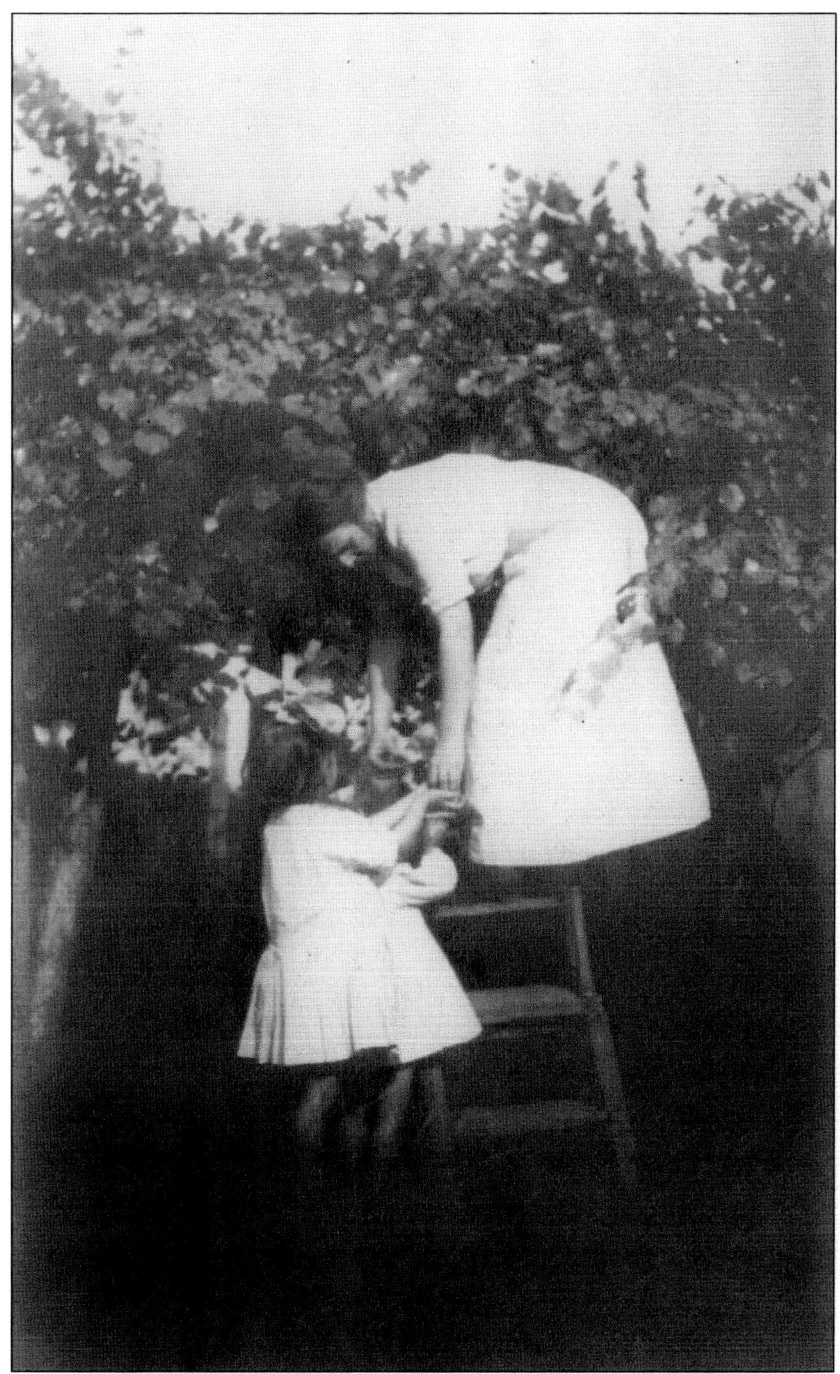

Harvesting Grapes, 1910s. Ann Wilkinson, Elizabeth Wilkinson, and Nannie Sturgeon are harvesting grapes at the Wilkinson farm. Muscadine grapes were used for making jams and jellies as well as wine and other tasty treats. Muscadine is a broad category of grape that includes many varieties of both bronze and black grapes. Scuppernong is one of the oldest and most popular varieties, so the name is used to refer to any bronze variety of muscadine (Courtesy of Mary Ann Rood.)

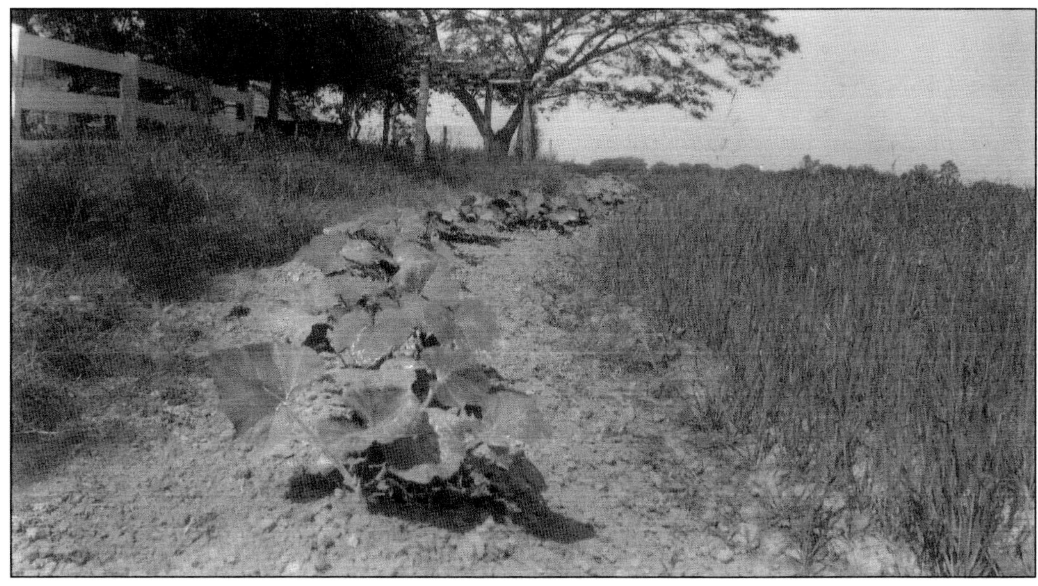

Nannie's First Planting and Harvest, 1930s. Ann "Nannie" Sturgeon Maynard first planted gourds in Cary in the mid-1930s. She and her husband had left North Carolina, and from 1920 through 1930, they resided in Fairfield, Virginia. Nannie returned, and she and her sister Mary did their first planting. With the success of one packet of seeds, the Sturgeon sisters formed the Gourd Village Garden Club, which later became the North Carolina Gourd Society. Nannie and Mary, along with Mary's daughters Ann and Elizabeth, were founding members of the society. (Both, courtesy of Mary Ann Rood.)

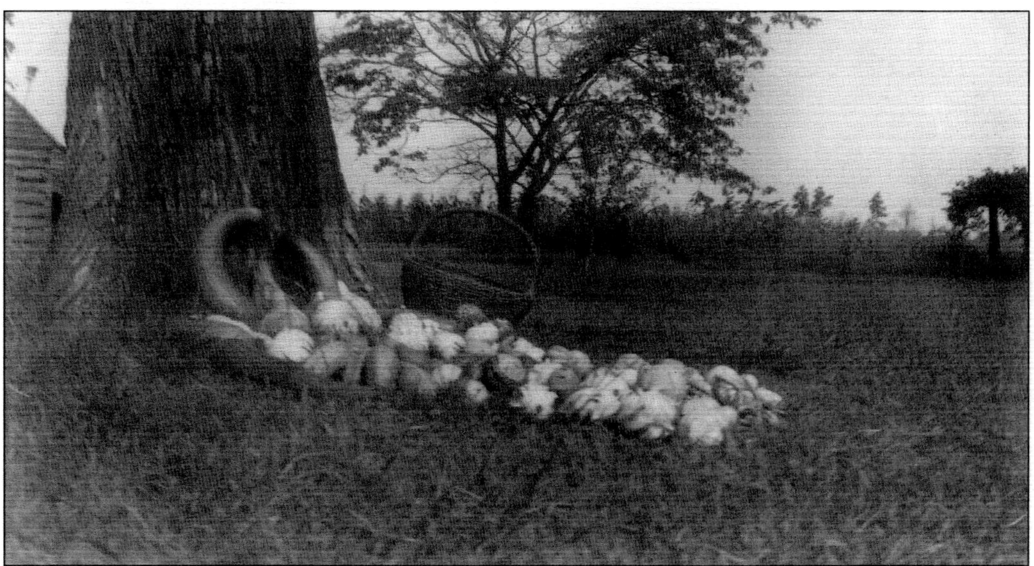

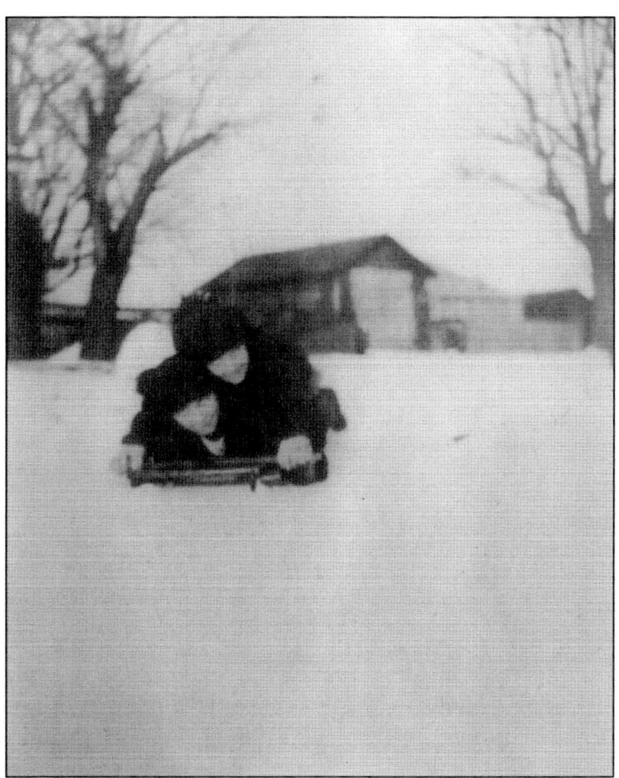

1920s Snow Storm. Elizabeth and Ann Wilkinson enjoy an unusual snowstorm in Cary. The sisters are having fun sledding down the sloping hills at the Wilkinson family home. Note the giant snowball in the background. Ann, who was born August 15, 1907, eventually married Graham McLean and moved to Lumberton, North Carolina. She passed away at the age of 61 in 1969. (Both, courtesy of Mary Ann Rood.)

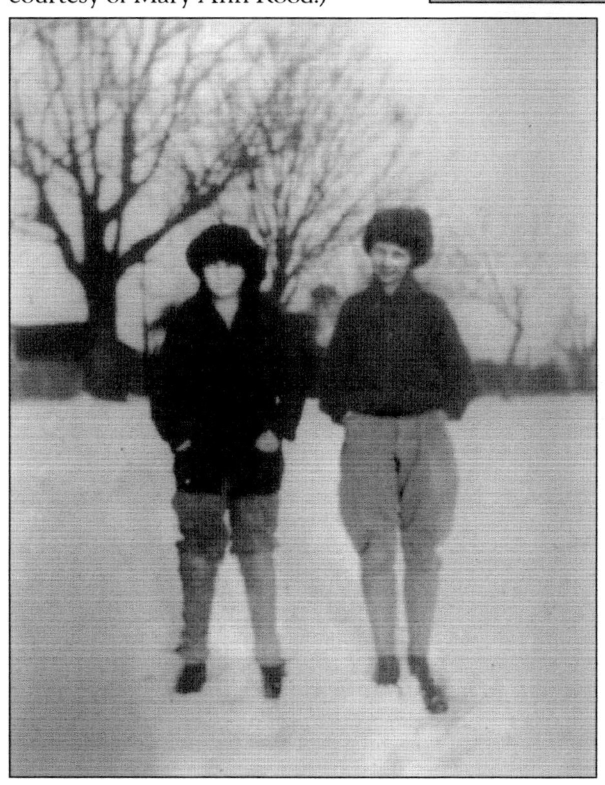

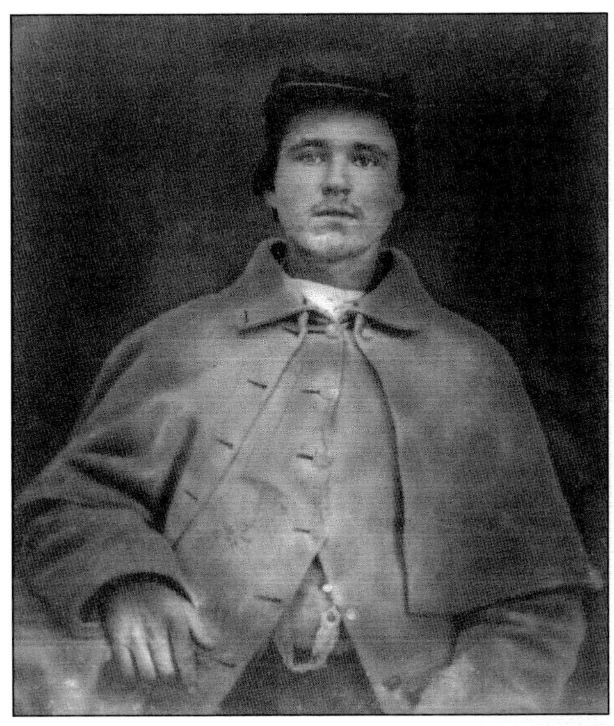

Samuel P. Waldo. Samuel Pierce Waldo was born in Hamilton, North Carolina, on March 15, 1845. After serving in the Civil War, Samuel received a degree in medicine from Washington University in Baltimore, Maryland, in 1868. Upon graduation, he established a medical practice in Cary around the time when Cary was incorporated. He then married Alice Margarette Owen on December 31, 1868, in Oxford, North Carolina. They went on to have five children, Ernest Owen, Pierce, Nathaniel Roan, Alice Lillian, and Maggie. He practiced medicine until his untimely death at the age of 46 on August 21, 1891. (Both, courtesy of Mary Ann Rood.)

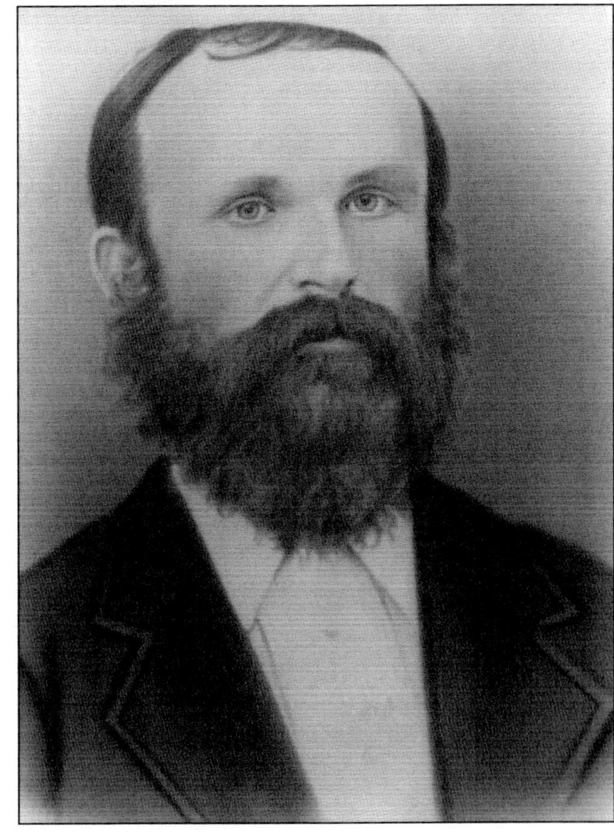

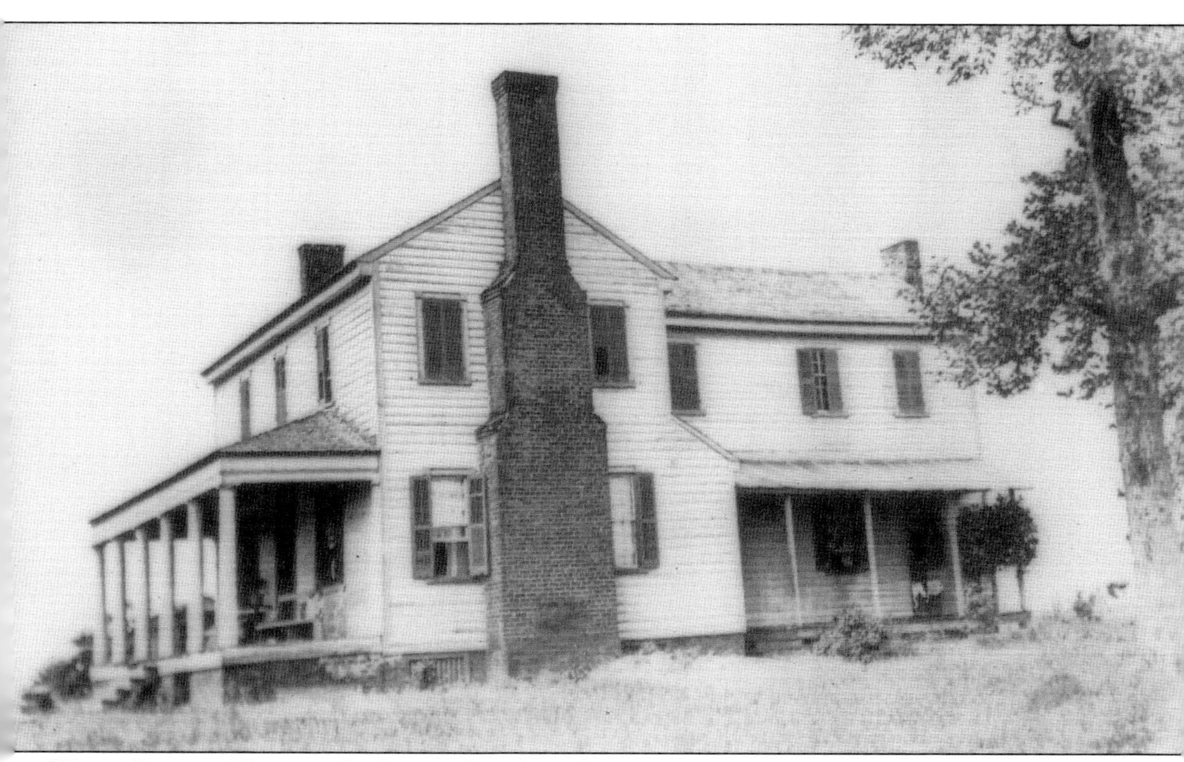

White Plains. This was the home of Nathaniel Jones, one of two men with that name who lived in Cary. Born in 1749, the Nathaniel Jones of White Plains opposed slavery and wanted to free his slaves, but North Carolina law prohibited him from doing so. He fathered 16 children by two wives and owned over 10,000 acres and a mill by 1811. The White Plains mansion stood near the present-day entrance to Greenwood Acres until it was demolished in the 1950s. In 1815, Jones died at the age of 66 from a "sore throat." He is buried in White Plains Cemetery, which is about one-quarter mile south of Cary Senior High School. (Courtesy of the North Carolina Office of Archives and History.)

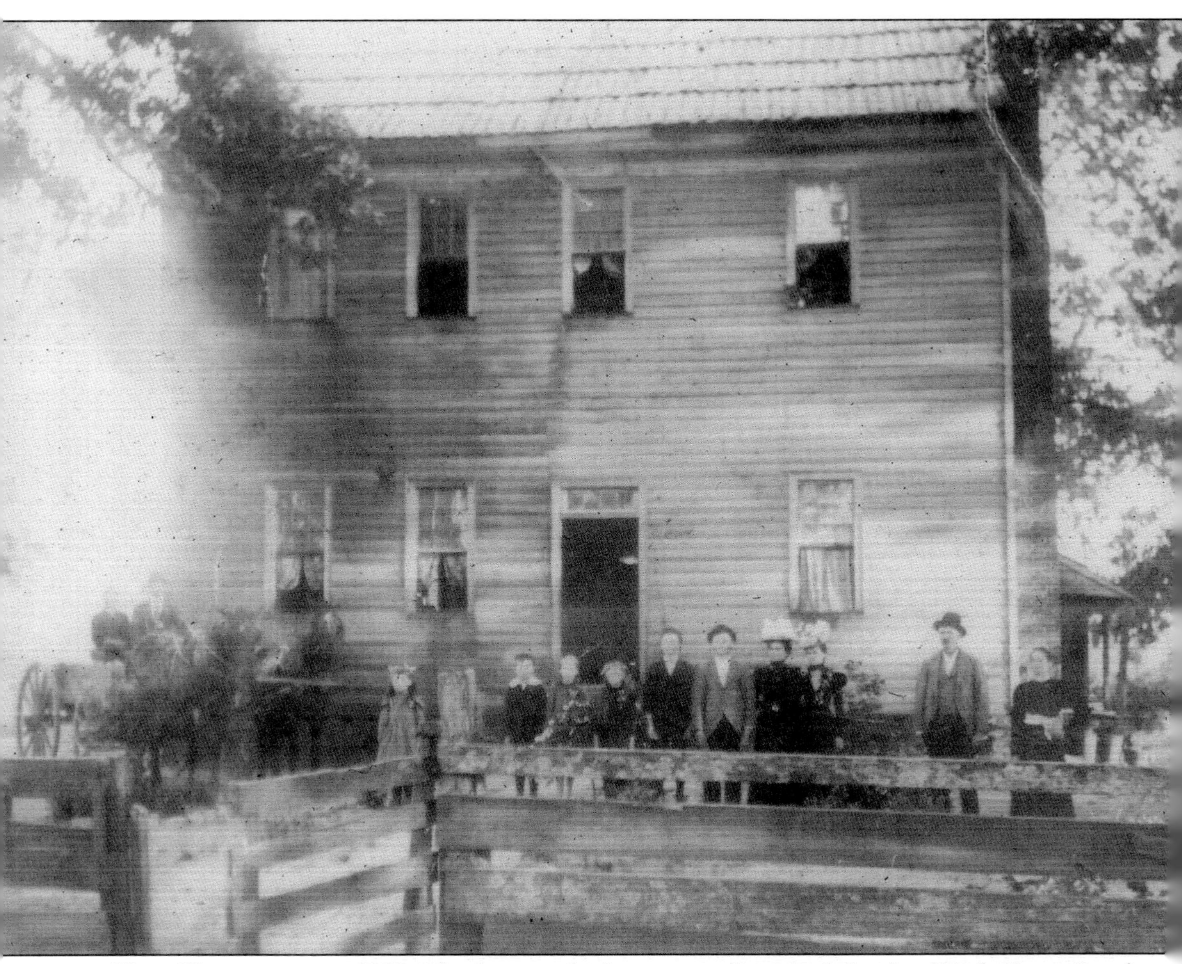

HIGH HOUSE AROUND 1897. This house, which once stood on the left side of High House Road, was built around the late 1700s. Fanning Jones was the owner, but he left Cary for Tennessee in 1822. It is believed the house was called the high house because it sat on a hill and was a tall, two-story structure with high ceilings. Some even said the house was haunted and had treasure buried around it. Farmer Nathaniel G. Williams bought the home, and it is believed he and his family are in this photograph. His sons Leander, Oscar, James, and Nathaniel; daughters Lovie, Allie, Sadie, and Mertie; and cousin Emma are in this picture. It is believed that Nathaniel and his wife, Minnie, are the couple on the far right. Only a small portion of the fireplace remains of this high house and a family cemetery. (Courtesy of the North Carolina Office of Archives and History.)

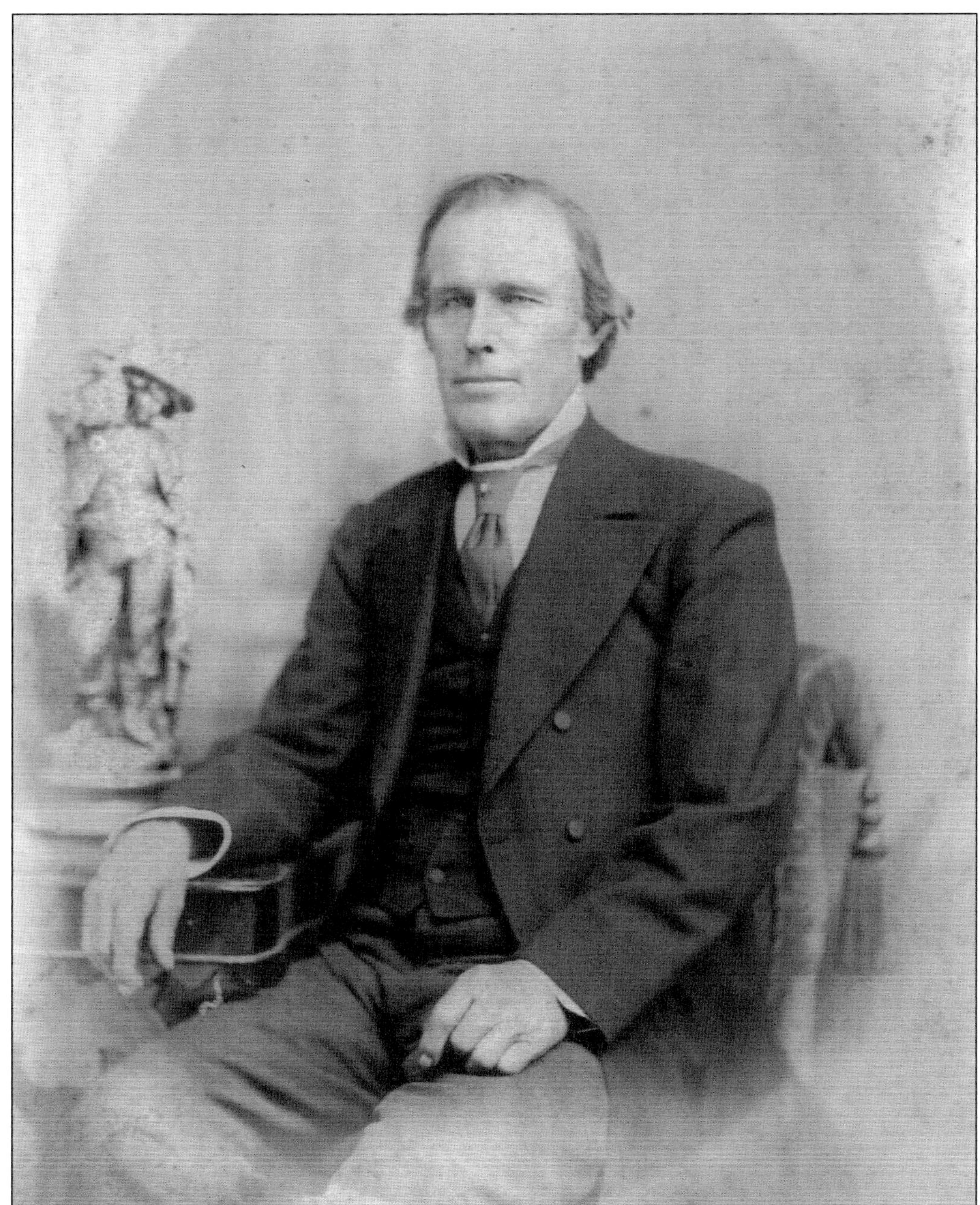

Carlos Yates, 1860s. Carlos Yates was born around 1816 and was a farmer and landowner in Wake County. Carlos, along with brothers Phares, Alvis, and Atlas, owned over 700 acres in Cary that were purchased by their father, Eli, around 1838. The property ran from a point south of Chatham Street and the present-day railroad tracks along Harrison Avenue past Maynard Road. Phares at one time owned and operated Yates Mill in Raleigh, and Atlas owned and operated a sawmill with Allison Frank Page in Cary. Carlos's farm was located near North Harrison Avenue and North Maynard Road. He married Mary Ann Marcom on December 17, 1839, in Chatham County. By 1870, they had moved to the Cary area, and they remained residents of Cary for the rest of their lives. (Courtesy of C.Y. Jordan.)

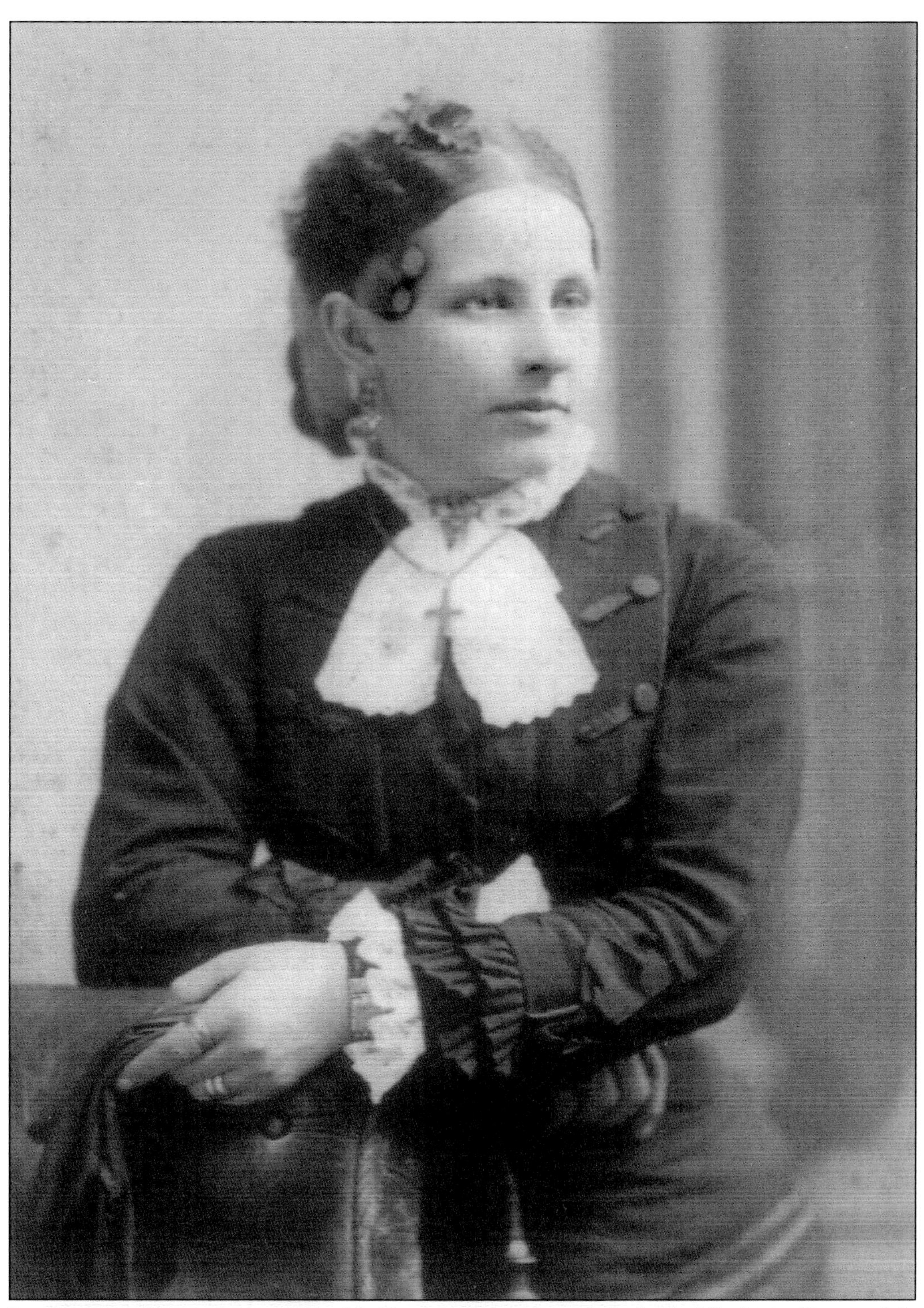

Ida Florence Yates, Late 1800s. Ida Yates was born the eighth child of Carlos in Cary on July 17, 1862. She married farmer James B. Jordan in 1882 and had nine children. She passed away on September 5, 1944, at the age of 82. (Courtesy of C. Y. Jordan.)

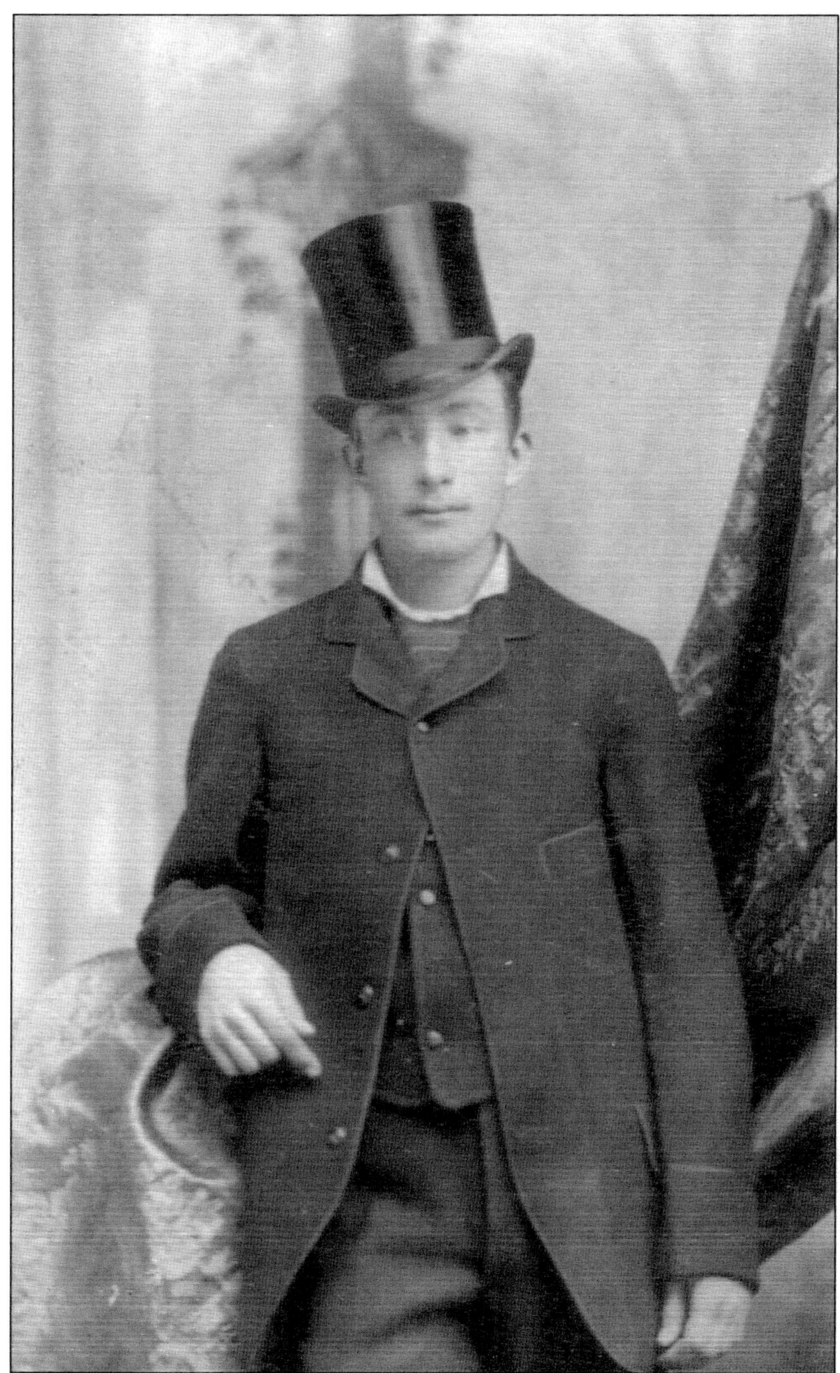

JAMES HENRY BELL JORDAN SR., 1880s. James B. Jordan was born on July 26, 1860, and was the husband of Ida Yates. James came to Cary in 1871 with his father, Henry B. Jordan, who served on the original Cary town council; his mother, Helen Crowder-Jordan; and his sister, Maggie Ida Jordan. In addition to being a farmer, James worked in the logging business and served for a number of years as a deputy U.S. marshal. He died in 1918 as a result of a gunshot wound suffered in the line of duty. (Courtesy of C. Y. Jordan.)

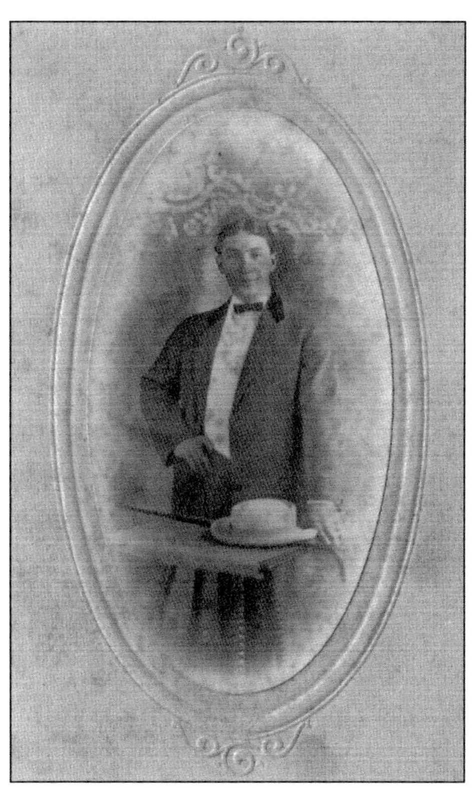

James B. Jordan Jr. around 1905. James B. Jordan Jr. was born in April 11, 1883, and was the eldest son of James B. Sr. and Ida. He died in October 18, 1918, at the age of 45. (Courtesy of C. Y. Jordan.)

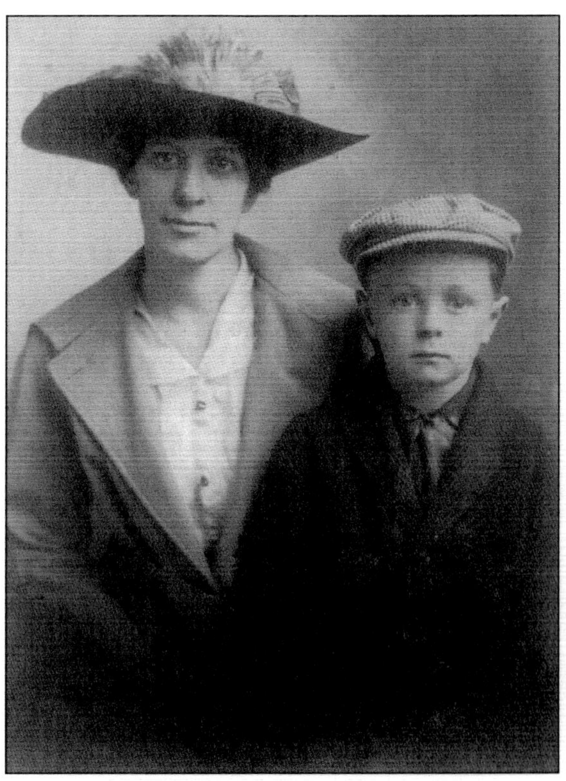

Mabel Lacy Jordan, 1900s. Not much is known about Mabel other than she was the wife of James B. Jordan Jr. She is pictured here with her nephew, Donald J Lacy. (Courtesy of C. Y. Jordan.)

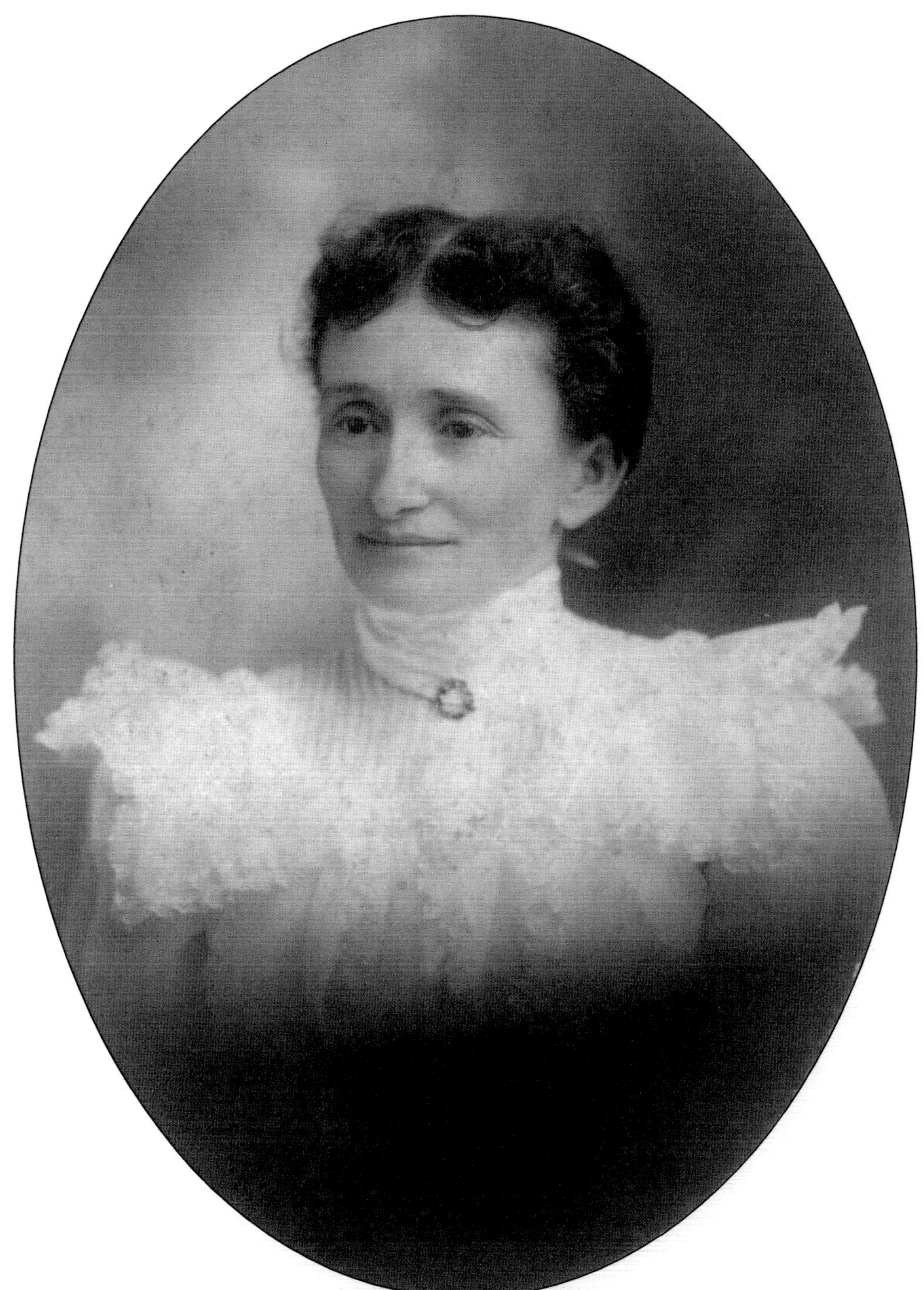

MAGGIE IDA JORDAN-ELLIS, 1900S. Maggie Ida Jordan was the daughter of Henry B. Jordan and the mother of schoolteacher Irma Ellis. By 1900, she was a widow and living in Wake Forest with her two daughters, Irma and Maud. In 1910, she and Irma moved back to Cary to live with Henry B Jordan at his home after the death of his wife, Helen Crowder Jordan. (Courtesy of C. Y. Jordan.)

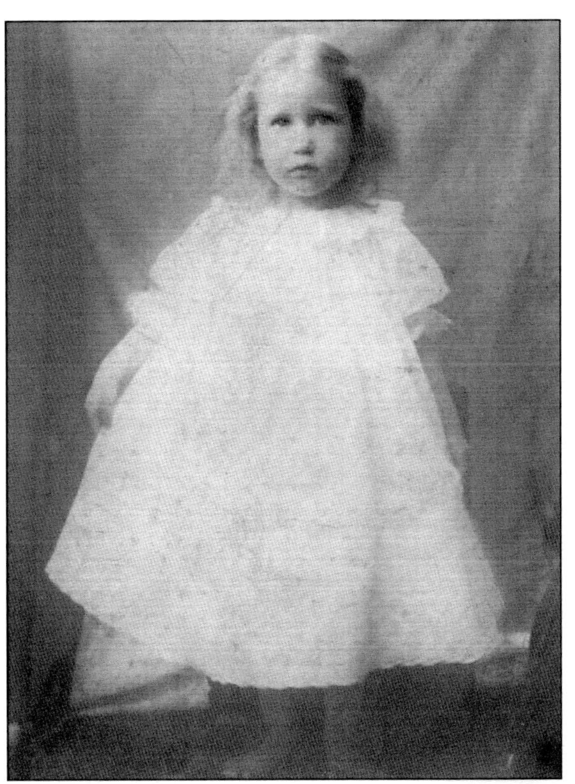

ANNIE MAY BEASLEY-JORDAN, 1900s. Annie Mae Beasley was born in Morrisville, North Carolina, on December 24, 1894. Annie came to Cary to attend school as a boarding student. She graduated around 1911. She married George H Jordan Sr., and they had four children: Marjorie, George H. Jr., James, and Carlos Y., also known as C. Y. (Courtesy of C. Y. Jordan.)

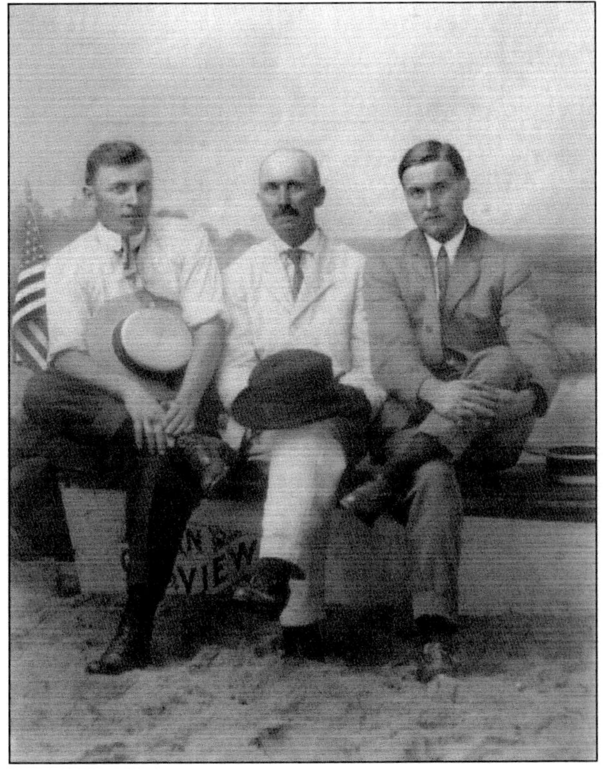

GEORGE H. JORDAN SR., 1920s. George Henry Jordan Sr. (center) was born on August 9, 1889. This photograph was taken with Ethel Holleman (left) and Alma Jordan (right). Anxious to work and be independent, young George quit school in 10th grade to work as a railroad brakeman. He worked in real estate and farming and was a merchant in a variety of businesses. He died on November 6, 1945, at the age of 56. (Courtesy of C. Y. Jordan.)

A Little Fun, 1910s. Carlos Y. Jordan was one of James B. Jordan and Ida Yates Jordan's sons. He was born in June 1892 in Cary. He is pictured here with a family friend, Alma Trader. The present-day C. Y. Jordan is named for both his uncle Carlos Yates Jordan and his great-grandfather Carlos Yates. (Courtesy of C.Y. Jordan.)

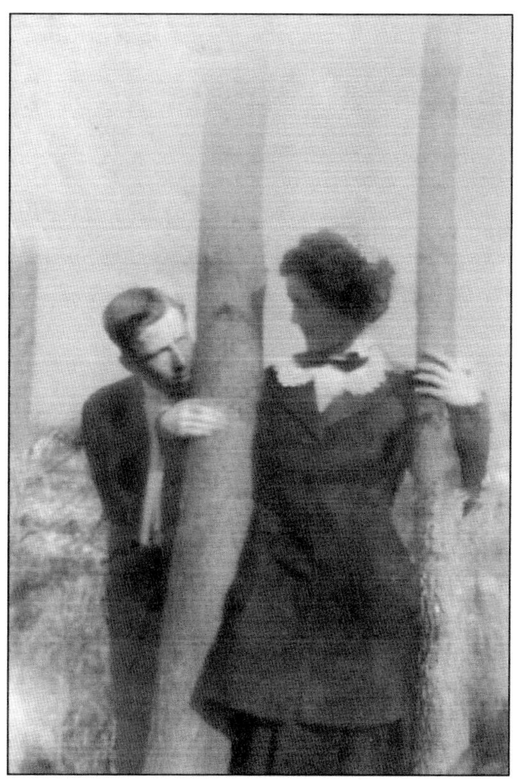

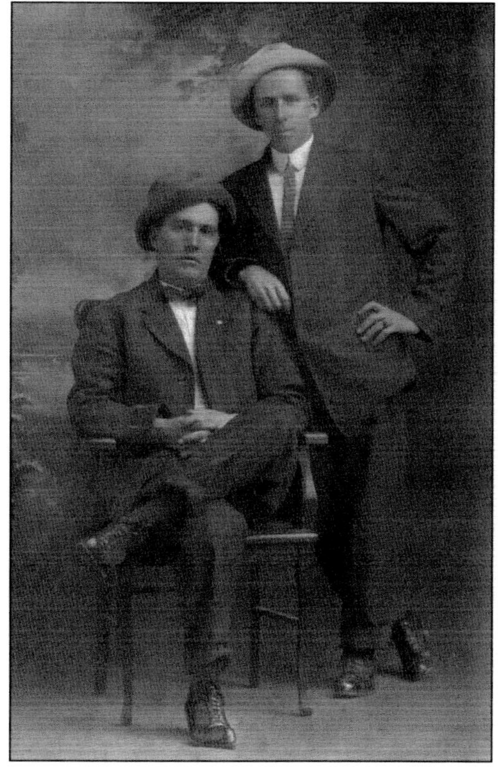

Friends in the 1910s. Carlos Y. Jordan poses with his seated brother-in-law, Dearing F. Stone, in their finest suits. Carlos was killed on September 21, 1912, at the age of 21 in a railroad accident that occurred between Garner and Clayton, North Carolina. (Courtesy of C. Y. Jordan.)

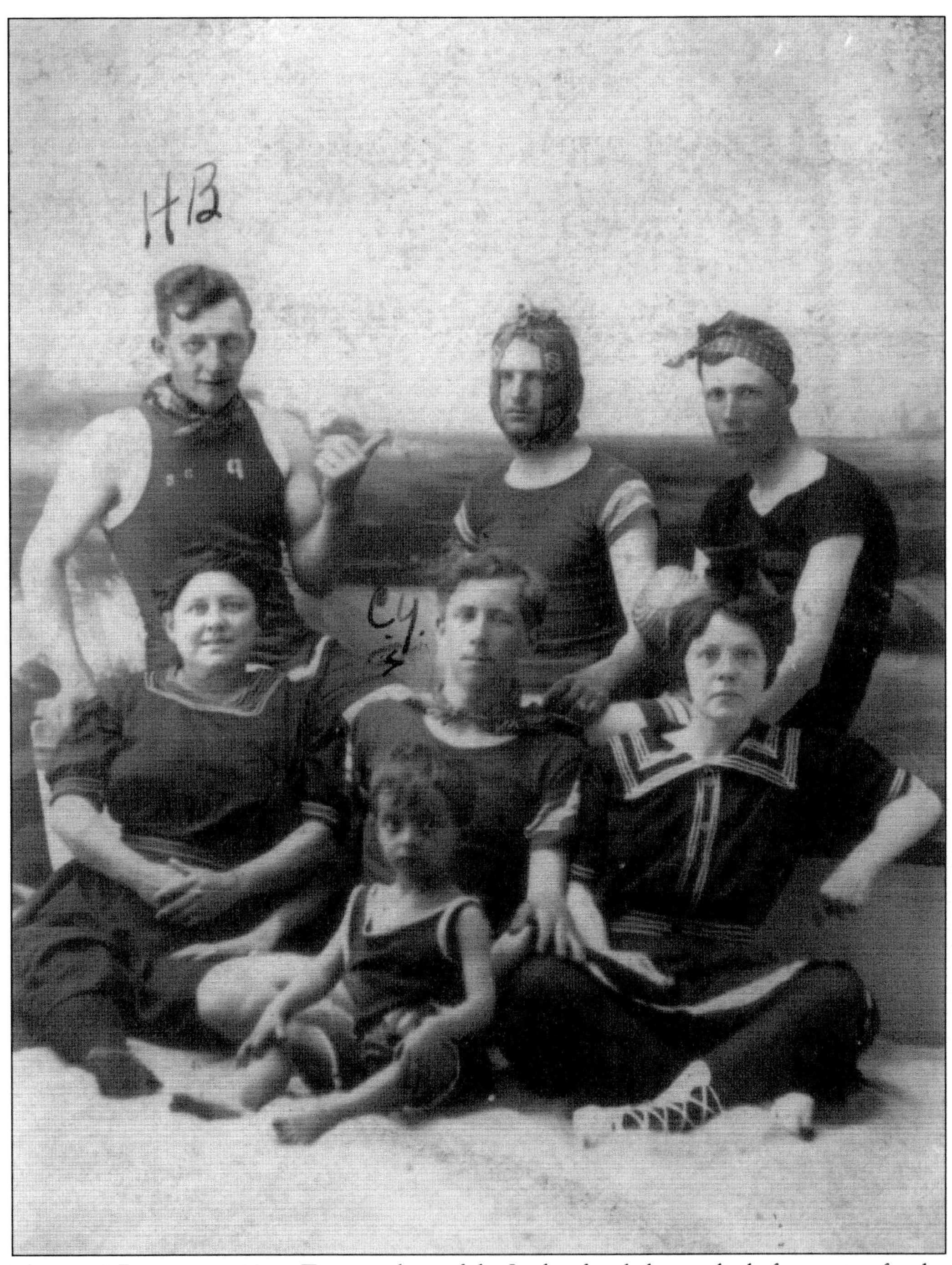

"SEASIDE" PORTRAIT, 1920S. Two members of the Jordan family have a little fun posing for the photograph in their bathing suits. The man at left in the second row is Hubert Jordan, and the man in the first row is Carlos Jordan. Hubert and Carlos Jordan were sons of James B. Jordan Sr. and Ida Jordan. Hubert was born on July 4, 1885. He married Lila Westbrook, and they had two children: Hubert B. Jr. and Bettie W. Jordan. Hubert B. Sr. passed away on March 12, 1925. (Courtesy of C. Y. Jordan.)

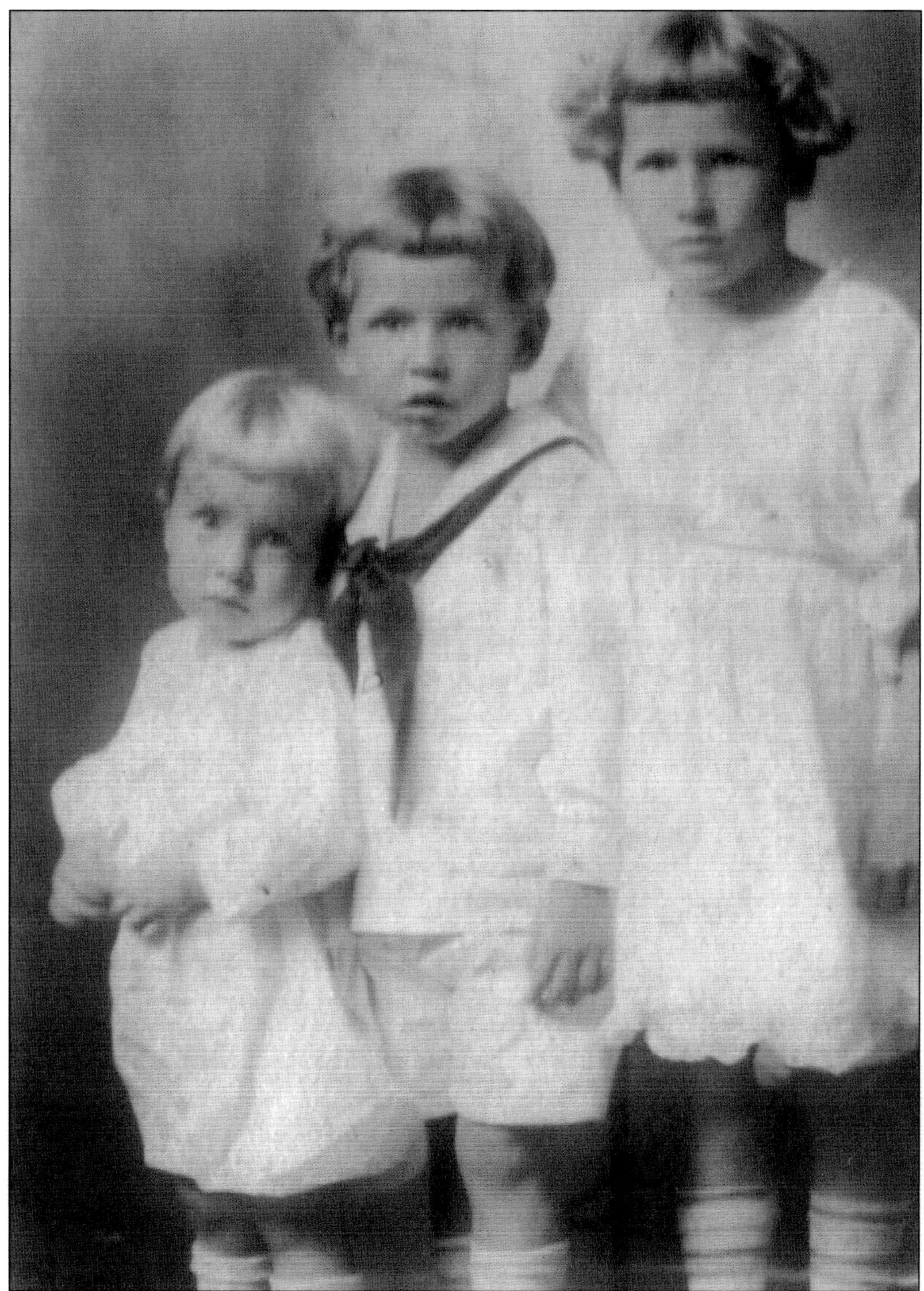

JORDAN GRANDCHILDREN, 1920S. Posing for a nice little family portrait are grandchildren of James and Ida Jordan. From left to right are James, George, and Marjorie Jordan. (Courtesy of C. Y. Jordan.)

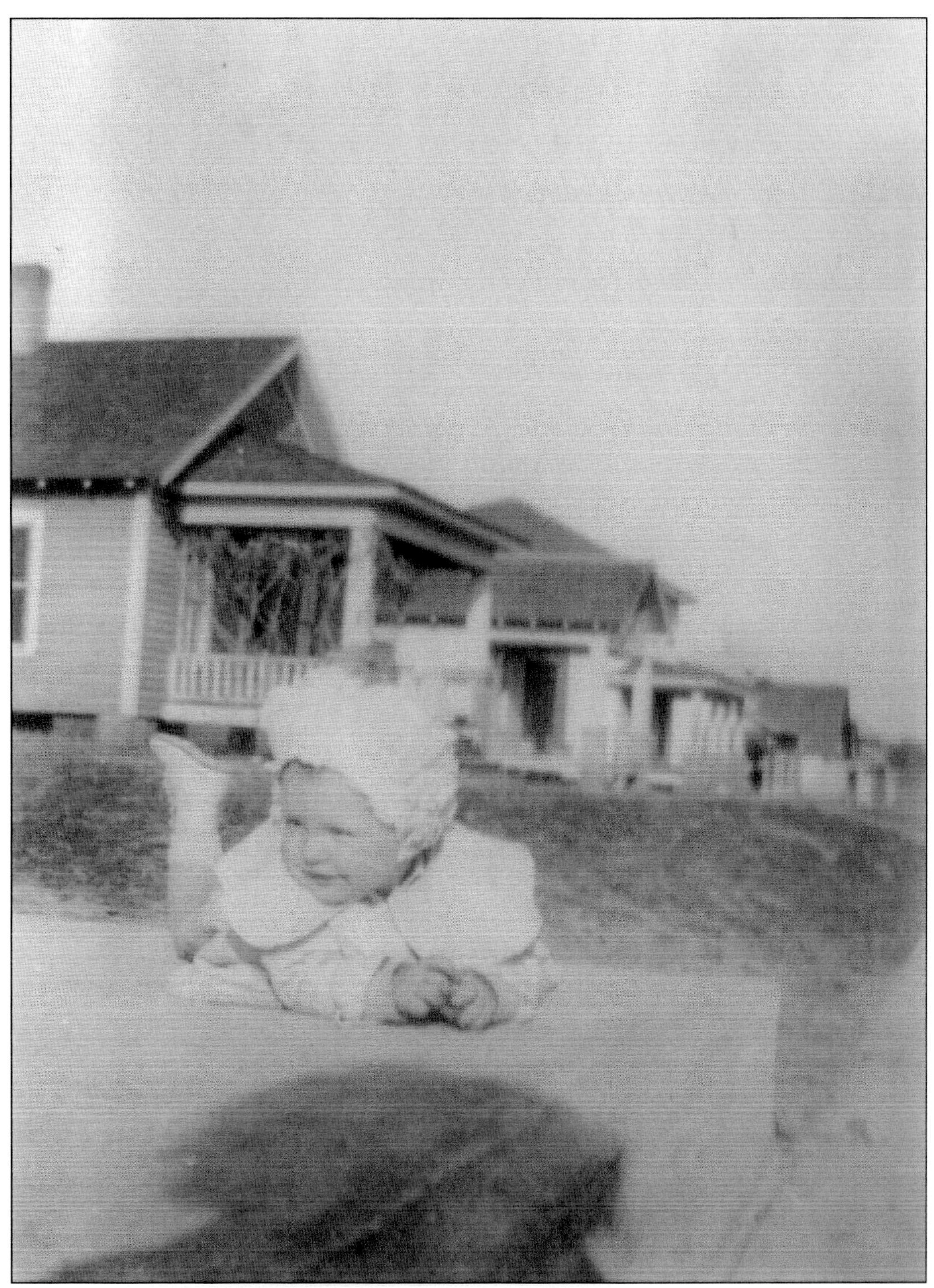

1920s View of East Chatham Street. This photograph of one of the Jordan babies is taken from the Jordan home on East Chatham Street. Cary's 1920 population was about 645. The village mayor, W. G. Crowder, passed away on September 28, 1921. In October 1921, W. H. Atkins was appointed to replace Crowder. (Courtesy of C. Y. Jordan.)

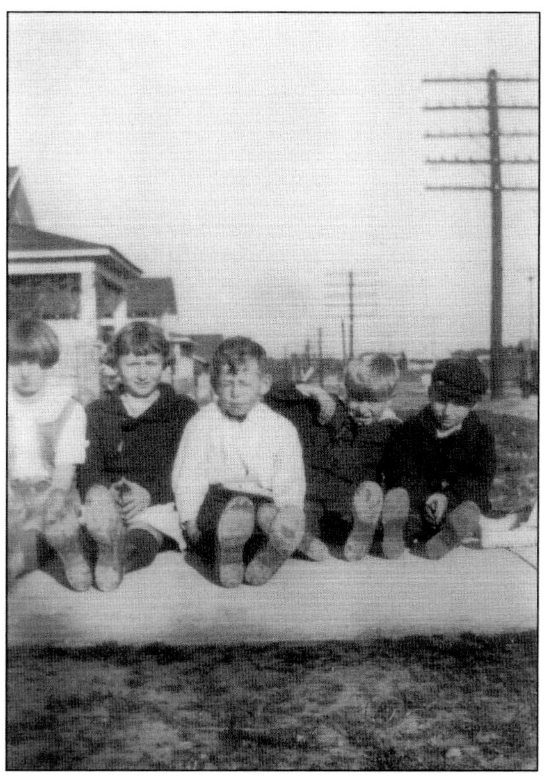

Jordans on Chatham Street, 1920s. Pictured here in the front of the Jordan family home are, from left to right, Dorothy Phillips, Marjorie Jordan, George H. Jordan Jr., James Jordan, and Hubert S. "Squeaky" Jordan. (Courtesy of C. Y. Jordan.)

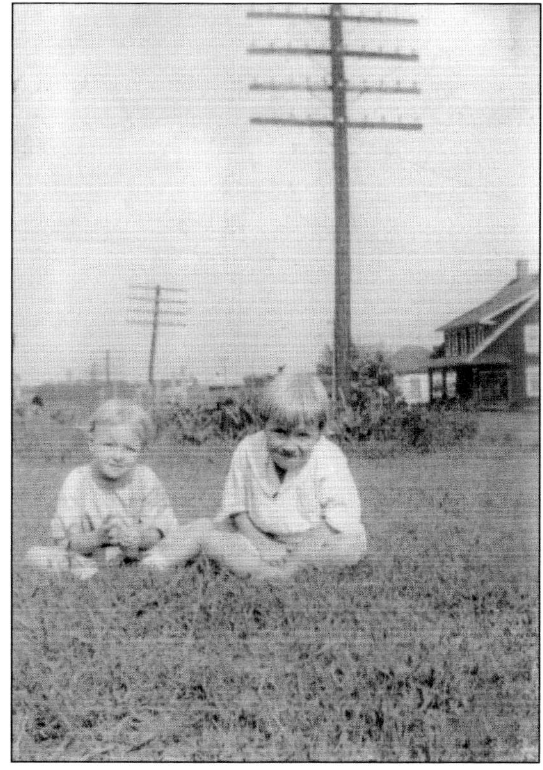

200 Block East Chatham Street, 1920s. This photograph shows that Cary was still very rural in the 1920s—but it had power lines. Pictured here are Bettie Jordan (left) and James Jordan. (Courtesy of C. Y. Jordan.)

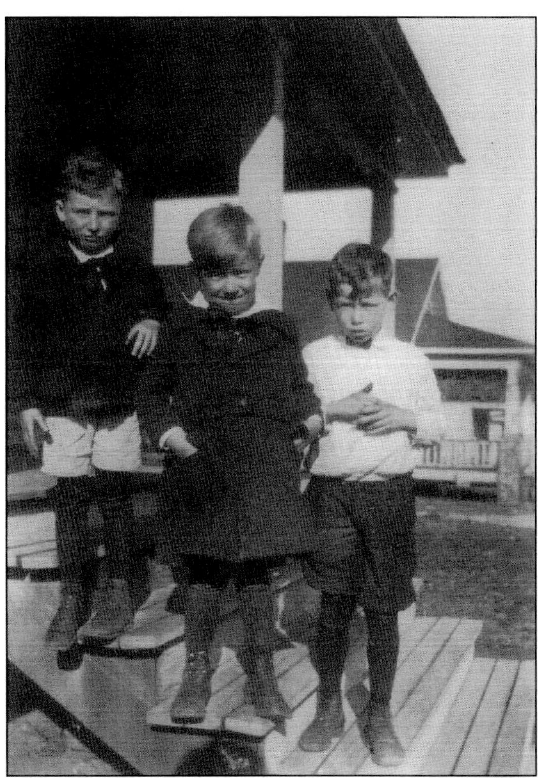

Jordan Cousins, 1920s. This photograph was taken on East Chatham Street and shows, from left to right, cousins Hubert Jr., James, and George Jr. (Courtesy of C. Y. Jordan.)

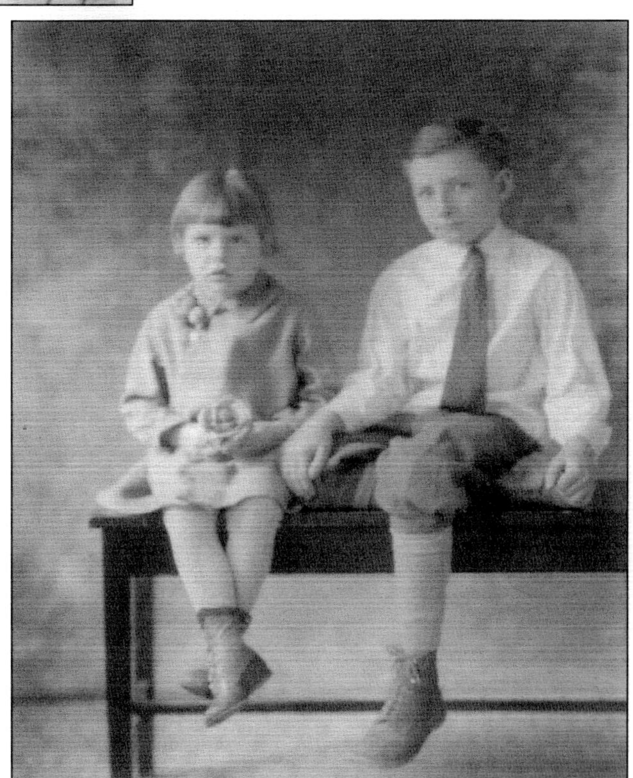

Betty and Squeaky, 1930s. Brother and sister pose for this professional portrait in the 1930s. Betty was born around 1924, five years after her brother, Hubert Jr. (Courtesy of C. Y. Jordan.)

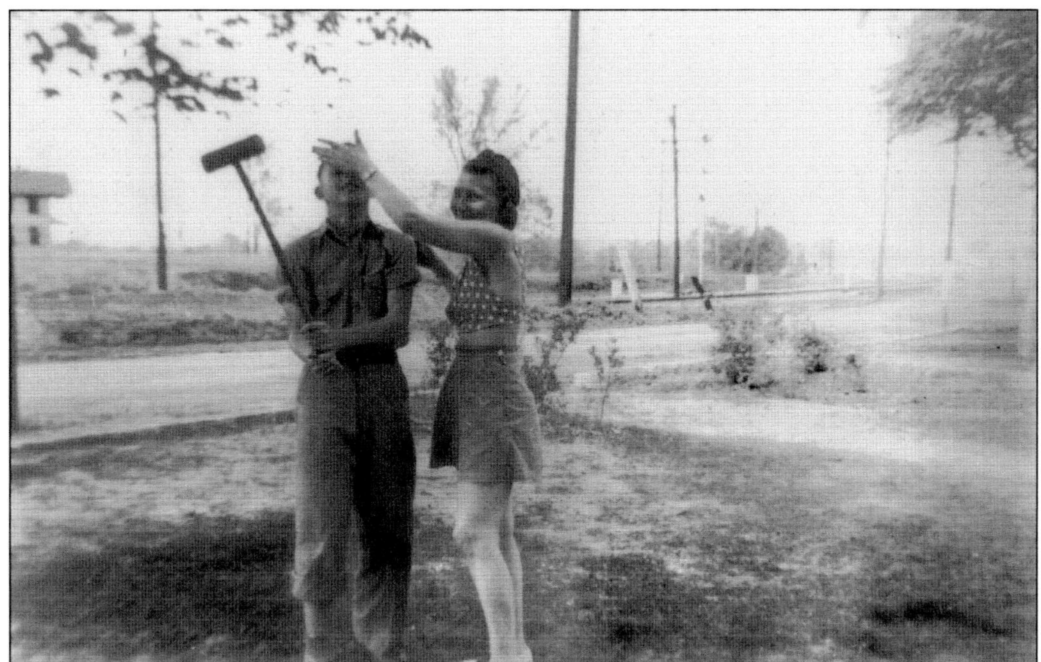

PLAYING CROQUET, 1940S. This fun photograph shows C. Y. Jordan, who was born in 1927, having fun with his aunt Lula Helen, whose nickname was "Doodie." Lula Helen was born on December 31, 1900, and in 1930, she was employed as a saleslady in a women's clothing store in downtown Raleigh. (Courtesy of C. Y. Jordan.)

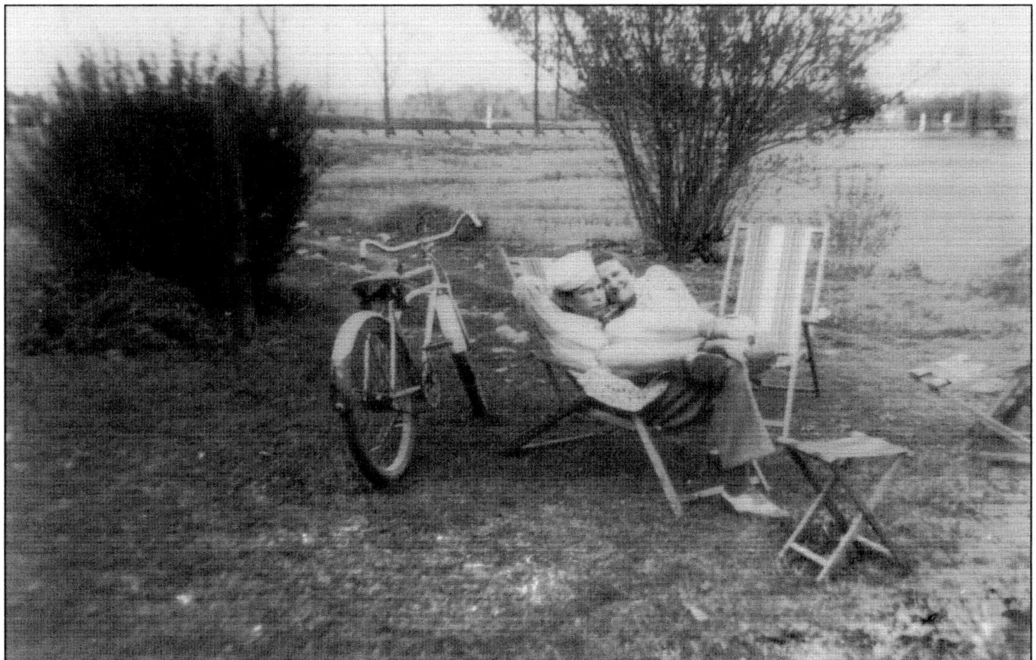

GEORGE H. JORDAN JR. AND LULA HELEN JORDAN, 1940S. George and his aunt Lula Helen pose together for a photograph in the backyard of the family home on Railroad Street, later renamed Cedar Street. (Courtesy of C. Y. Jordan.)

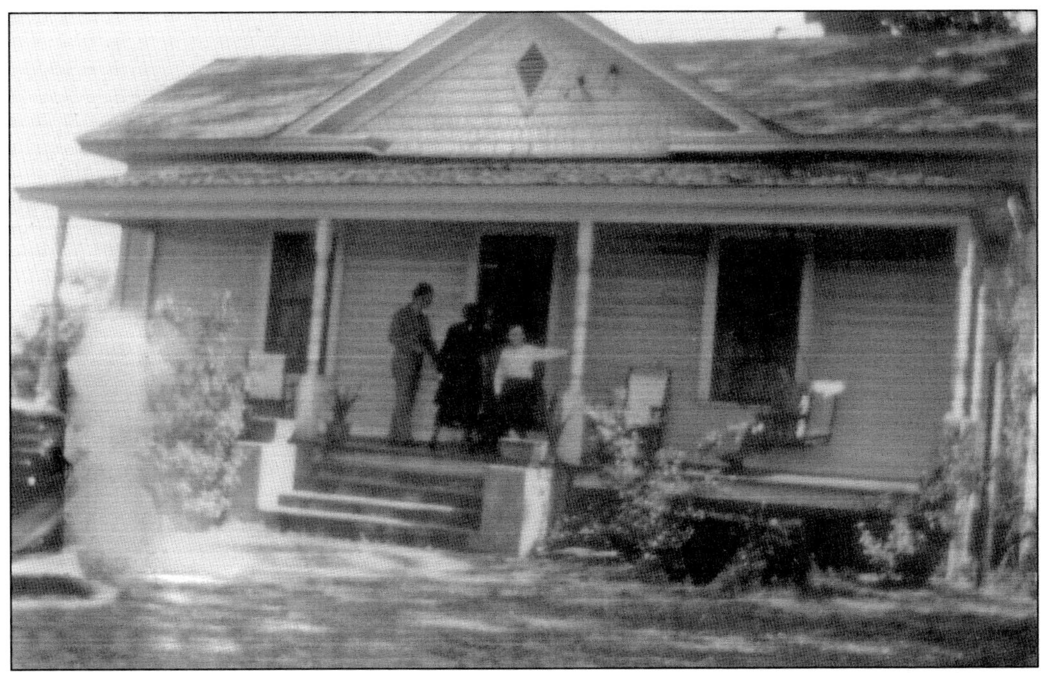

Ida Yates Jordan House, 1930s. Jordan family members pose for a picture on Railroad Street. C. Y. Jordan, George H. Jordan Sr.'s son, is the little boy in the white shirt. (Courtesy of C. Y. Jordan.)

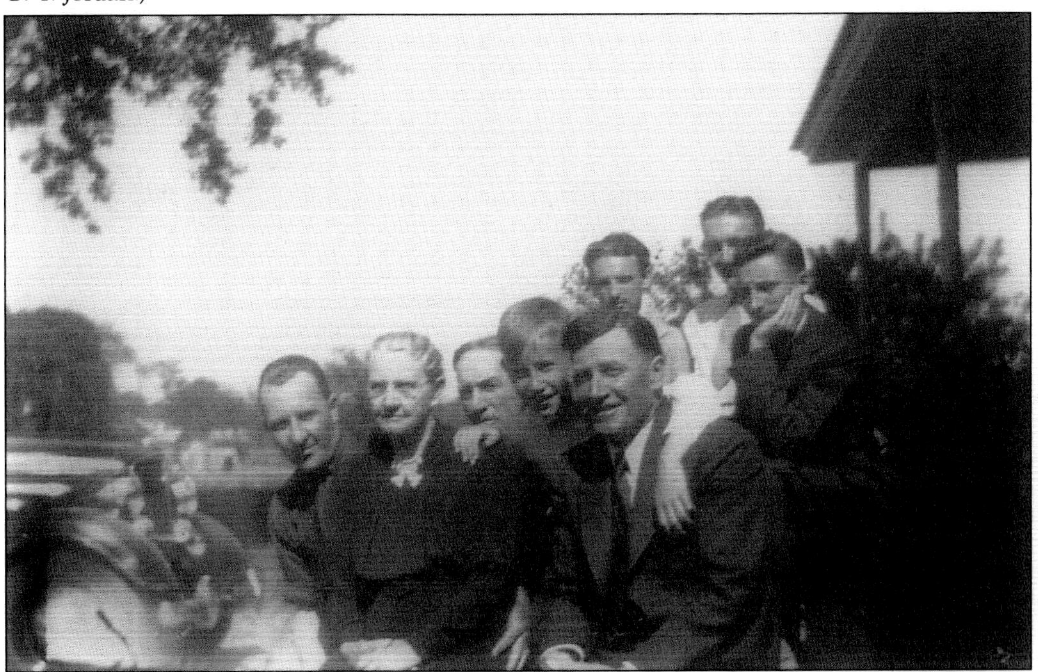

Ida Yates Jordan Family, 1930s. This photograph was taken at Ida Jordan's home, From left to right are (first row) son John Raymond, Ida, Dearing F. Stone (husband of Alma Jordan, Ida's daughter) grandson C. Y. Jordan, and son George H. Sr.; (second row) grandson-in-law Jack Martin and grandsons Francis Stone and Hubert B. Jordan Jr. (Courtesy of C. Y. Jordan.)

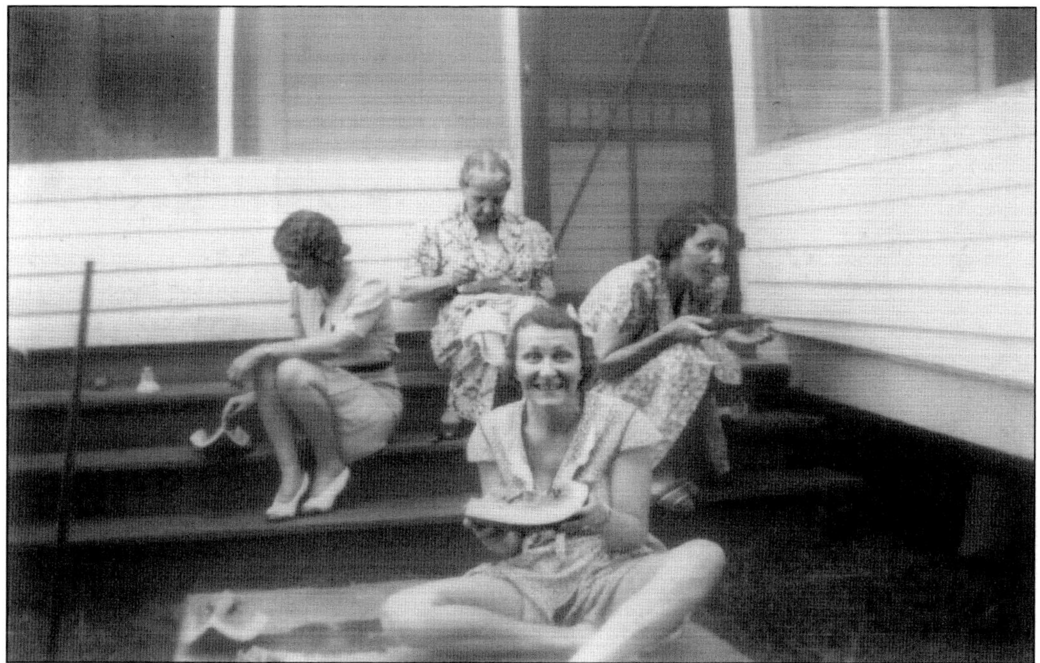

Summer Watermelon, 1930s. The Jordan gals enjoy some cool watermelon on a warm summer day in Cary. In front is Lula Helen. Pictured in the back, from left to right, are Betty Jordan, Ida "Granny" Jordan, and Lily Jordan. (Courtesy of C. Y. Jordan.)

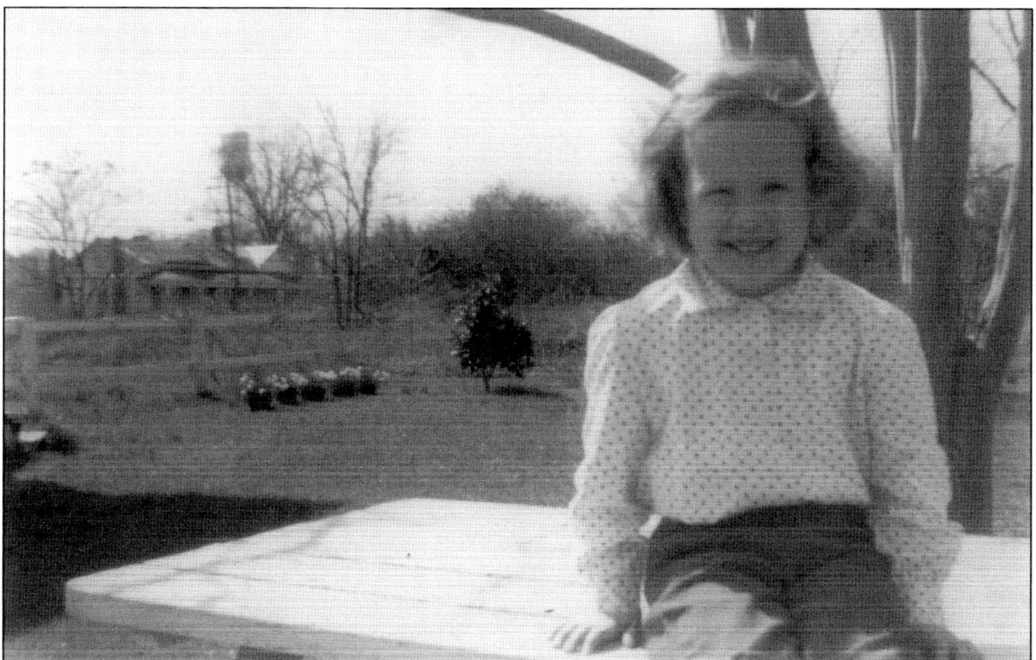

Carla Jordan around 1959. Carla is the daughter of C. Y. and Dollie Jordan and the granddaughter of George H. Jordan Sr. She poses here on a picnic table in the backyard of Lila Westbrook Jordan, her great aunt, looking south onto Chatham Street. Note in the background the Cary water tower, which has since been removed. (Courtesy of C. Y. Jordan and Carla Jordan Michaels.)

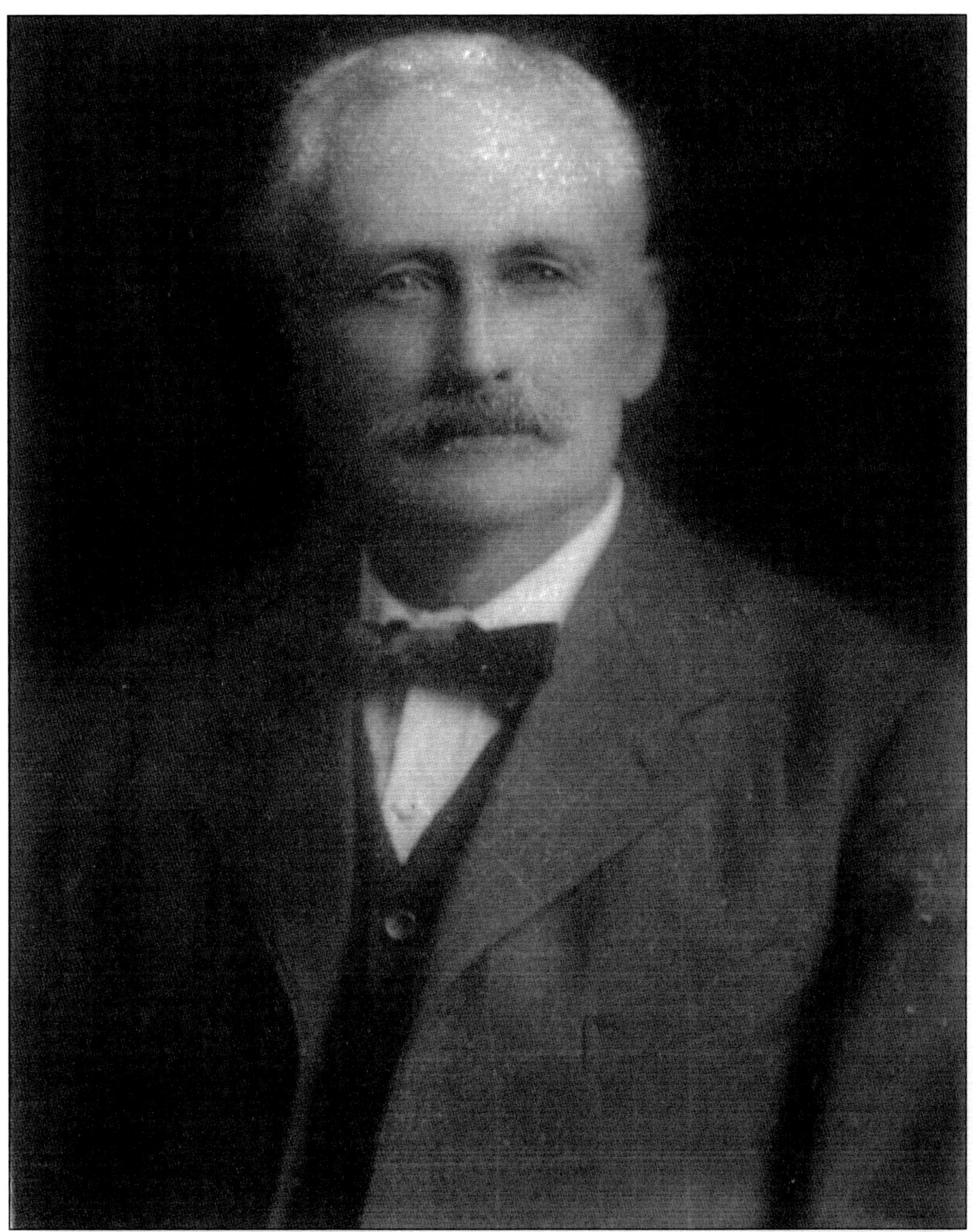

James Pickney Henry Adams. J. P. H. Adams was born on October 2, 1845, in Cary. In 1874, Adams was elected as the first church clerk of the Missionary Baptist Church of Cary. He married his second wife, Cora Reavis, on December 23, 1879. James had three children with his previous wife, Claude A., Hattie A, and Alpheus. He also had eight children with Cora: Lillian, Effie, Laurie, Cleo, Lucy, Gussie, Mabel, and Henry R. He was a farmer and held many jobs, but the one most residents disliked was that of U.S. deputy collector. When J. P. H. Adams came to their door, it was time to pay their taxes. James died on May 1, 1916. (Courtesy of Charlie Adams.)

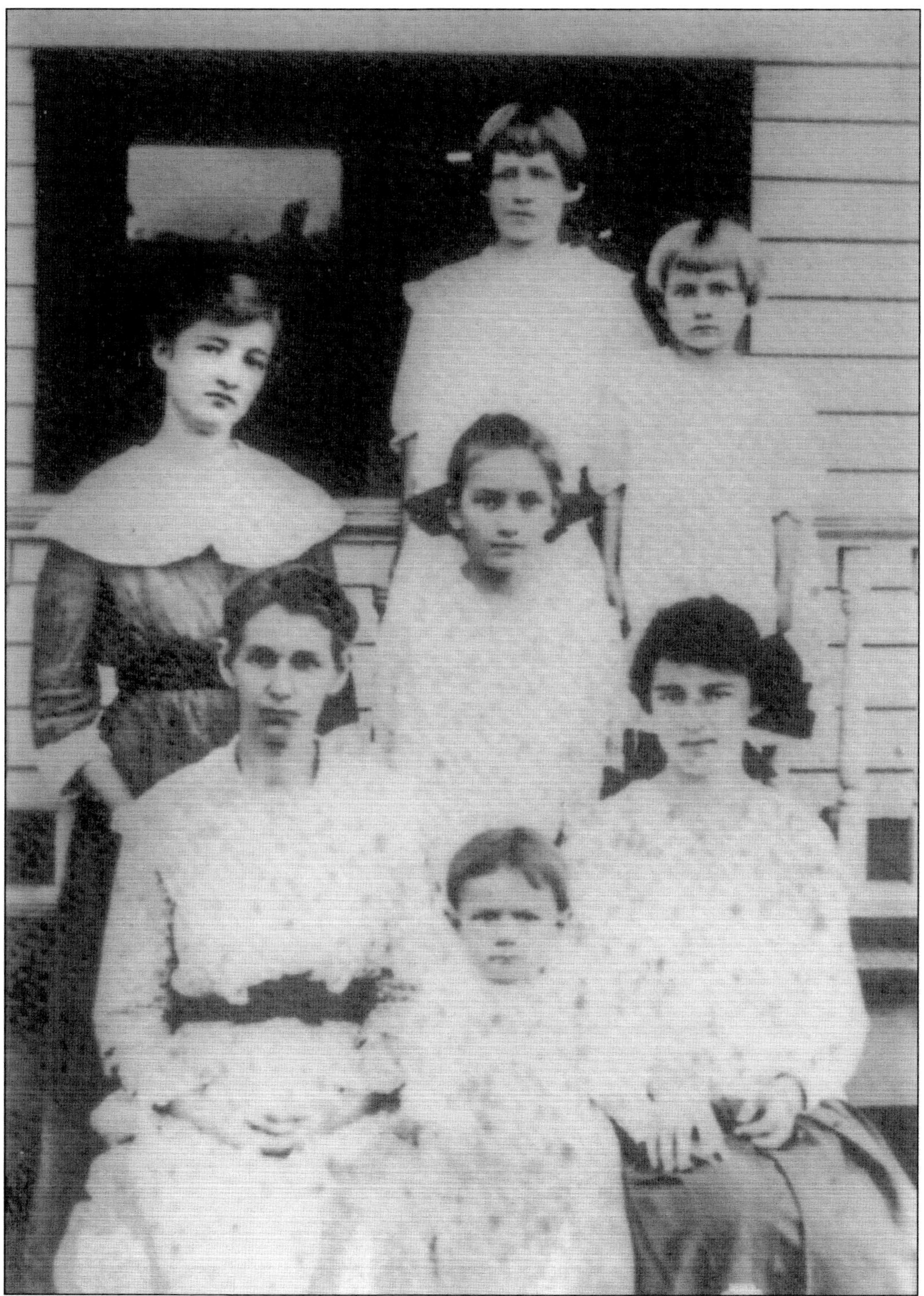

Ethel Gladys Copeland Adams around 1905. Ethel Adams is the girl in the black dress, and the little boy is Bill Rogers. Ethel was born on Valentine's Day in 1908. She taught school in Cary for over 40 years and died in 2004 at the age of 96. (Courtesy of Charlie Adams.)

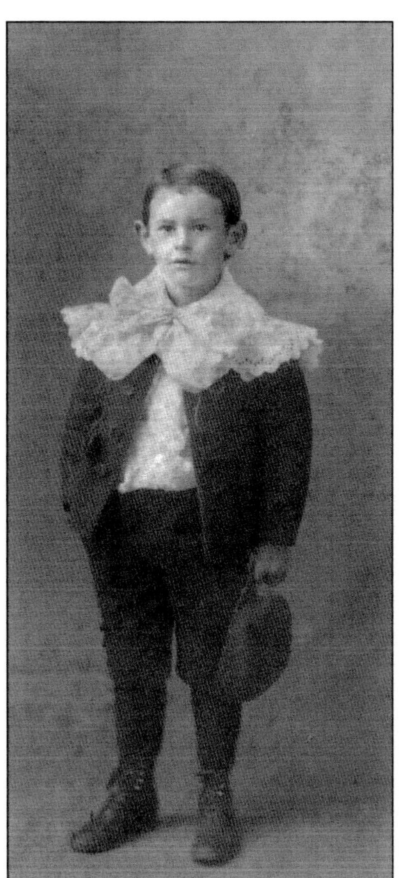

Henry Reavis Adams around 1913. This photograph of Henry was taken when he was 13 and lived on Adams Street, off Academy Street. Henry was born to J. P. H. Adams and Cora Reavis-Adams on March 21, 1900, and graduated from Cary High School. He married Ethel Copeland. Henry's older sister Cleo, who owned a drugstore in Durham, sent him to Bay School of Pharmacy in Massachusetts. He worked for her in Durham until she helped him buy Adams Drugs in Cary, which he owned for 25 years. He sold the drugstore to the Ashworths when he discovered that his son had other interests. (Courtesy of Charlie Adams.)

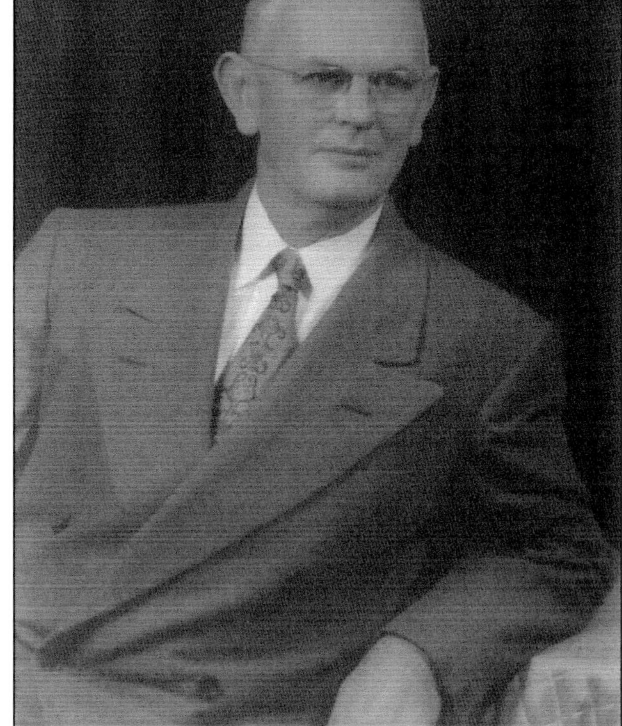

Henry Reavis Adams around 1962. As the town pharmacist, Henry got the honorary title of "Doc" Adams because he administered assistance to residents when the doctor wasn't available. Henry was a big fan of sports and a Duke diehard. He passed away on August 30, 1968, at the age of 69. (Courtesy of Charlie Adams.)

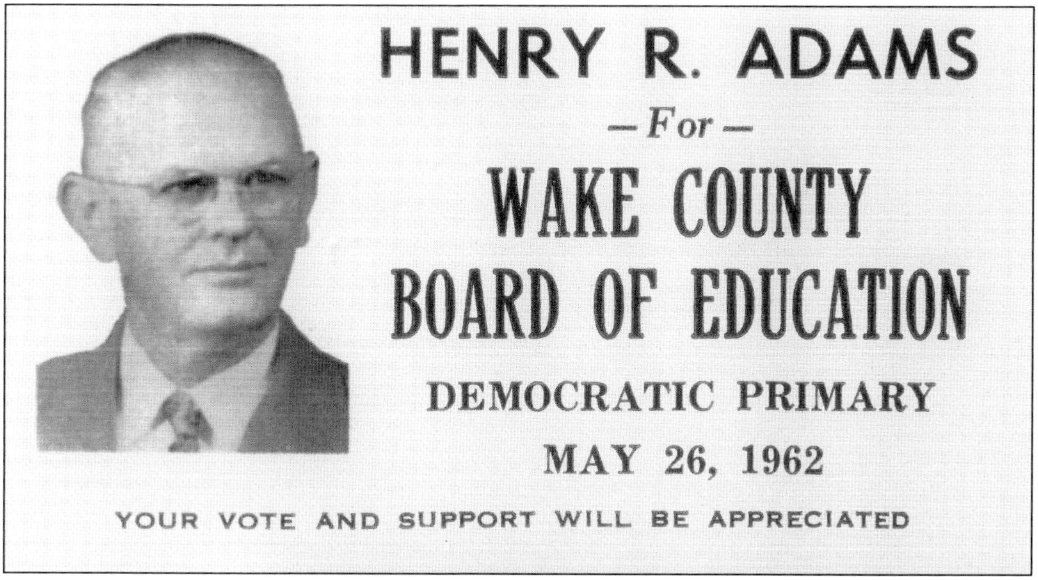

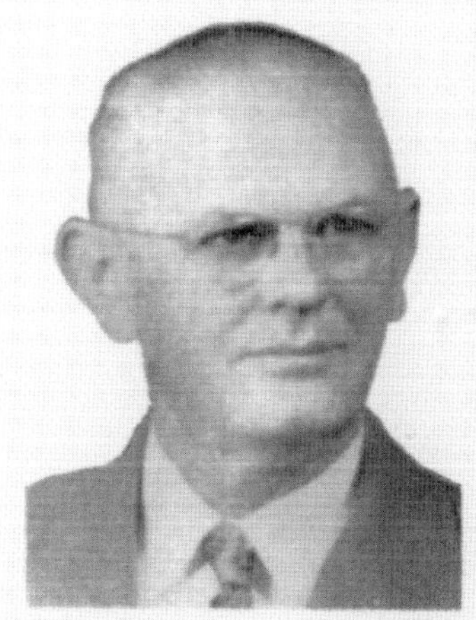

HENRY R. ADAMS

— For —

WAKE COUNTY BOARD OF EDUCATION

DEMOCRATIC PRIMARY

MAY 26, 1962

YOUR VOTE AND SUPPORT WILL BE APPRECIATED

HENRY R. ADAMS AROUND 1962. Born on March 21, 1899, Henry was nominated to the Wake County Board of Education. (Courtesy of Charlie Adams.)

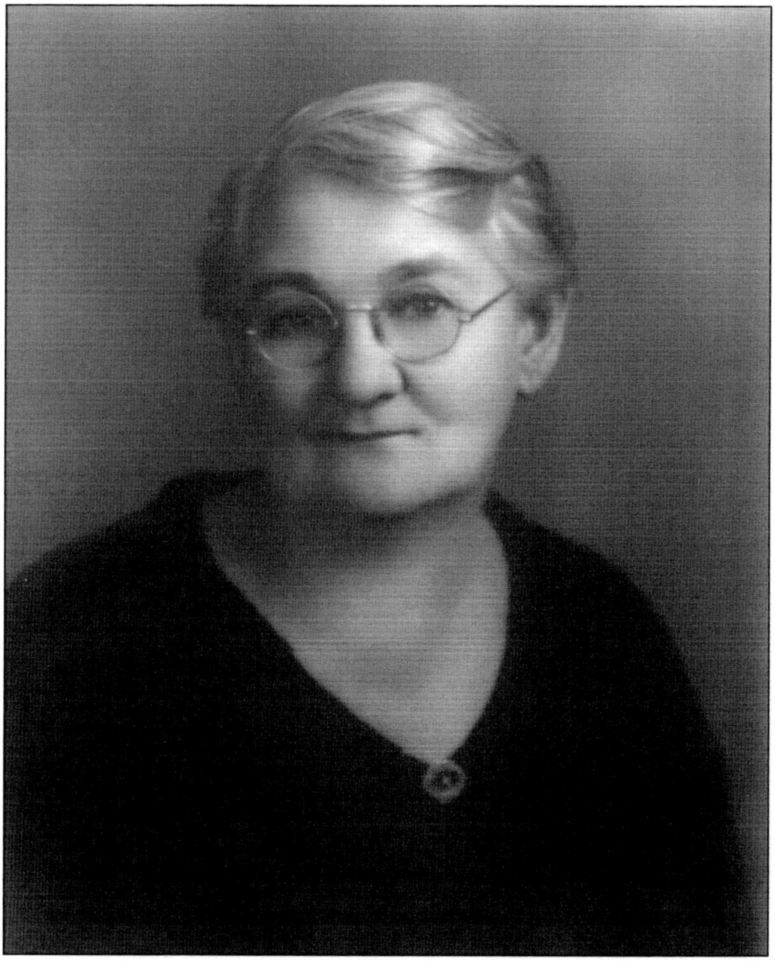

IDA COPELAND. Henry R. Adams's mother-in-law and Ethel Copeland Adams's mother, Ida Copeland is remembered by her grandson as a very sweet, kind woman. After Henry died, she stayed with different family members. Her father was Charles Copeland, who ran a nursery in Cary. She lived into her 80s. (Courtesy of Charlie Adams.)

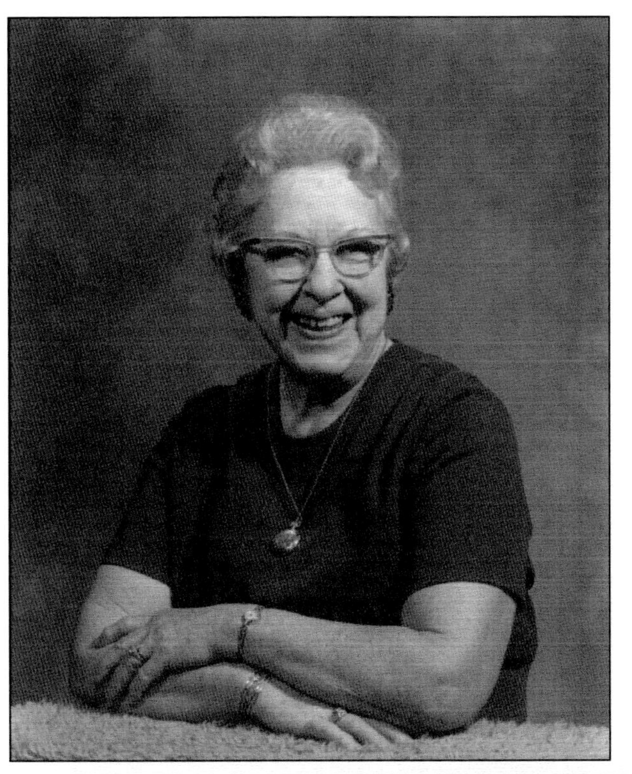

ETHEL GLADYS COPELAND-ADAMS. Ethel Copeland graduated from Cary High School in 1922 with studies in home economics. She soon married Henry Adams and bore their only child, Charlie Adams, in 1937. Ethel was one of the most beloved teachers at Cary High School. Ethel also took care of the patrons at the lunch counter in her husband's drugstore. She prepared all the deviled eggs, tuna, chicken, and pimento cheese salads. They were prepared in her home and then brought to the drugstore. Freshly squeezed orangeade was popular with boys, while lemonade and limeade were popular with the girls. The men usually drank Coke. (Both, courtesy of Charlie Adams.)

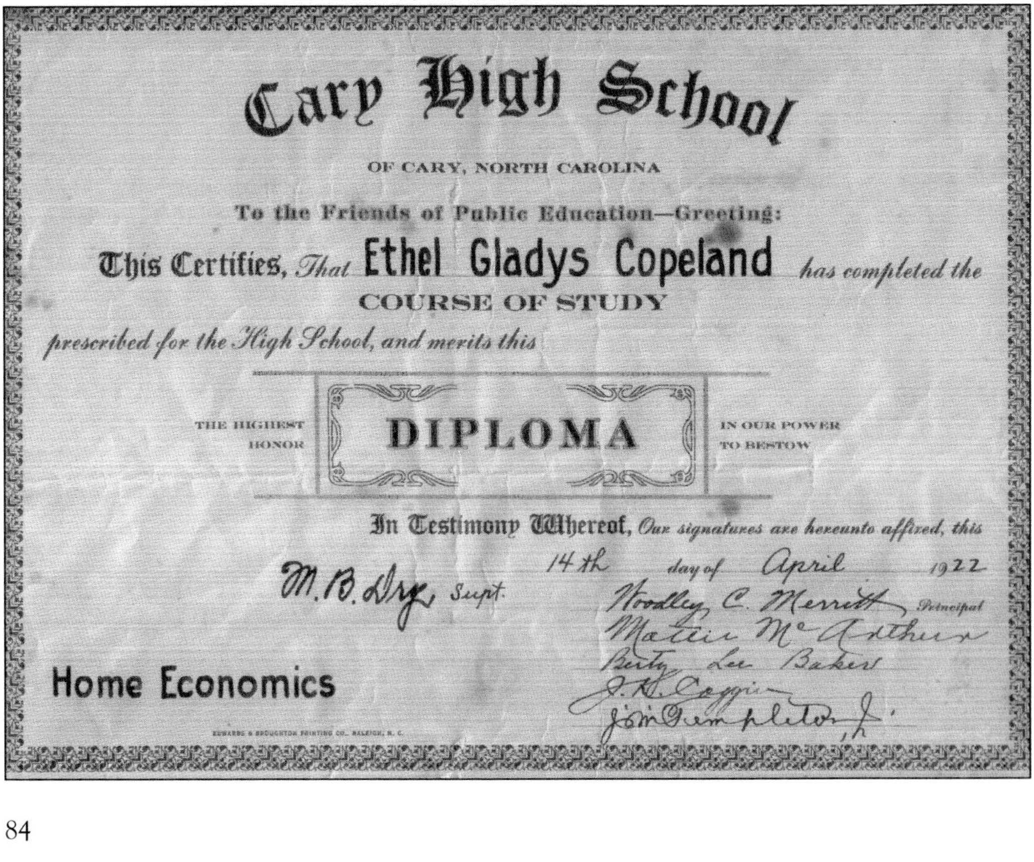

Cary High School

OF CARY, NORTH CAROLINA

To the Friends of Public Education—Greeting:

This Certifies, *That* Ethel Gladys Copeland *has completed the*

COURSE OF STUDY

prescribed for the High School, and merits this

THE HIGHEST HONOR **DIPLOMA** IN OUR POWER TO BESTOW

In Testimony Whereof, *Our signatures are hereunto affixed, this* 14th *day of* April 1922

M. B. Dry, Supt.

Woodley C. Merritt, *Principal*

Mattie McArthur

Betty Lee Baker

J. H. Coggin

J. M. Templeton, Jr.

Home Economics

EDWARDS & BROUGHTON PRINTING CO., RALEIGH, N. C.

Friends and Relatives Posing for a Picture. From left to right are Marjorie Adams, Lula Helen Jordan, and Mary Lou Stone. In the front is Hubert Jordan Jr. (Courtesy of C. Y. Jordan.)

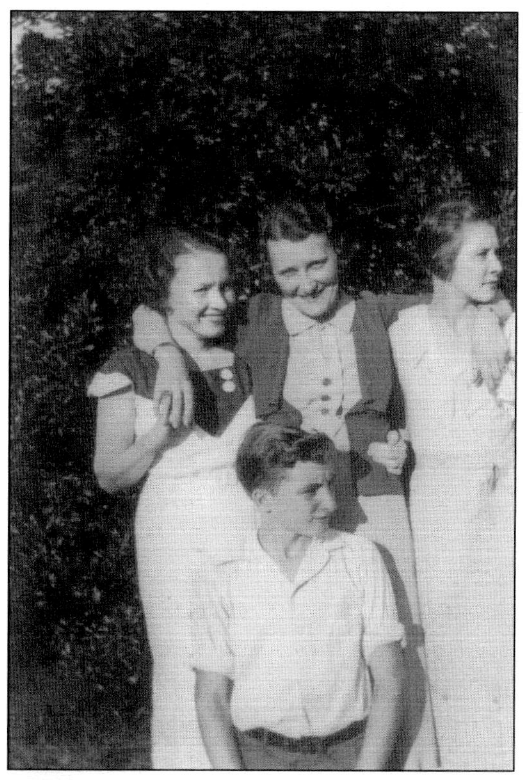

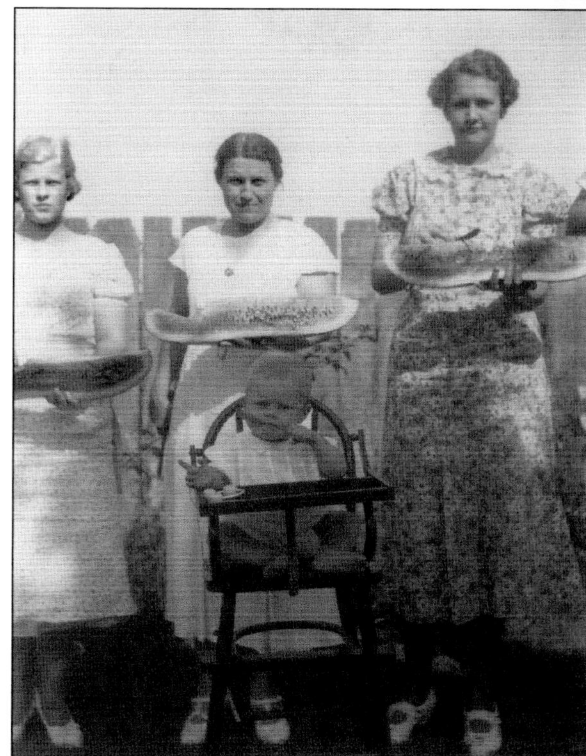

Baby Raoul and the Watermelon, 1940s. These three ladies are showing off large pieces of watermelon. From left to right are Esther McCauley, Grace Holleman Maynard, and Mildred Holleman Sanford. The baby is Grace's son, Raoul Maynard. (Courtesy of C. Y. Jordan.)

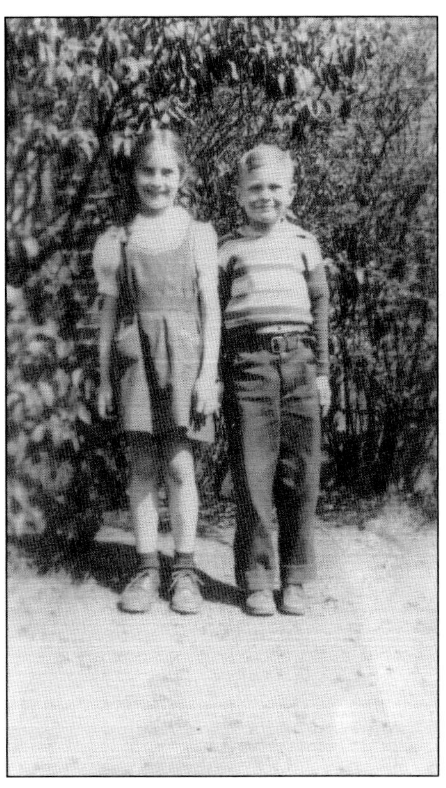

Tommie Womble and Jane Maynard. This photograph shows Tommie Womble and Jane Maynard-Bowers at their first-grade class in 1942 on Academy Street. Jane played basketball, graduated from Meredith, and is a teacher and counselor today. Tom played football, was a legislator for the state of North Carolina, and is a minister today. (Courtesy of Charlie Adams.)

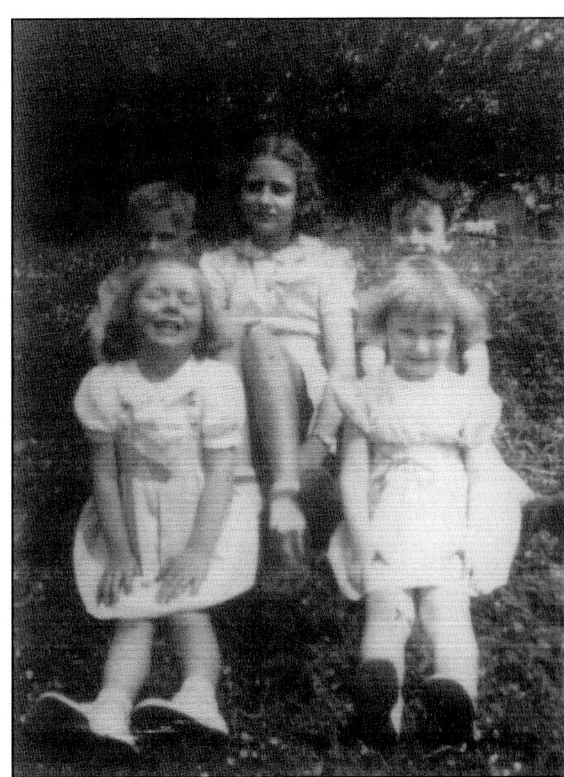

Rogers Family. This 1940s photograph shows members of the Rogers family. They owned the restaurant and motel in Cary in the 1960s. (Courtesy of Bill Rogers.)

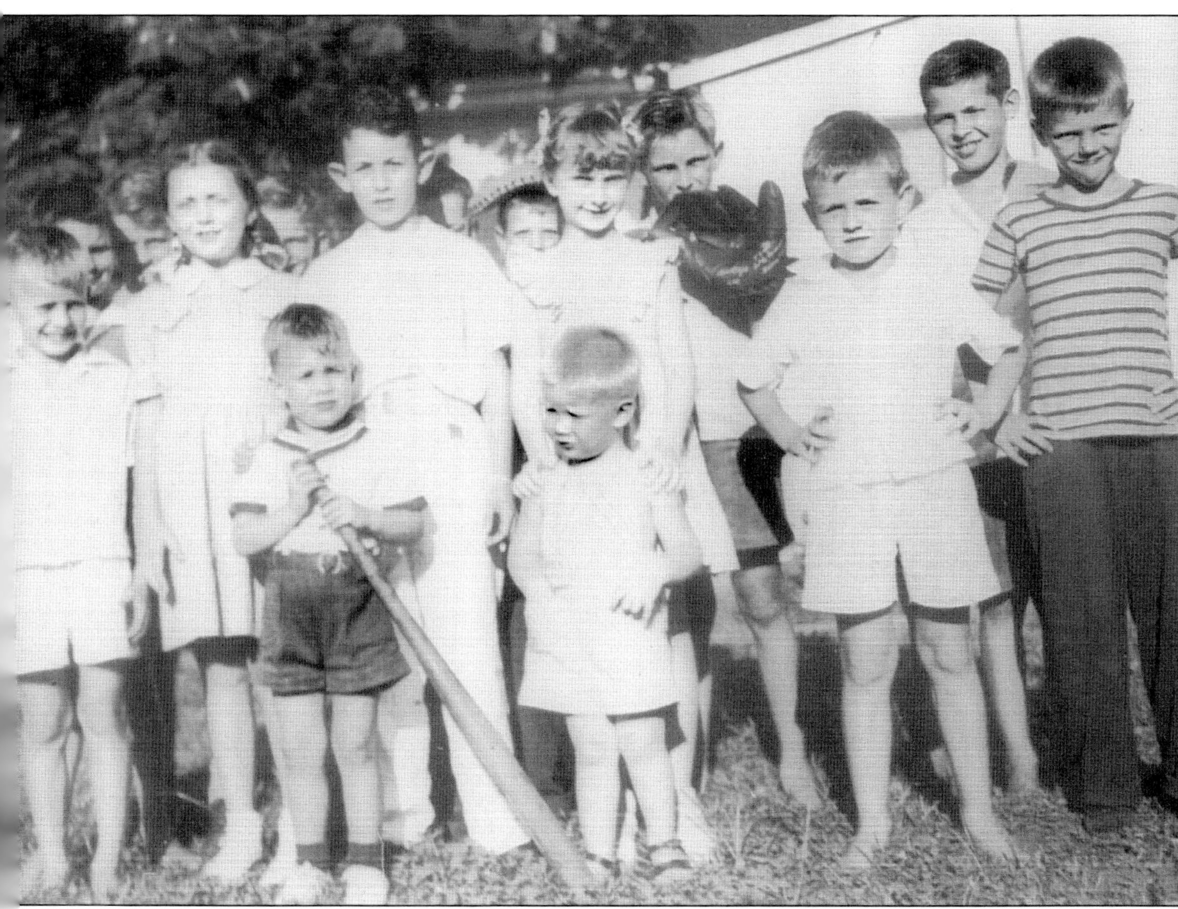

Adams and Rogers Clan. A photographer captured this picture for Charlie Adams's birthday party at 320 South Academy Street. Pictured from left to right are (first row) Jimmy Copeland and Johnny Walf; (second row) Nelson Fry, cousin Doris Rogers, Charlie Adams, cousin Jean Setzer, and John Yarborough (hands on hips); (third row) five unidentified, cousin Bill Rogers (with glove), A. G. Bullard, and Linville Midgette (striped shirt). (Courtesy of Charlie Adams and Bill Rogers.)

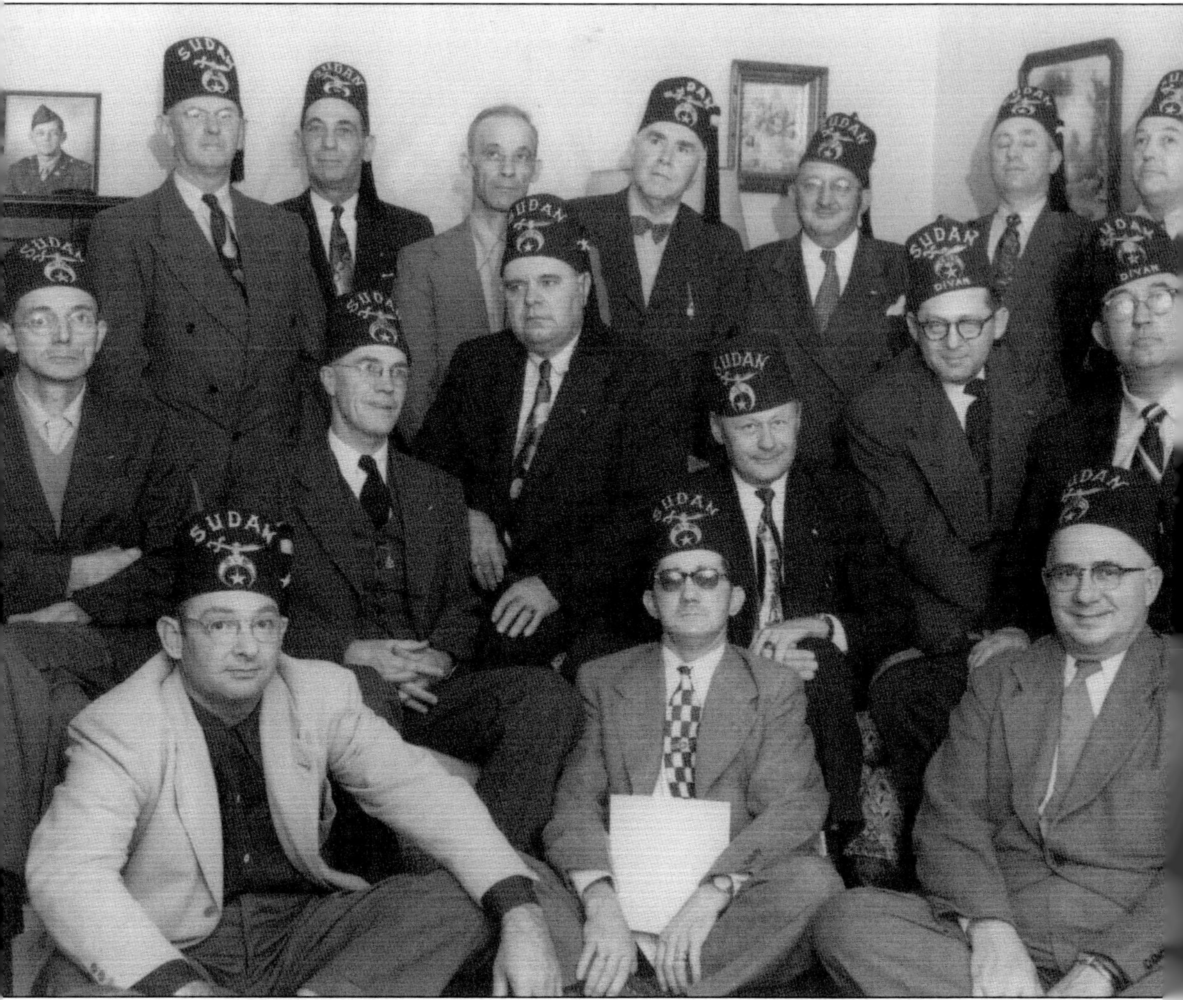

E. Sanderford Home. The photograph shows Shriners assembled at the home of E. Sanderford. The 13 Masons who organized the first Shrine Temple in New York City in 1872 knew that they needed an appealing theme for their new order, so they chose an Arabic theme. The most noticeable symbol of Shrinedom is the distinctive fez or hat that all Shriners wear at official functions. (Courtesy of Charlie Adams.)

JESSIE MERIEL CONNER-HEATER AROUND 1920. Jessie was born around 1900, and by 1930, she had married Russell Heater. Jess was in World War I as a yeoman third-class provisional. While she wanted to serve her country, she was discharged on December 8, 1920, because as a woman, she could not go out to sea. Her son Robert recalls hearing his mother say this about Cary: "The street that brought you here will take you away." (Courtesy of Robert B. Heater.)

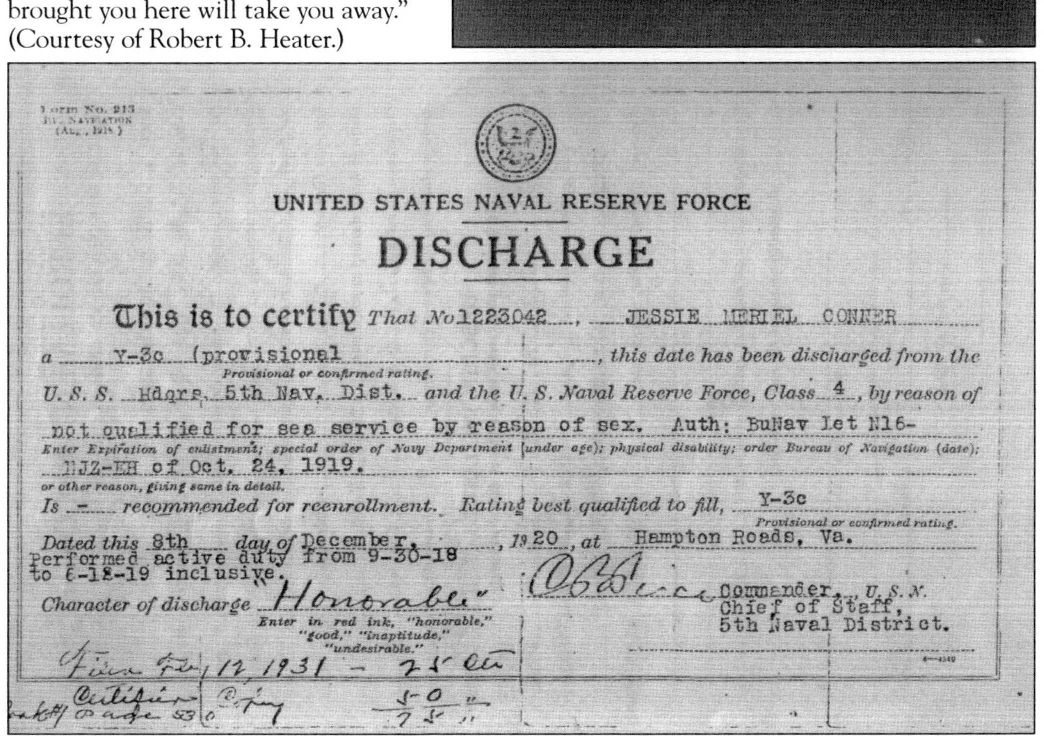

Form No. 213
Bu. Navigation
(Aug., 1918)

UNITED STATES NAVAL RESERVE FORCE

DISCHARGE

This is to certify That No1223042, JESSIE MERIEL CONNER a Y-3c (provisional *Provisional or confirmed rating.*, this date has been discharged from the U. S. S. Hdqrs. 5th Nav. Dist. and the U. S. Naval Reserve Force, Class 4, by reason of not qualified for sea service by reason of sex. Auth: BuNav Let N16- *Enter Expiration of enlistment; special order of Navy Department (under age); physical disability; order Bureau of Navigation (date);* NJZ-EH of Oct. 24, 1919. *or other reason, giving same in detail.*

Is - recommended for reenrollment. Rating best qualified to fill, Y-3c *Provisional or confirmed rating.*

Dated this 8th day of December, 1920, at Hampton Roads, Va.
Performed active duty from 9-30-18 to 6-18-19 inclusive.

Character of discharge "Honorable" *Enter in red ink, "honorable," "good," "inaptitude," "undesirable."*

Commander, U. S. N.
Chief of Staff,
5th Naval District.

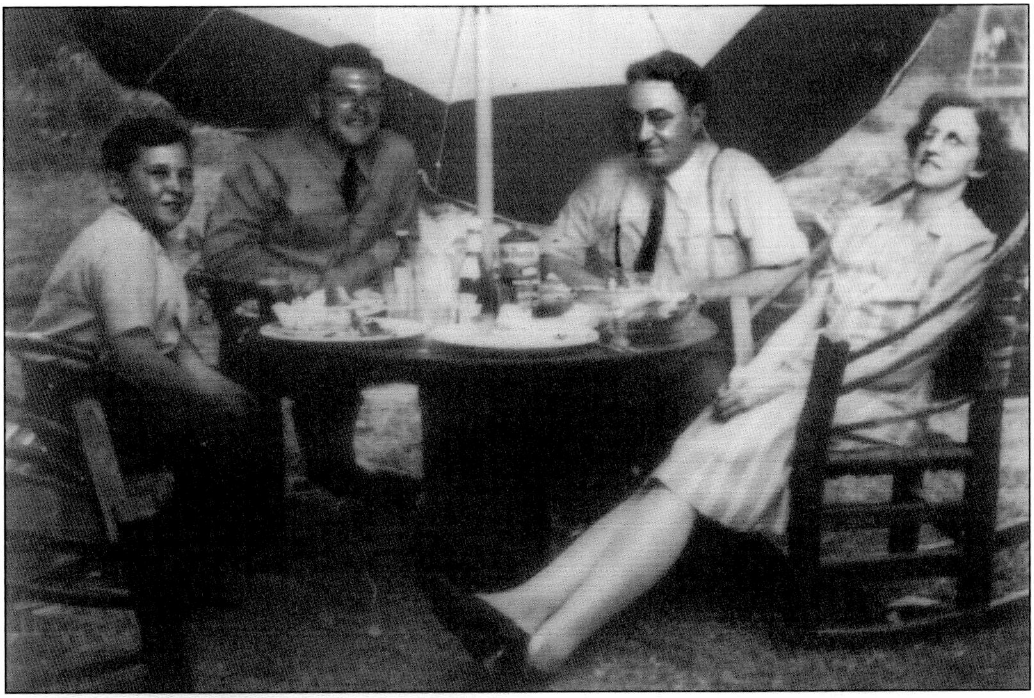

RUSSELL AND JESSIE HEATER, 1940S. The Heater family is enjoying a backyard picnic. Pictured from left to right are son Bob Heater, Hurk Kelly, Russell Heater, and Jess Heater. (Courtesy of Robert B. Heater.)

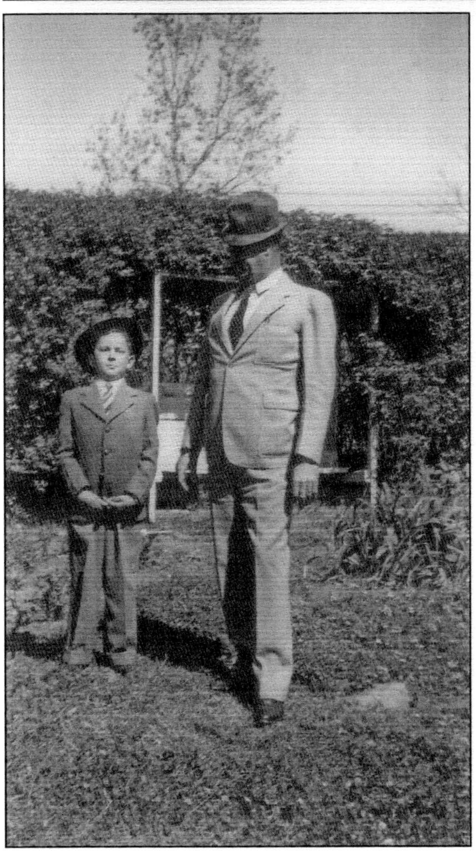

EASTER, AROUND 1939. Bob Heater and his father are all dressed up in their finest Easter clothes. (Courtesy of Robert B. Heater.)

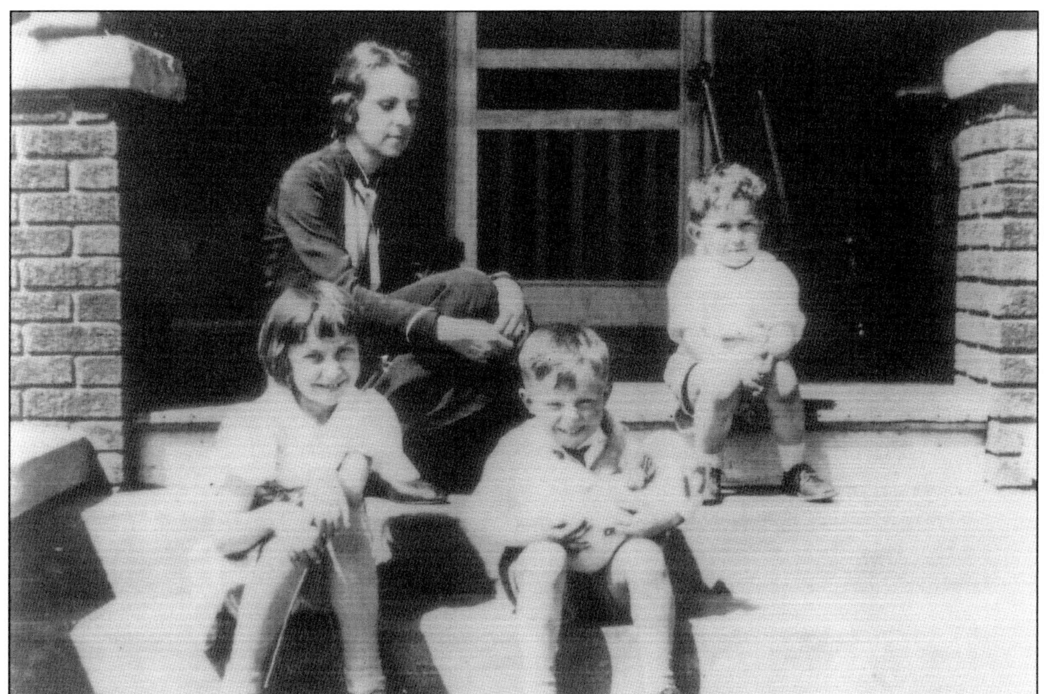

PORCH GRINS, 1930S. From left to right, Barbara Gertz, Dorothy, Bob Heater, and Mills Gertz are caught sitting in the sun on the front porch. (Courtesy of Robert B. Heater.)

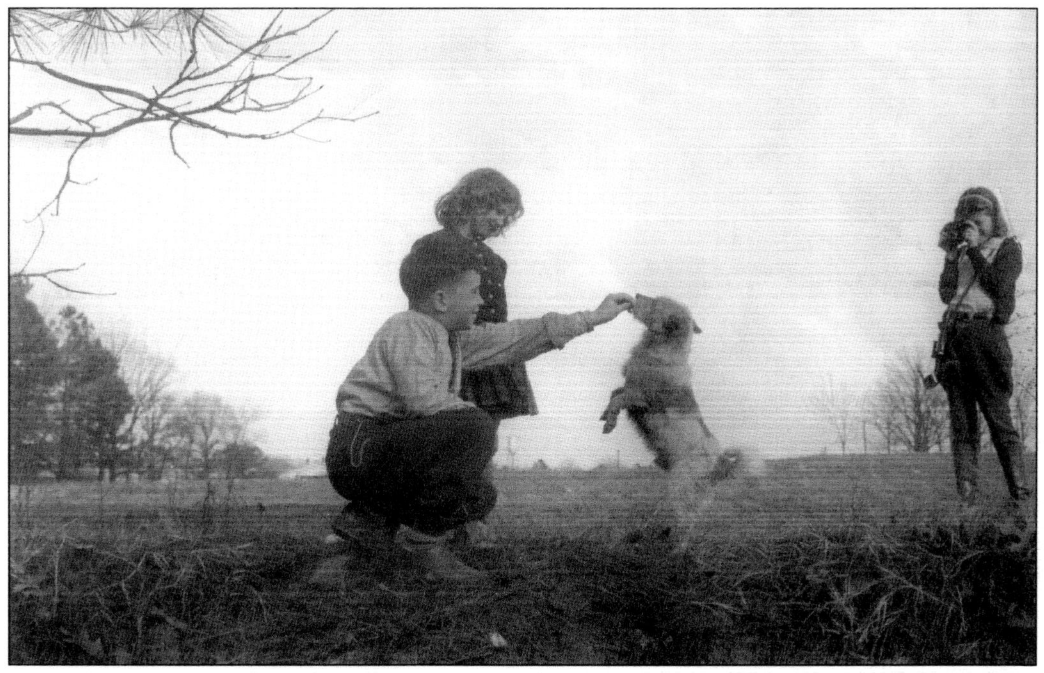

FEEDING THE DOG, 1940S. Bob Heater feeds the family dog while Ann Heater looks on. Jane Coggins is snapping the photograph. (Courtesy of Robert B. Heater.)

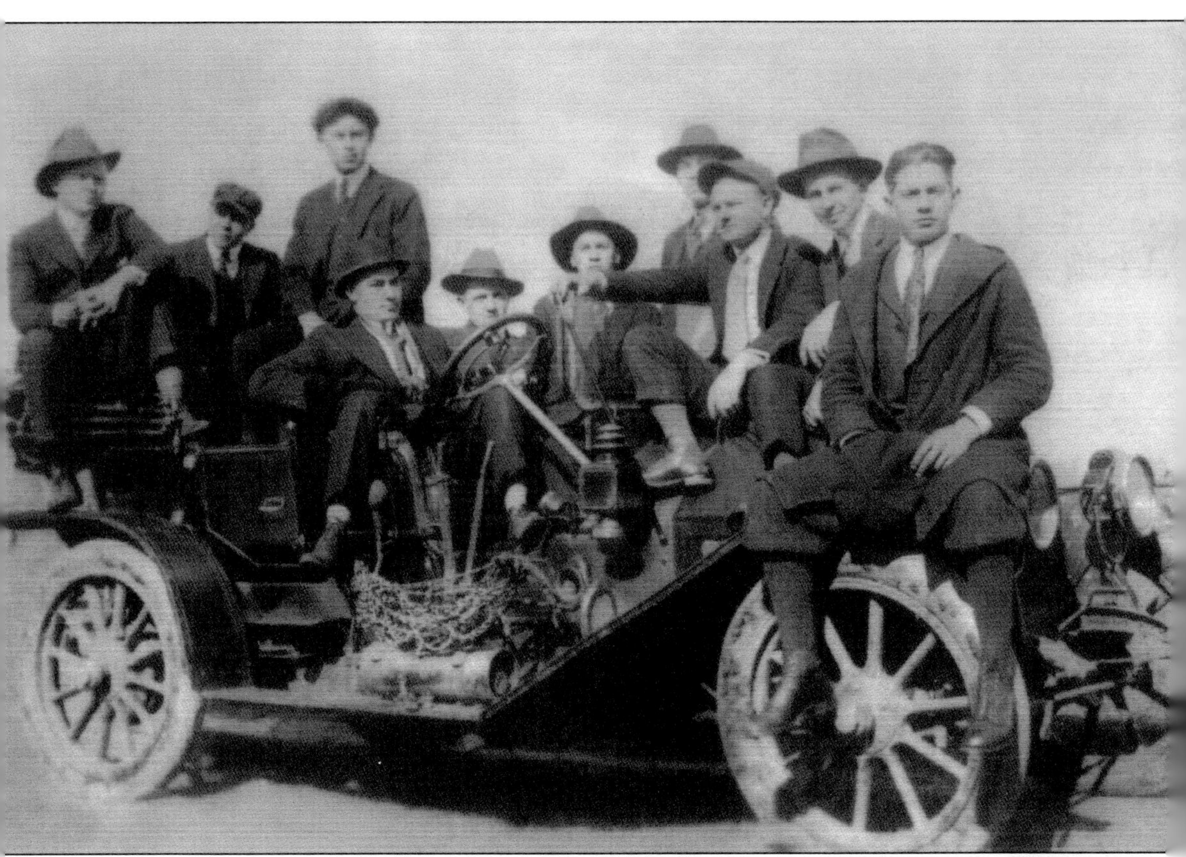

Russell Heater and His Car, 1920s. Russell (behind the wheel) and his friends pose with his car. From left to right are Worth Williams, Harvey Waddell, unidentified, C. L. Beddingfield, Johnny Breeze, unidentified, Harold Atkins, and two more unidentified friends. (Courtesy of Robert B. Heater.)

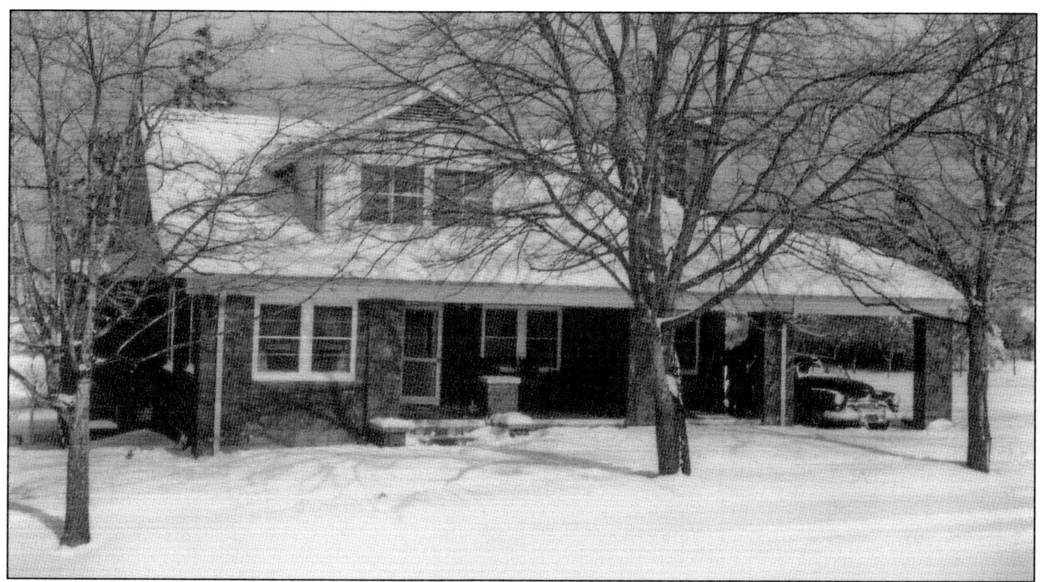

RUSSELL HEATER HOME AROUND 1932. This photograph shows the Heater home in 1932 after a snowstorm had dusted the house with white powder. (Courtesy of Robert B. Heater.)

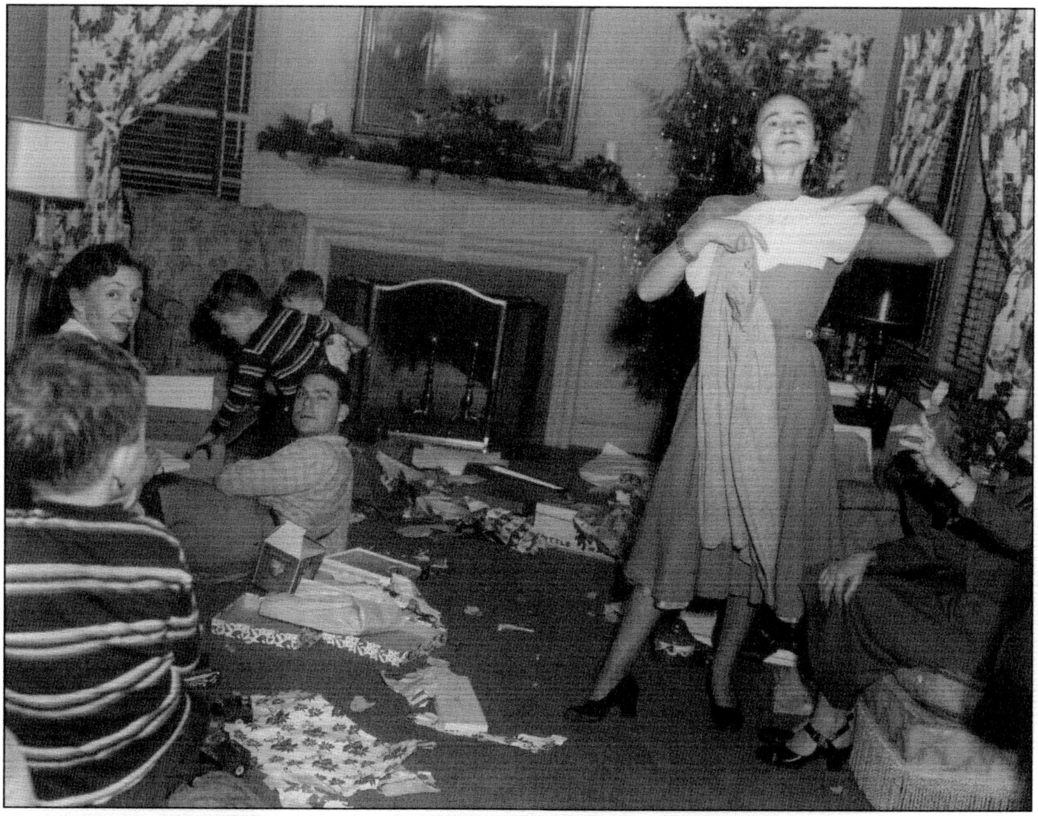

CHRISTMAS IN THE 1950S. The Heater family enjoys opening their presents on Christmas. Pictured from left to right are Marjorie Heater-Herring, Fred Herring, twins Tom and Bill Bland, and their mother, Dorothy Bland. (Courtesy of Robert B. Heater.)

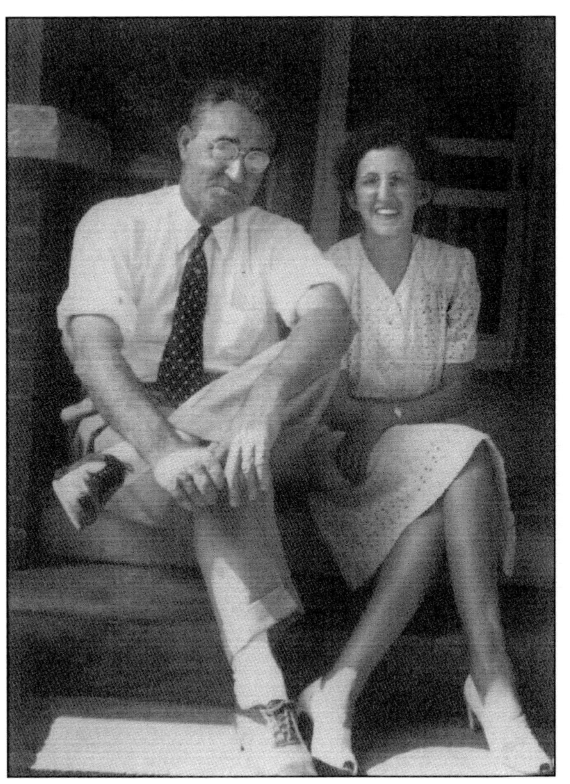

Russell and Jessie Heater, 1930s. Russell and Jessie were happily married and had three children: daughters Dorothy and Marjorie and son Robert. B. Heater. (Courtesy of Robert B. Heater.)

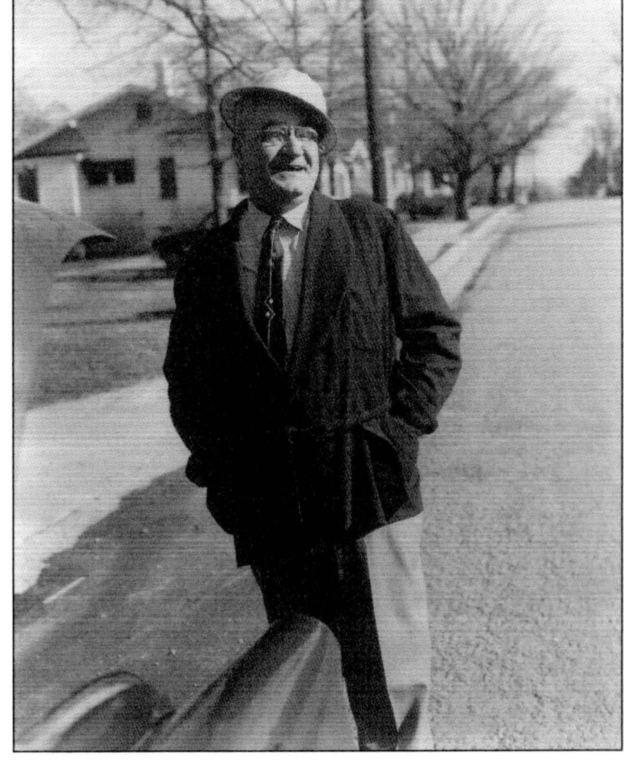

Russell Oran Heater. Russell was the owner of Heater Well Company, which dug wells not only in Cary but all over North Carolina. Russell headed up war bond drives, was a county commissioner, received the Boy Scouts' Beaver Award as Scoutmaster for fund-raising, and was the vice president of the exchange club. He was often referred to as "Mister Cary," because he promoted Cary whenever he could. Russell was the second chairman of the committee to promote the state college; the committee is now the Wolf Pack Club. He passed away at 75. (Courtesy of Robert B. Heater.)

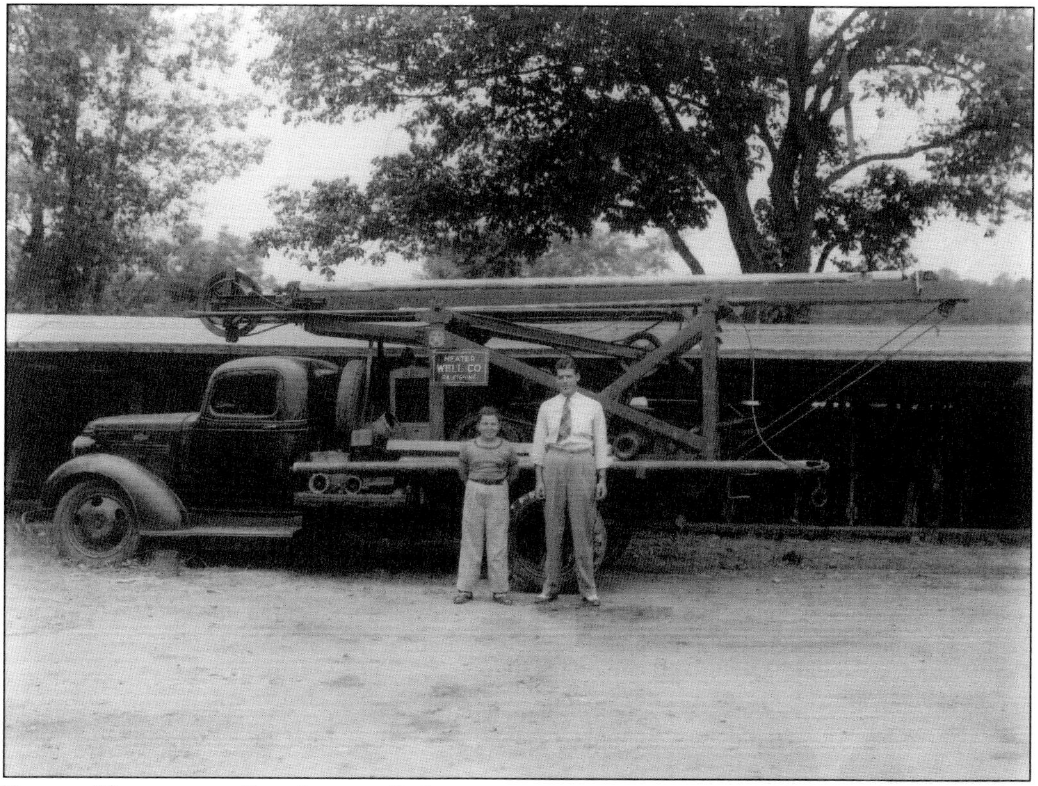

ROBERT HEATER AND BUD INGOLD. Robert remembers working as helper for Bud drilling wells for his father's company. He carried pipes and swung a sledgehammer on hot bits, or as he says, "It swung me as much as I swung it." The Heater Well Company was running 24 machines in the late 1940s. (Courtesy of Robert B. Heater.)

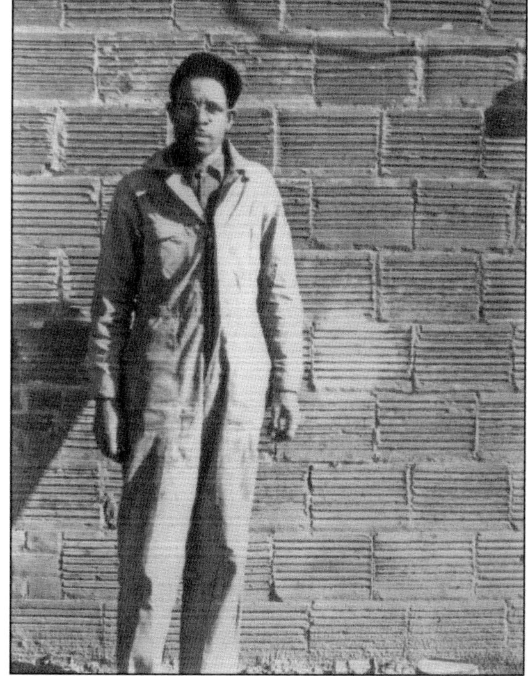

HERMAN EDWARDS. A longtime employee of the Heater Well Company and family friend of the Heaters, Edwards did everything for the company, including opening and closing the shop and drilling. On his way to work one day, a truck struck and killed him. (Courtesy of Robert B. Heater.)

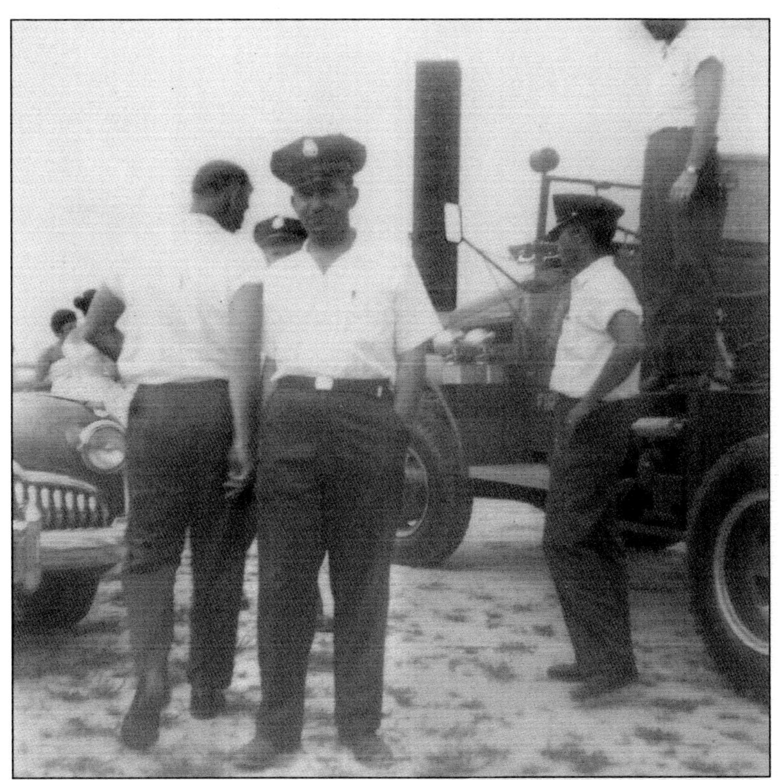

Robert B. Heater, Fireman. Bob joined the fire department when it was an all-volunteer group. During World War II, when there was a shortage of available young men, 12-year-old Bob Heater trained with the fire department. He answered his first fire call when he was 15. The chief sent him through the window with a hose, and he was able to put out the fire. In April 1956, he was appointed assistant chief, and by September that same year, he made chief. (Courtesy of Robert B. Heater.)

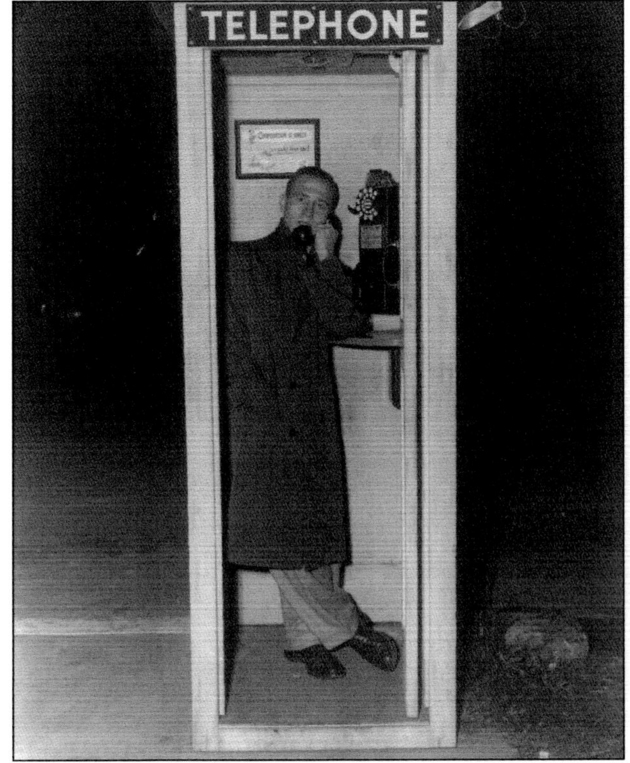

Lynn Banks. This was snapped by Bob Heater while Lynn was trying to score a date with a Meredith College student in a Cary phone booth. Lynn's parents came to Cary around 1919, and he was born in a house on the corner of East Chatham Street and Walker Street in 1928. He graduated from Cary High School in 1944 and from Wake Forest College in 1948. He was a realtor and appraiser for many years. Lynn says, "Living and being educated in Cary gave you a feeling of belonging . . . everybody knew everybody." (Courtesy of Robert B. Heater.)

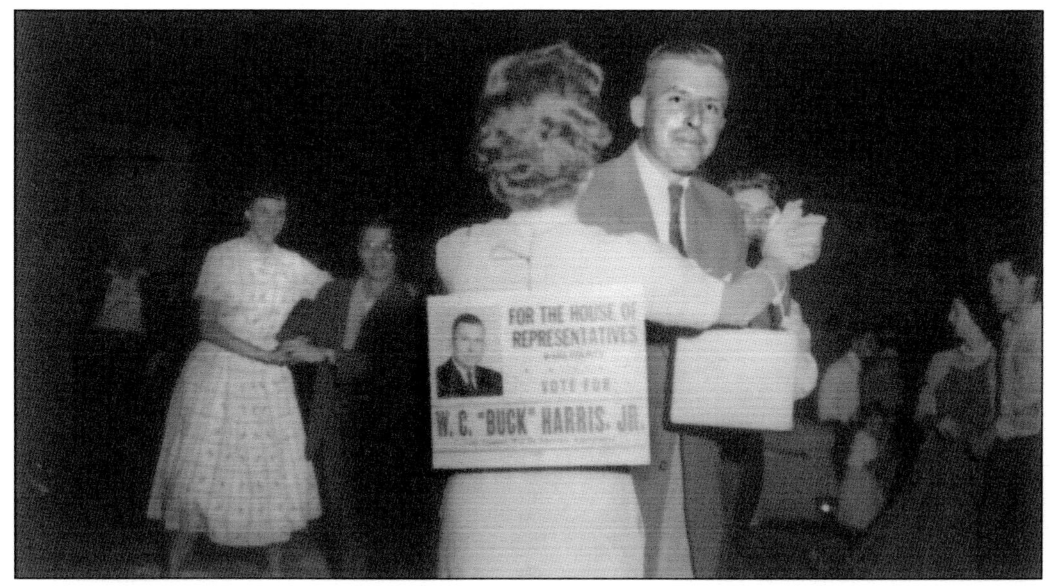

Fireman's Day Dance. The Cary Fire Department relied heavily of fund-raising events to pay for all of its equipment. The dance was held after a day of festivities. In 1956, Fireman's Day concluded with a street dance and the music of the Mills Brothers Hillbilly Band. (Both, courtesy of Stanley Lorren.)

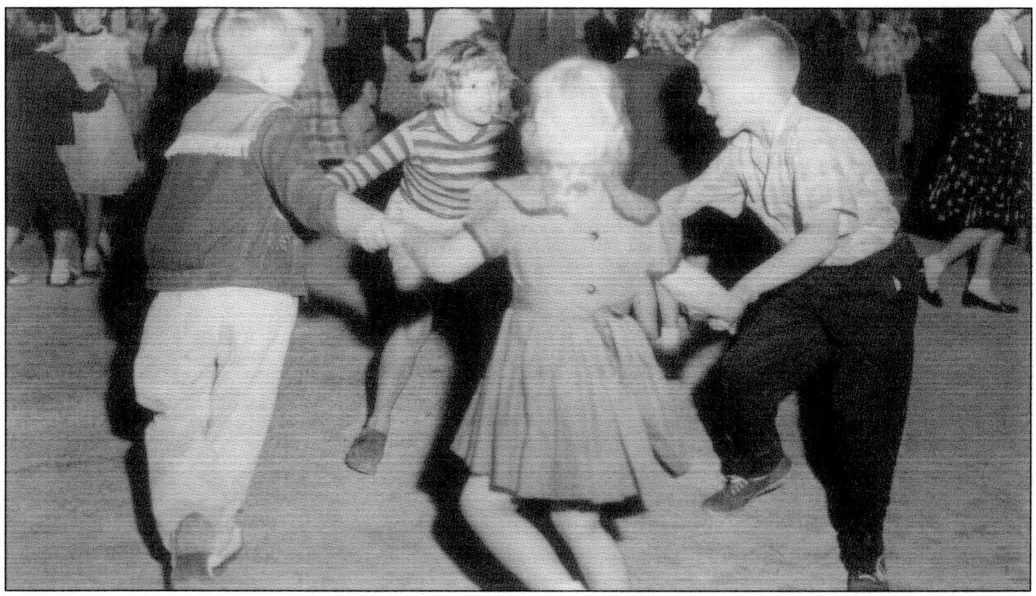

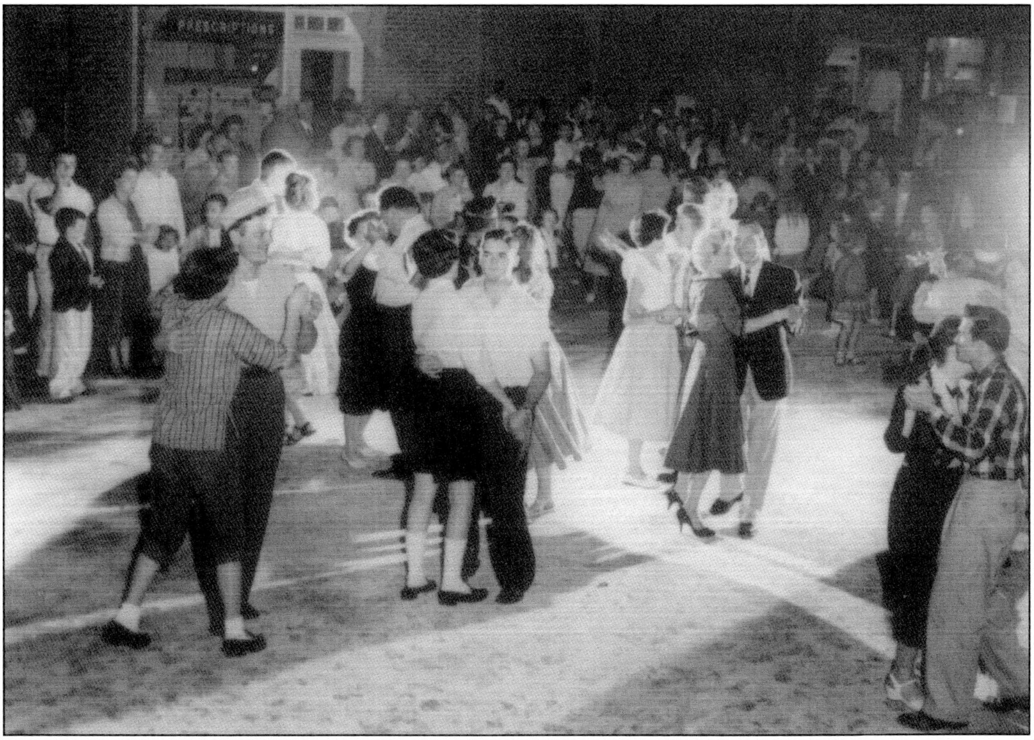

FIREMAN'S DAY DANCE AROUND 1960. The eighth annual Fireman's Day was held on May 7, 1960. The schedule included a parade at 3:30 p.m., supper at the high school cafeteria from 5:00 p.m. until 8:00 p.m., games from 6:30 p.m. until 8:00 p.m., and a street dance from 8:00 p.m. until midnight. Fried fish was served in the cafeteria, prepared by firefighters, their wives, and members of the Fire Auxiliary Association. Drawings were held for various prize merchandise, and an open house was held at the emergency shelter set up at the Cary Methodist Church from noon until 4:30 p.m. (Both, courtesy of Stanley Lorren.)

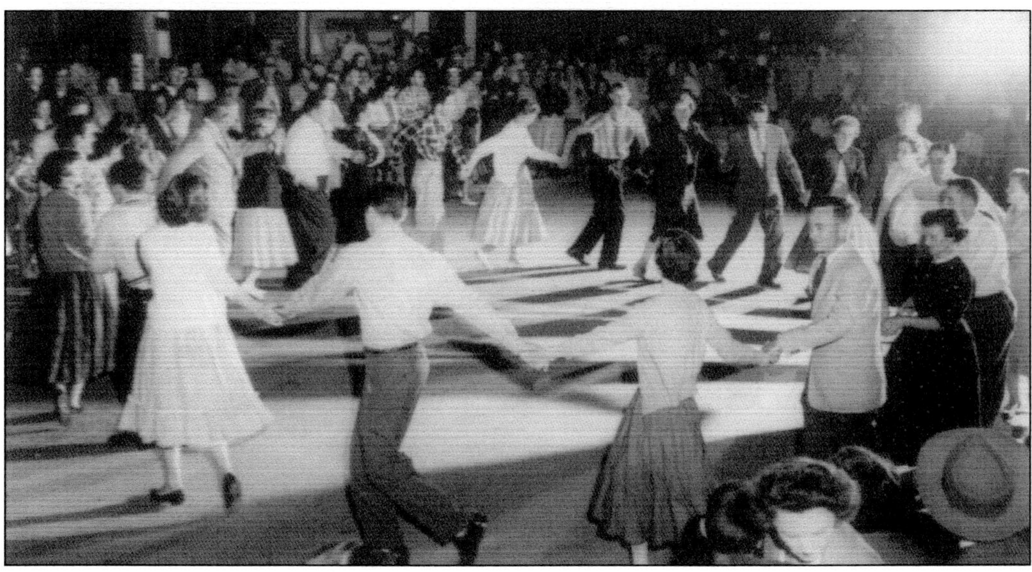

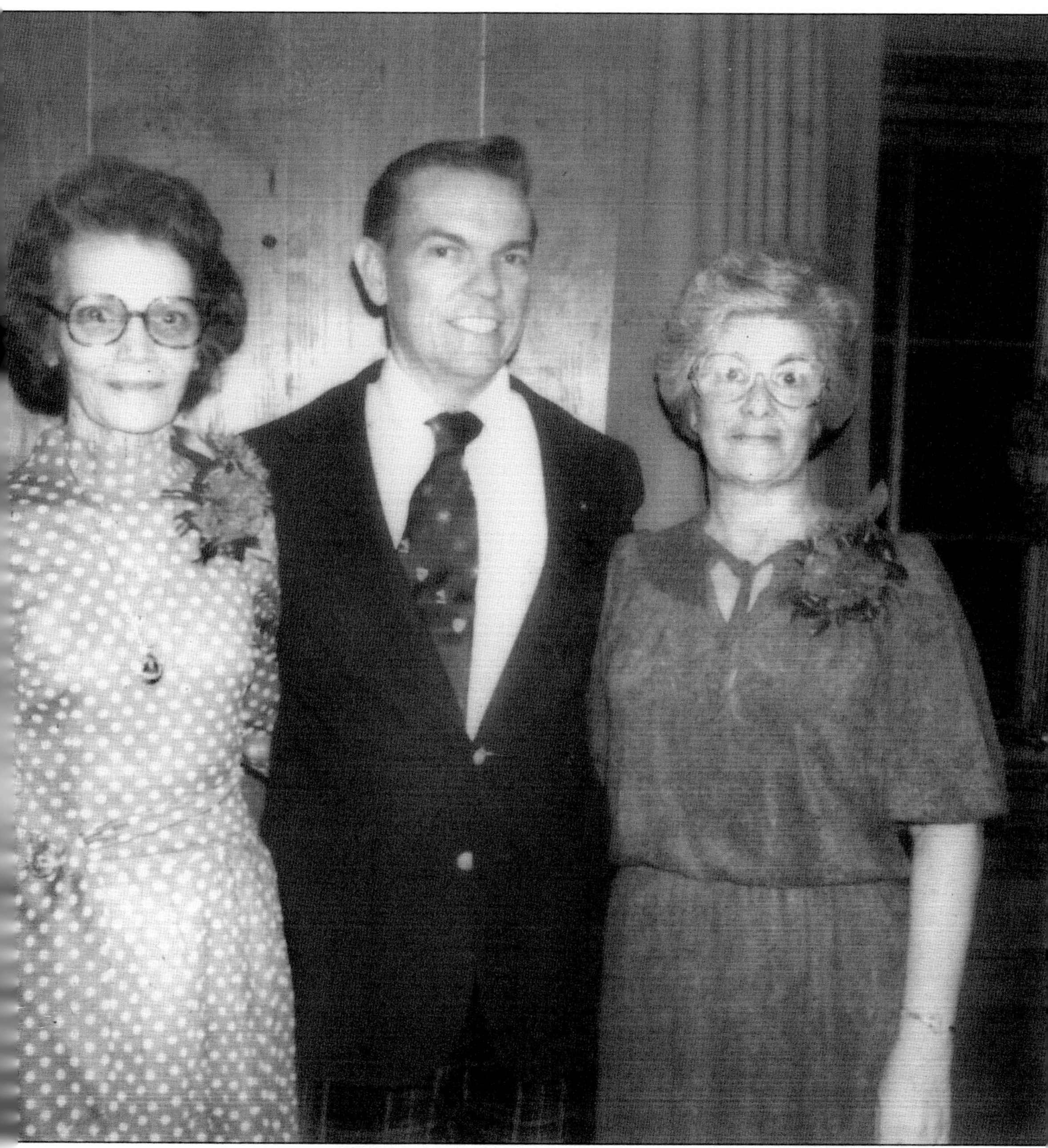

Ashworth's Drug Store Counter Lady. Edna Cyrus worked behind the Ashworth's lunch counter for 23 years serving chicken, tuna, and pimento cheese sandwiches. Pictured from left to right are Edna Cyrus, Ralph Ashworth, and Peggy Cannady in 1970. (Courtesy of Ralph Ashworth.)

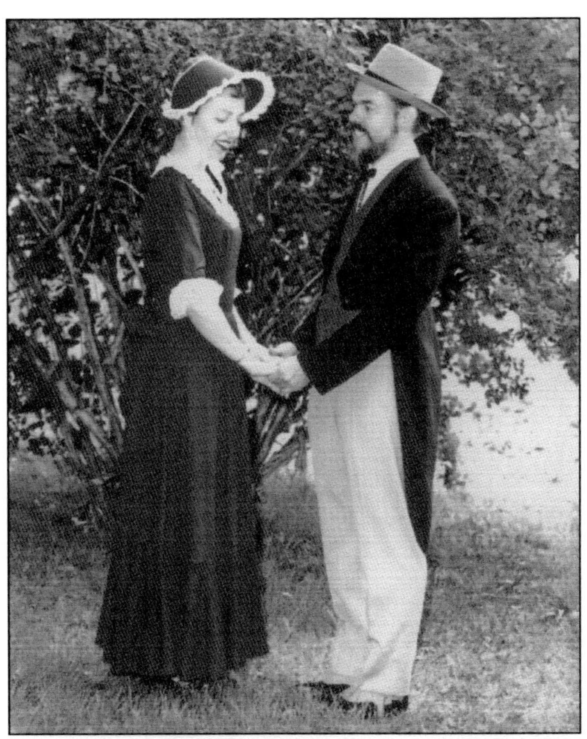

The Ashworths. Ralph and Daphne Ashworth are the owners of Ashworth Drugs in Cary. They are pictured here in costume for Cary's centennial celebration in 1971. (Courtesy of Ralph Ashworth.)

1971 Men's Costumes. Many of the local residents decided to dress in period costumes for Cary's centennial. Mayor Waldo Rood is one of the men in this photograph. (Courtesy of Mary Ann Rood.)

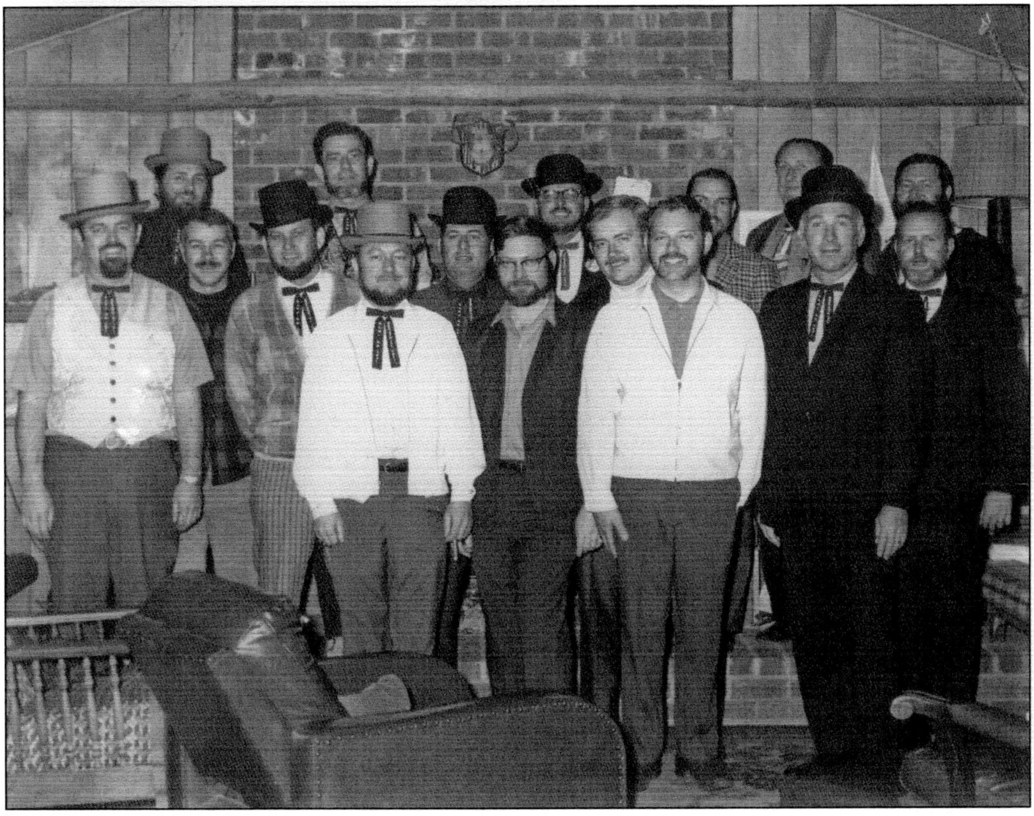

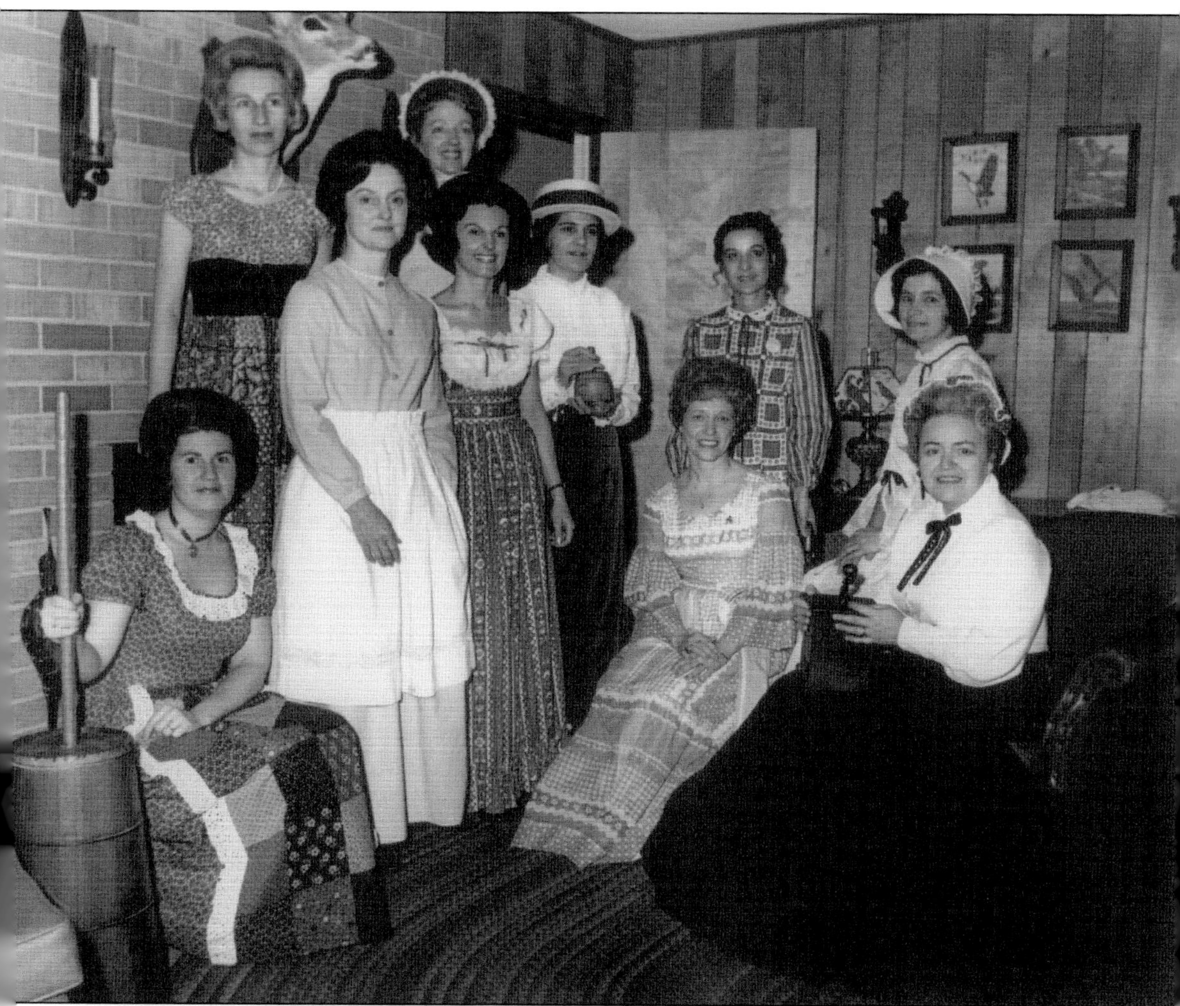

1971 WOMEN'S COSTUMES. Cary's female residents also dressed for the centennial celebration. From left to right are (first row) Mary George Brewer, Barbara Thomas, and Jane Thompson; (second row) Joan Sibley, Jean Ladd, Anne Hedgecock, Sue Gordon, and Carita Clayton; (third row) Blair Hatcher (left) and Daphne Ashworth. (Courtesy of Ralph Ashworth.)

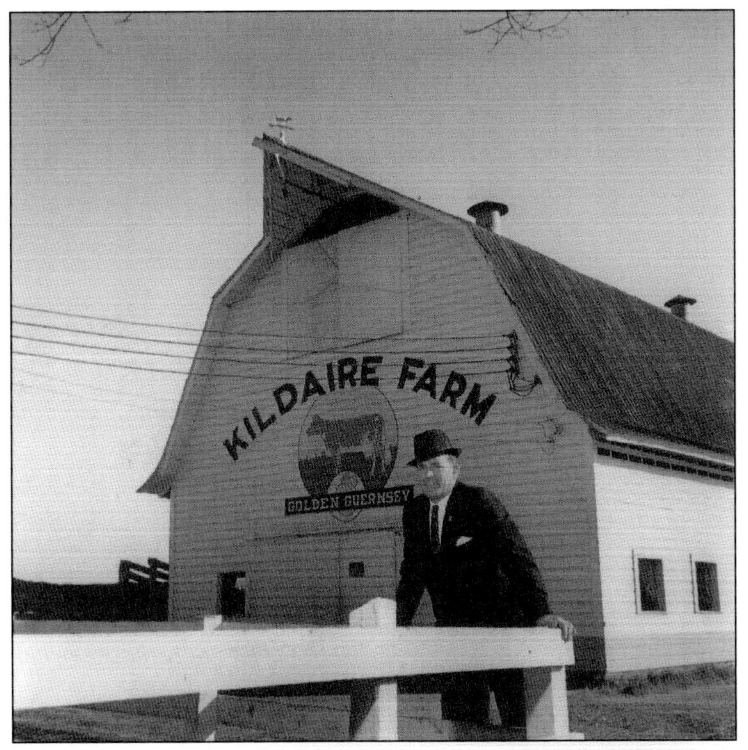

KILDAIRE FARM. Begun in the 1920s or 1930s, Kildaire Farm in 1941 was a working 1,000-acre farm. Manager Clyde Keisler rented an additional 500 acres. About seven families lived and worked on the farm until around the early 1970s. It was a self-sufficient facility: people grew their own vegetables and baked their own bread. All the dairy products produced on the farm were sold to the Kilgore family, who owned Pine State Dairy. (Both, courtesy of Sally Keisler.)

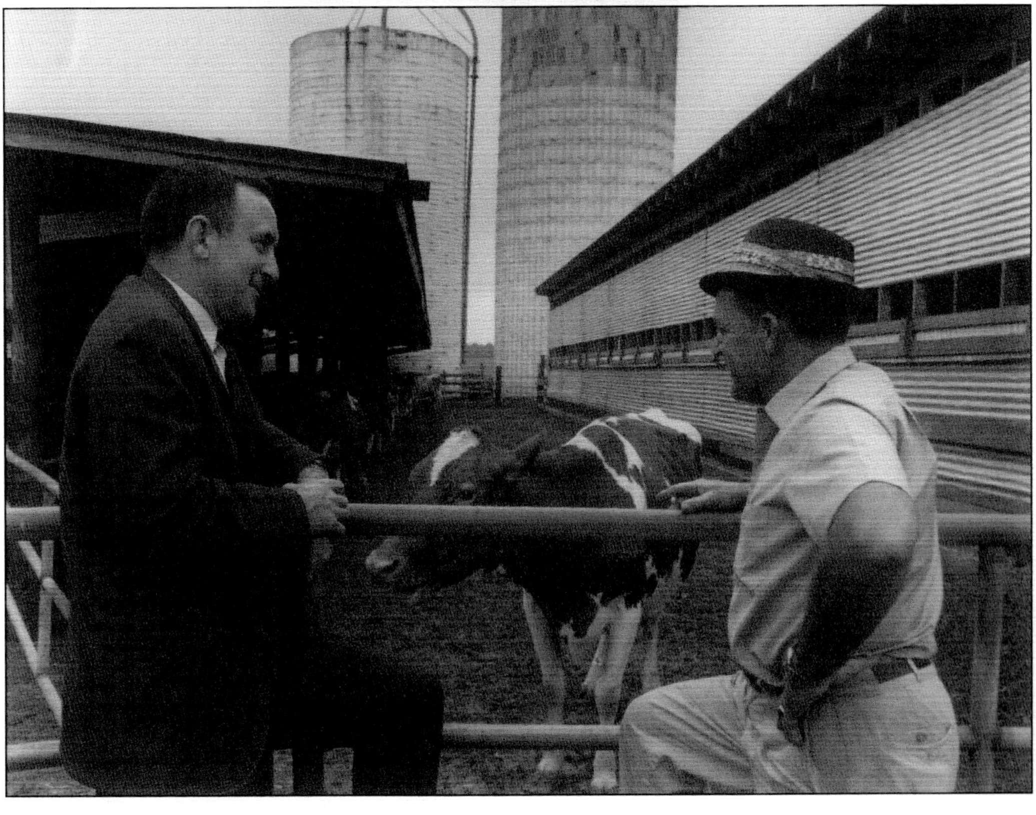

Clyde Keisler. Clyde moved to the Cary area in 1941, and he ran Kildaire Farm. In the 1950s, Kildaire Farm Road was paved. The farm operated until around the 1970s, when it was sold. The land was converted to subdivisions. (Courtesy of Sally Keisler.)

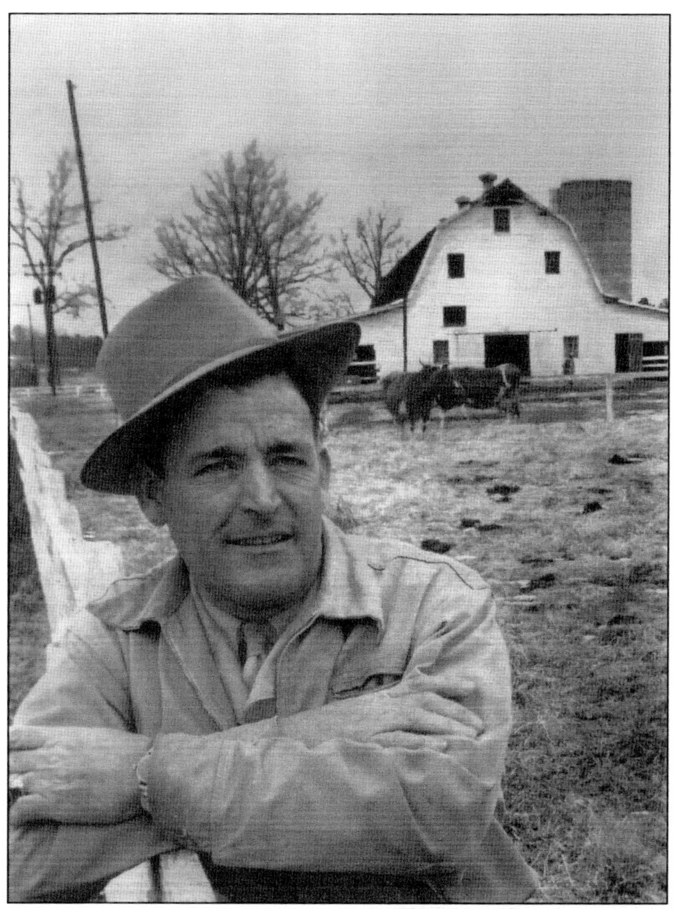

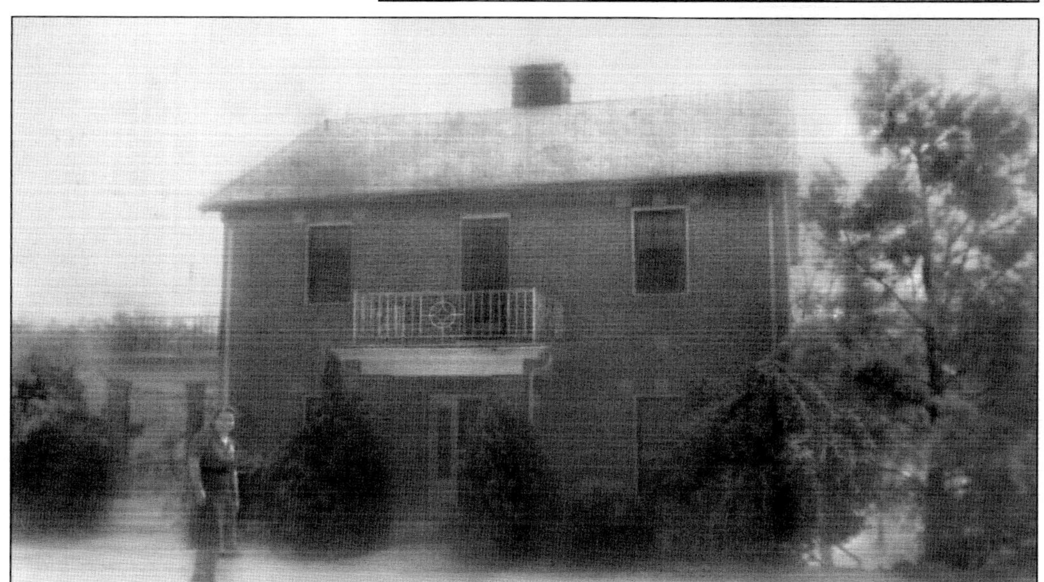

Morris Dairy Farm, 1930s. This Morris-Dixon farm was another working farm in Cary. (Courtesy of C. Y. Jordan.)

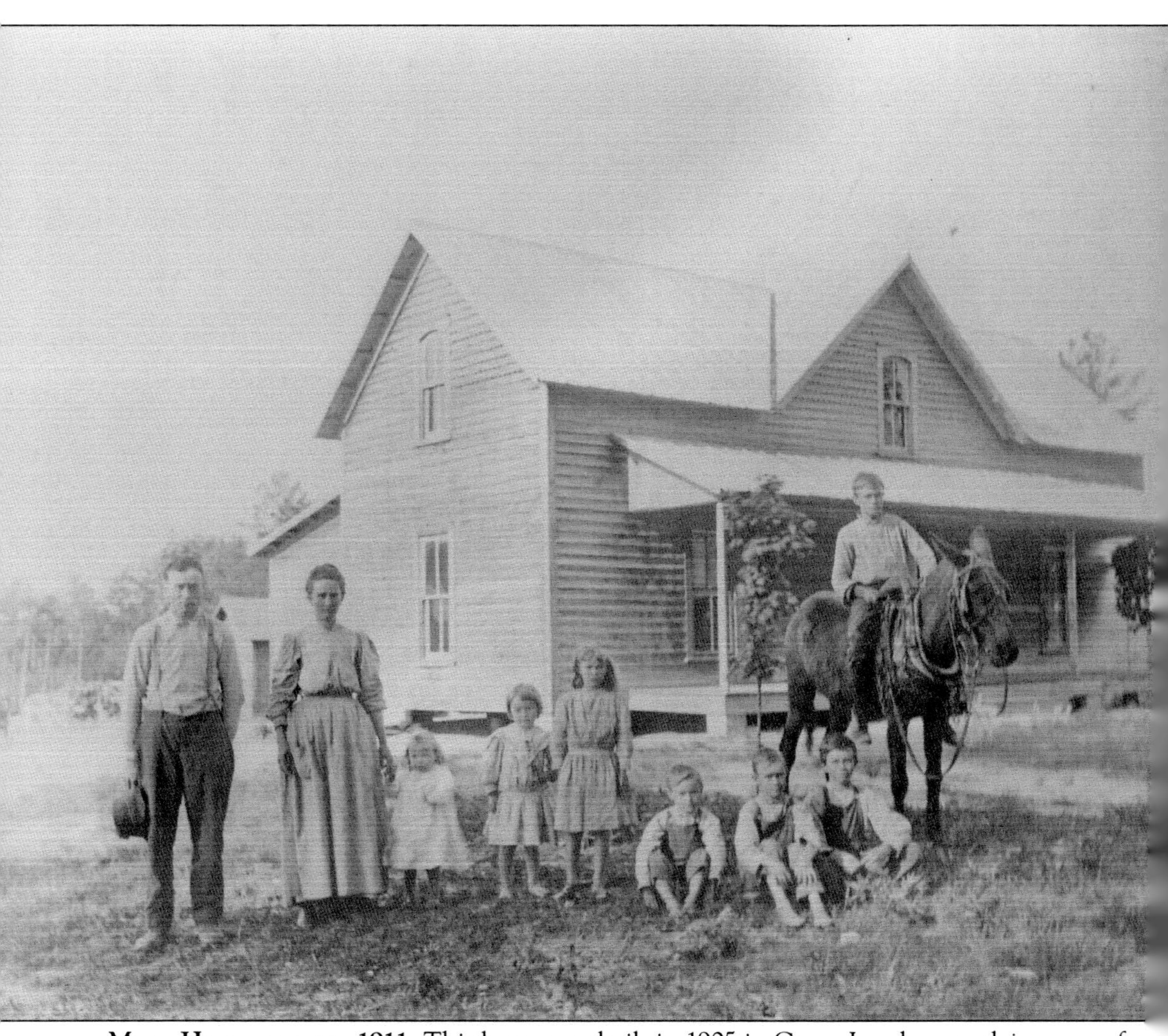

Mills House around 1911. This house was built in 1905 in Green Level, an outlying area of Cary. From left to right are William Henry Mills, his wife Ora Estella B. Mills, Mary Katherine Mills, Ruby Estella Mills, Maggie Reba Mills, Earnest Leon Mills, Joseph Monroe Mills, and James Rex Mills. Ollie Theodore Mills is sitting on the mule. (Courtesy of David Faircloth.)

Four

Fire and Brimstone

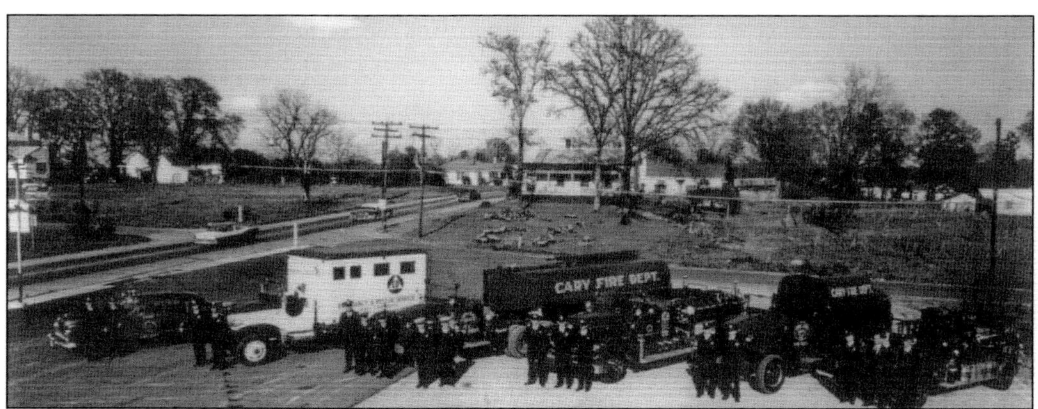

Cary Fire Department. In 1921, Cary made arrangements with Raleigh for a fire truck and crew of firemen to answer any alarms within the town of Cary. In 1922, Cary's first fire inspector, Lloyd Matthews, was appointed, and the first fire company was organized. The town's board also passed a resolution to purchase a fire engine. In 1923, the fire engine, an American LaFrance chemical engine on a Ford Model T chassis equipped with two 35-gallon chemical tanks, was delivered. H. H. Waddell and D. C. Page were appointed as fire chief and assistant chief, respectively. In 1925, the first water lines and fire hydrants were placed in service. In 1927, the town's six firefighters were W. L. Jones, L. E. Sturdivant, T. F. Wilkinson Jr., Royce Ellington, Marvin Breeze, and Robert Atkins. In 1935, the fire station was moved to a new location in back of the Masonic lodge at the corner of Chatham and Academy Streets. (Courtesy of Jim Matthews.)

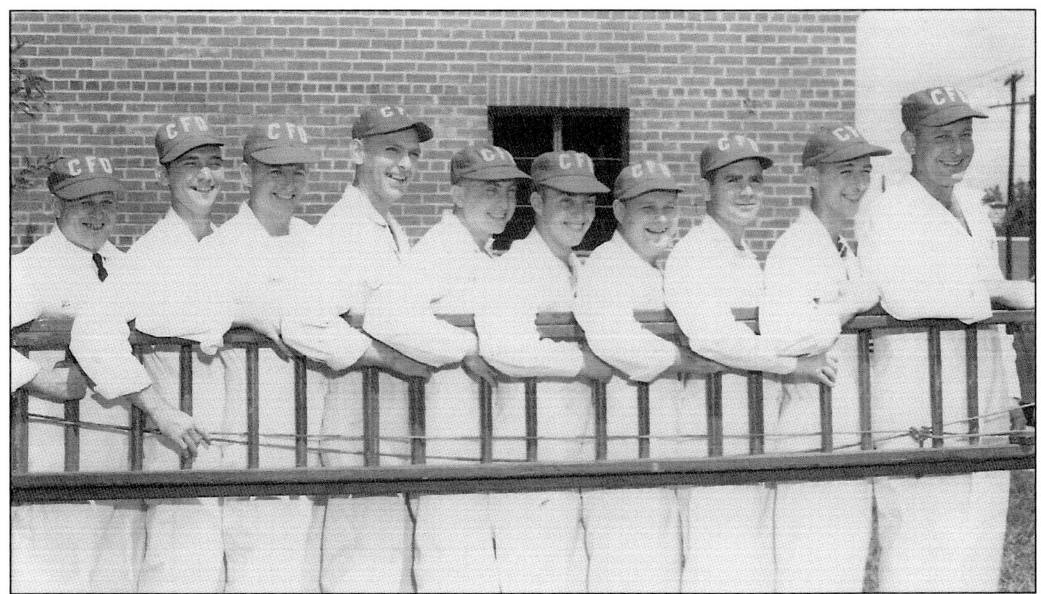

Cary Fire Department, 1950s. Before Cary got its new fire station, the town had some changes. In 1936, a new team of firefighters was named: chief M. R. Conner, assistant chief L. E. Midgette, Ivan Ruth, A. Pleasants, Clyde B. Hawkins, C. R. Craddock, W. R. Matthews, Walter Pendegraph, Alvin Sloan, Clarence Oakley, Norwood Northcutt, and C. R. Penny. In 1952, the fire station on Academy Street was demolished after the lot was sold to J. G. Hobby to raise funds for a new fire station planned at the corner of Cedar and North Academy Streets. (Both, courtesy of Jim Matthews.)

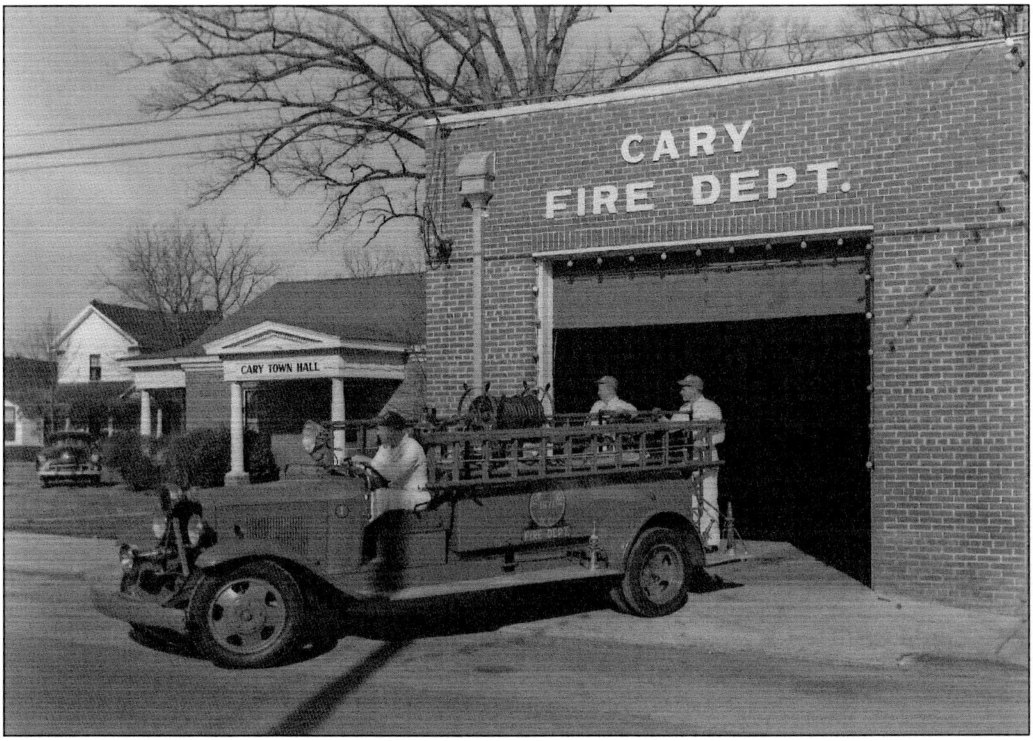

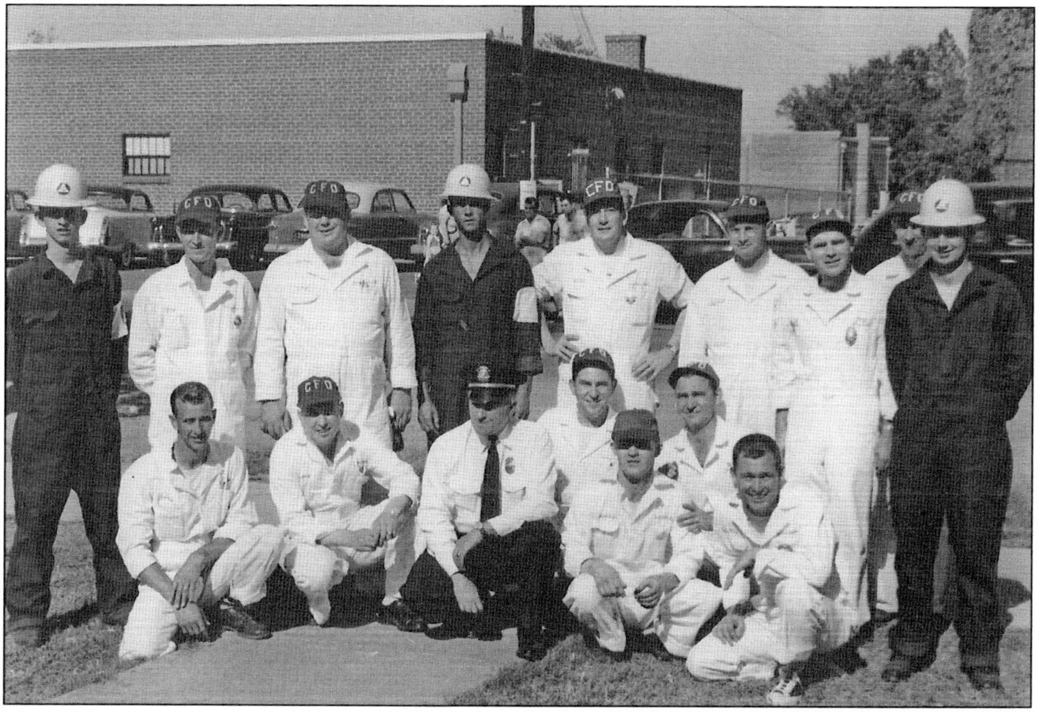

NEW CARY FIRE HOUSE. In the summer of 1953, the new fire station at 100 West Chatham Street was completed. It was a 30-foot-by-20-foot brick veneer and cinder block building. It had one apparatus bay and was adjacent to town hall. The building cost about $4,000. The following, a second station, was built on the 100 block of Cedar Street. It occupied a 20-foot-by-65-foot tin shed on a town-owned lot behind Rogers Motel. Firefighters furnished the labor and obtained the materials for building. (Both, courtesy of Stanley Lorren.)

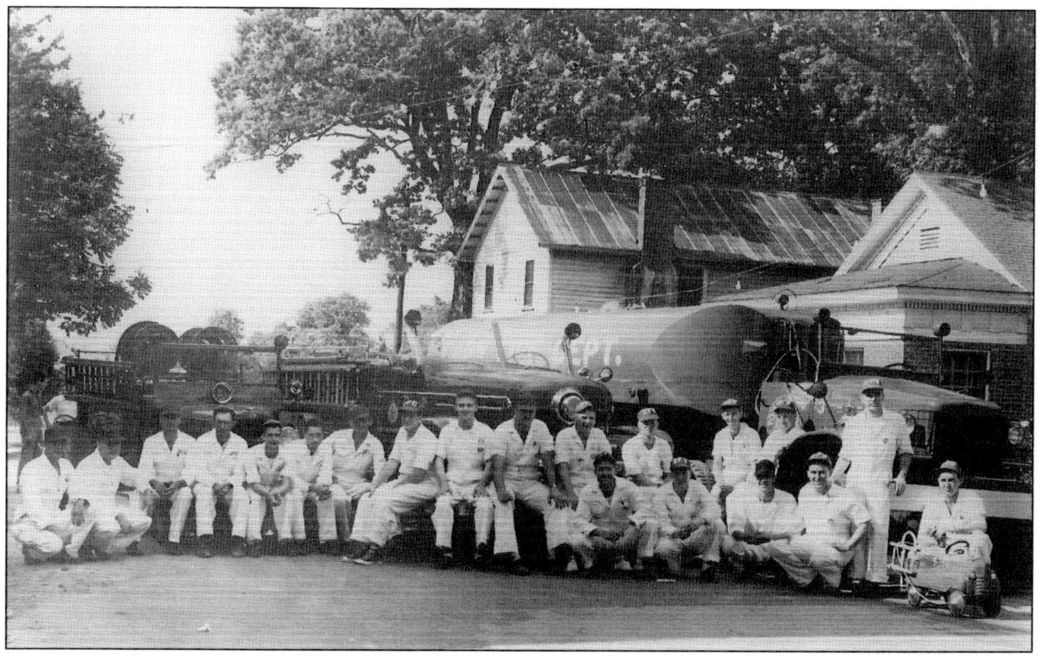

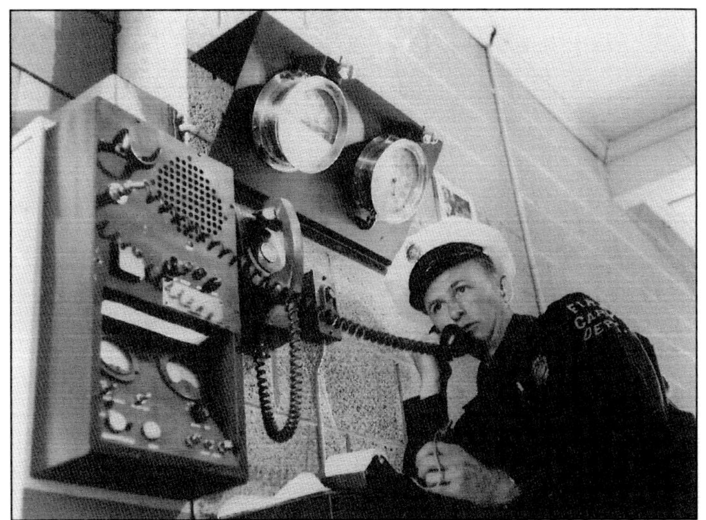

Linville Midgette. This photograph shows Linville during his term as Cary's fire chief. (Courtesy of Stanley Lorren.)

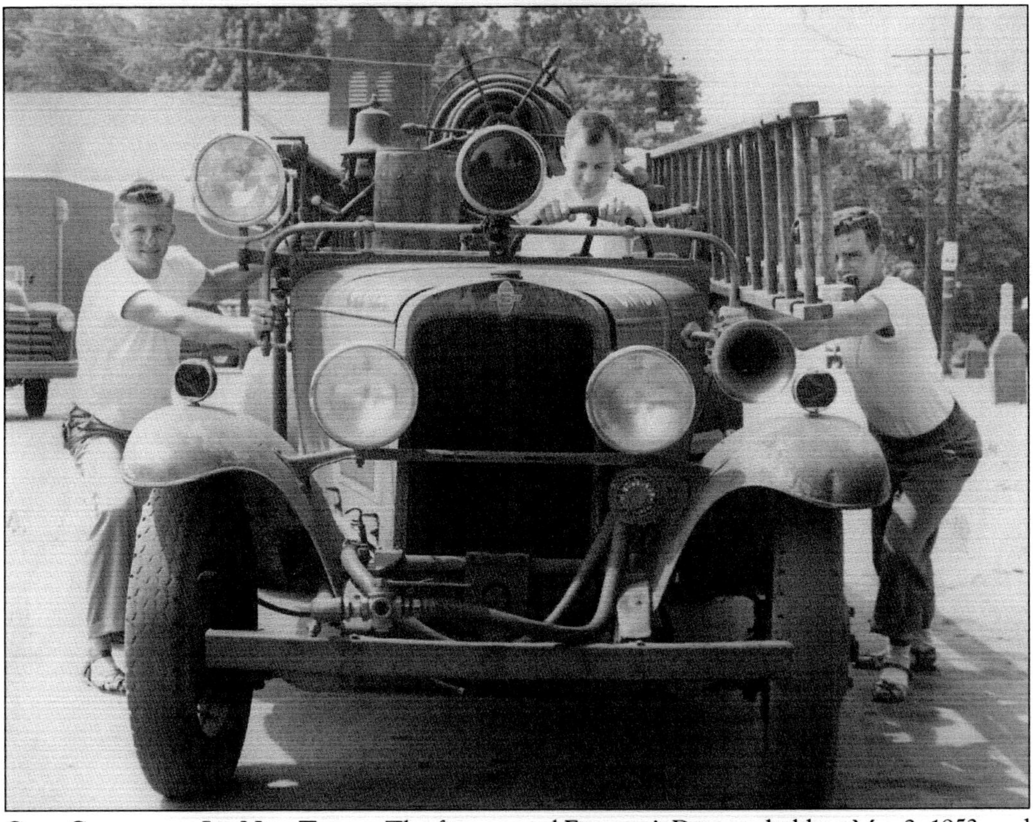

Cary Celebrates Its New Truck. The first annual Fireman's Day was held on May 2, 1953, and was expected to attract more than 5,000 people. The mile-long parade started at 3:00 p.m. along Highway 1, beginning at Russell Heater's home on Harrison Street and concluding at Cary High School. A barbecue supper was held at the school cafeteria, and a square dance was held from 8:30 to midnight. Nearly $500 worth of prizes was donated by local merchants, and these prizes were displayed in the Adams Building between the Cary Bank and post office. Each store featured a special item for sale, and everyone was eligible for a prize. (Courtesy of Stanley Lorren.)

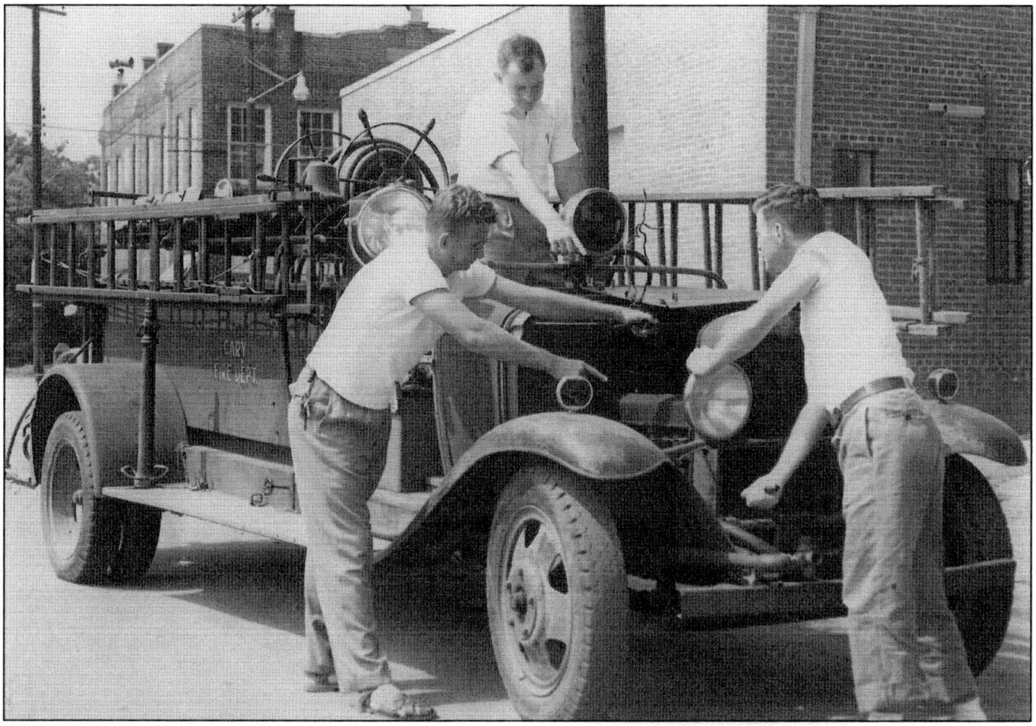

POLISHING AND DEMONSTRATING. In 1954, Cary held its second annual Fireman's Day, and a tractor-drawn tanker truck was displayed. The tractor shown here had a 1,500-watt AC generator mounted, 10 new tires and tubes, and a brilliant coat of red paint. The bell from Cary's first fire truck, a Model T purchased in 1924, was replated and placed on the truck. The entire project was completed by the fire department's 20 members without using any funds from the town treasury. Instead, the men were assisted by a host of individual donors. (Both, courtesy of Stanley Lorren.)

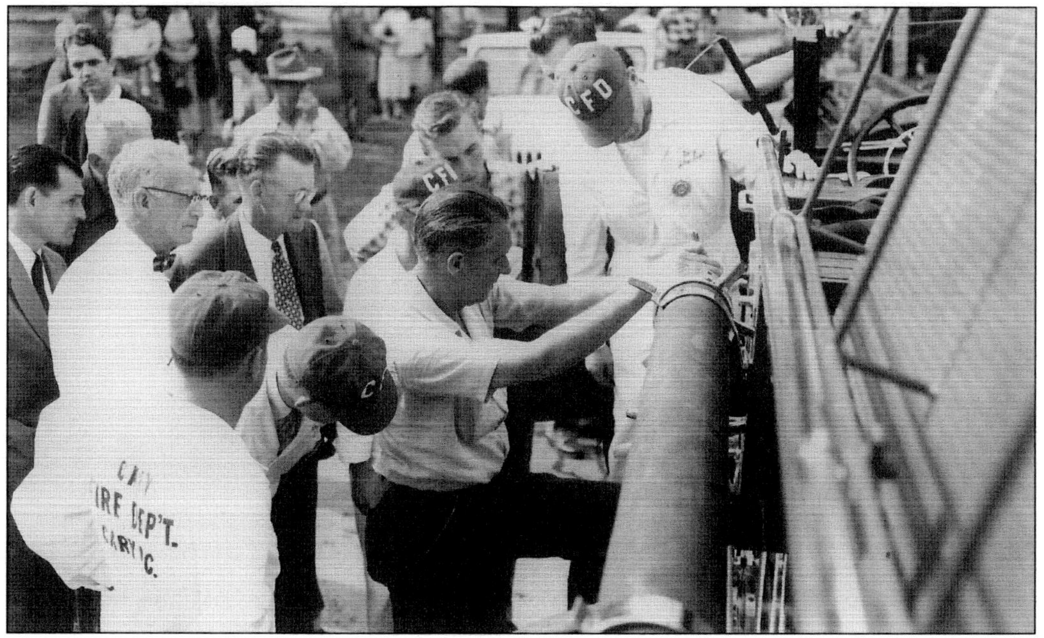

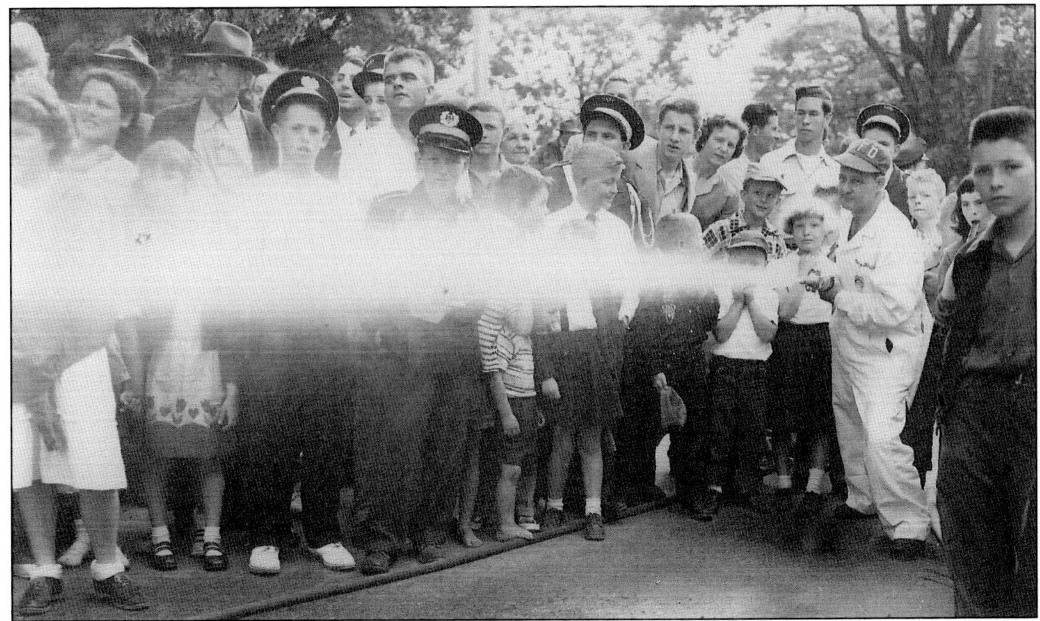

1955 Fireman's Day. The third annual Fireman's Day was held when the parade began at 3:00 p.m. Activities at 9:00 p.m. included a card and coin game in one quarter of the town. In honor of Mother's Day, moms were taken for rides on the fire truck. The kids took their turns from 8:00 to 9:30 p.m. The civil defense rescue truck carried $8,000 worth of equipment, including a 5,000-watt portable generator, a 2,500-watt generator, a two-way radio, a $600 resuscitator, block and tackle, ropes, and a portable oxygen-acetylene torch. (Both, courtesy of Stanley Lorren.)

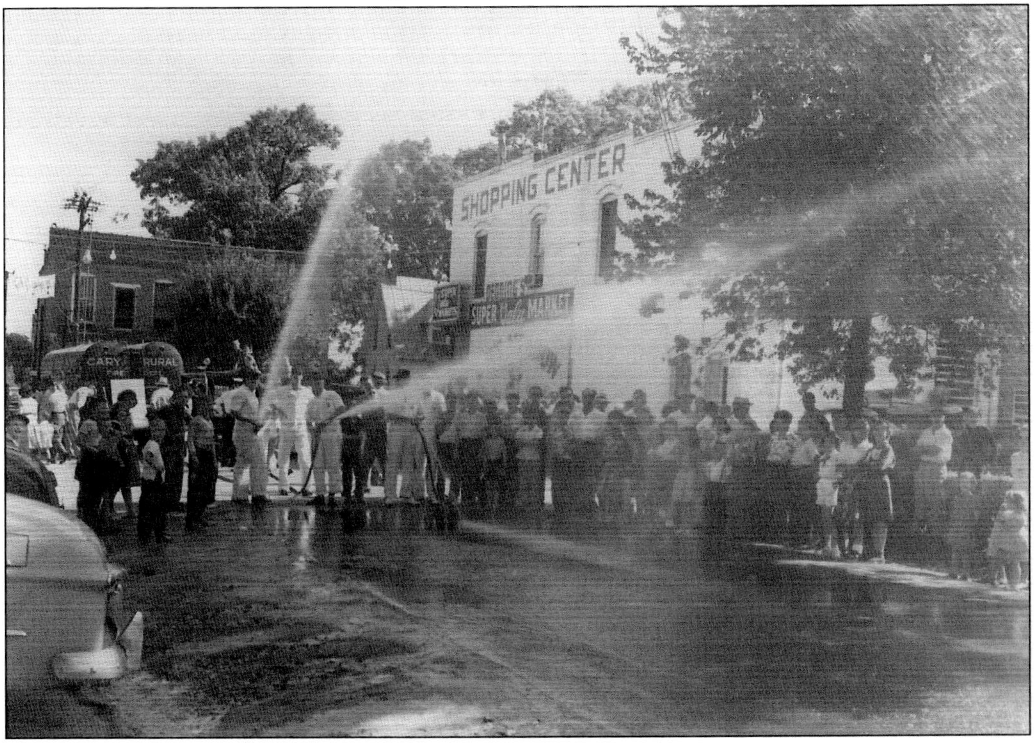

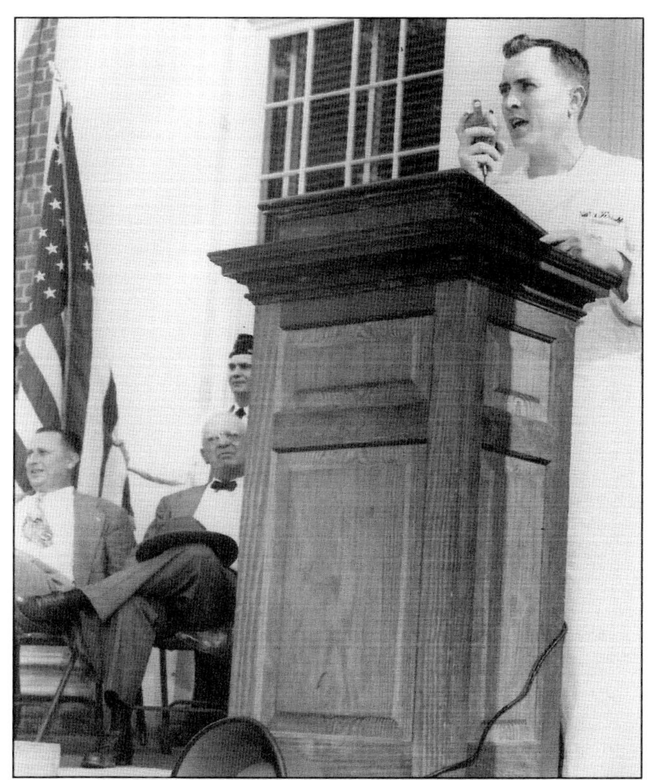

Fireman's Day Speeches. Many speeches were given during the annual Fireman's Day celebration. The gentleman in the suit is Mayor H. Waldo Rood. In 1960, Mayor Rood suggested the town establish its own fire department as a volunteer group to work under the direction of a paid chief, who would also be the new police chief. They would be separate from the present Cary Volunteer Fire Department, which served both the town and the surrounding rural area. Firefighters could choose whether to come with the town or remain where they were. The board subsequently adopted a resolution in support of the mayor. Townspeople and firefighters disagreed with the proposal, and a committee was appointed to work out the differences. (Both, courtesy of Stanley Lorren.)

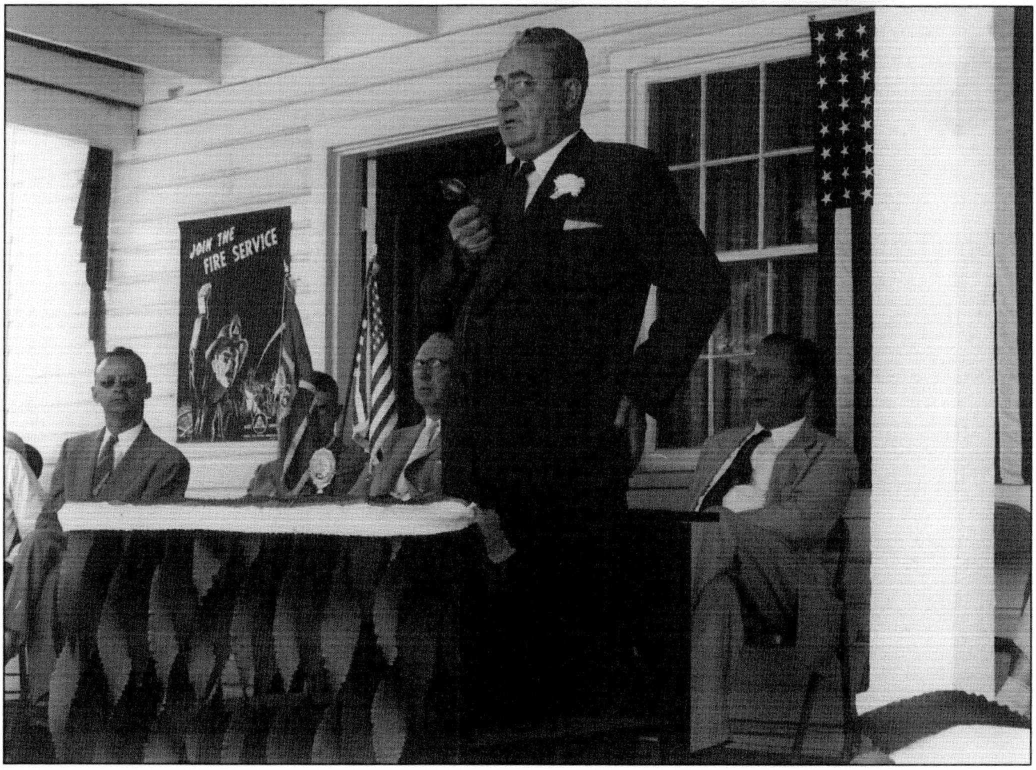

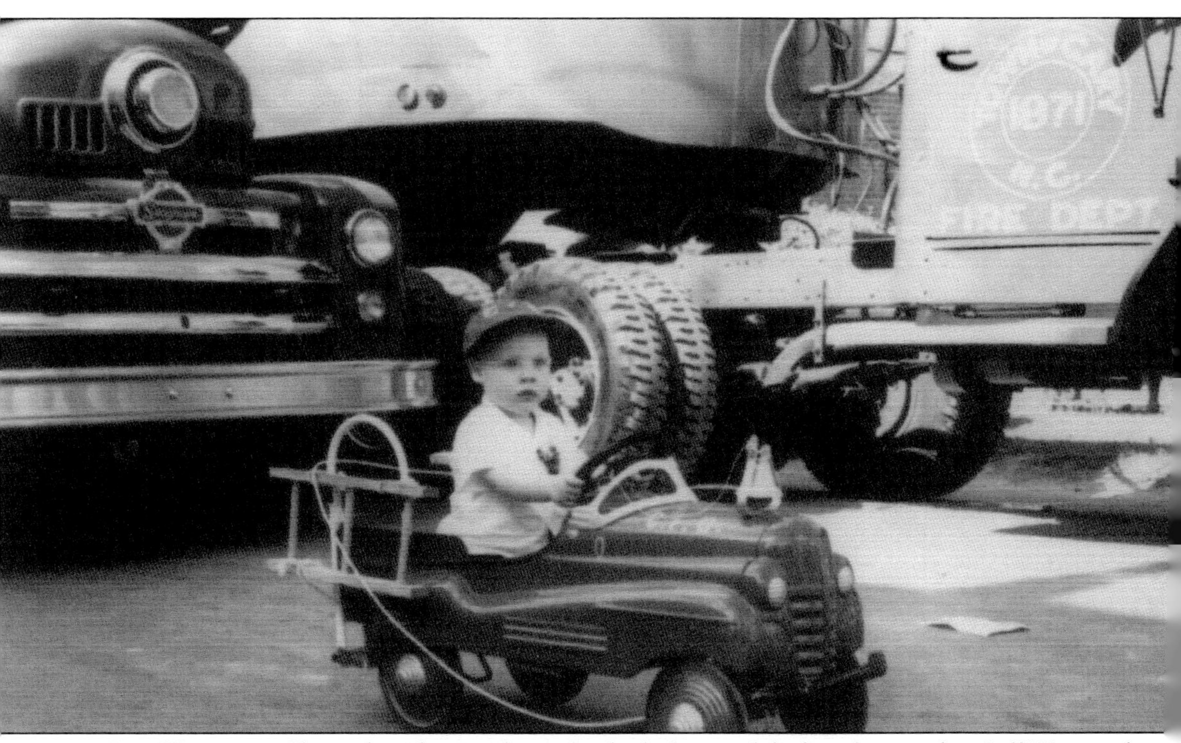

Jeff Winstead. Shown here having fun in his little fire truck before the parade is Jeff Winstead. (Courtesy of Stanley Lorren.)

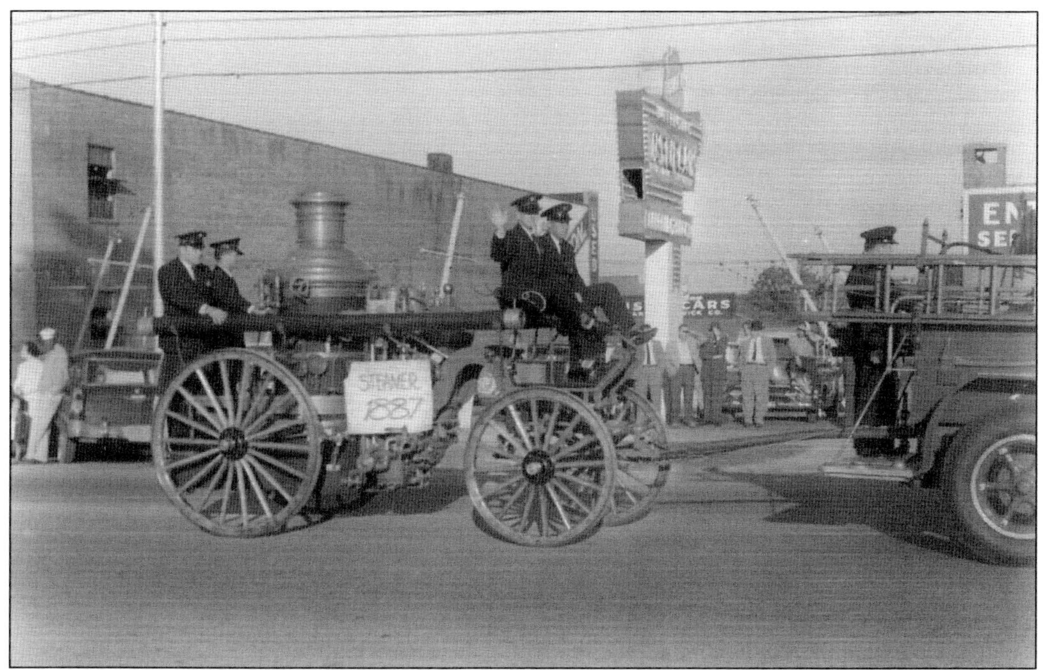

FIREMAN'S DAY, 1950S. In 1956, the fire department had 25 members. They held their fourth annual Fireman's Day in May. The festivities began at 3:00 p.m., and there were fire engines from Apex, Garner, Morrisville, Raleigh, and Cary. The music was played by the North Carolina State College Drum and Bugle Corps and senior and junior bands from Cary High School. The parade also featured Girl Scouts, the Wake County fire chiefs' cars, floats, and automobiles. Activities also included Quizno, a legal version of Bingo—then illegal. Fireman's Day concluded with a street dance and the music of the Mills Brothers Hillbilly Band. That same year, the department announced plans to build a $75,000 fire station on a 100-foot-by-120-foot site on the southeast corner of Cedar and North Academy Streets. Fund-raising began on Fireman's Day, with cornerstone bricks being auctioned off for a total of $2,035. (Both, courtesy of Stanley Lorren.)

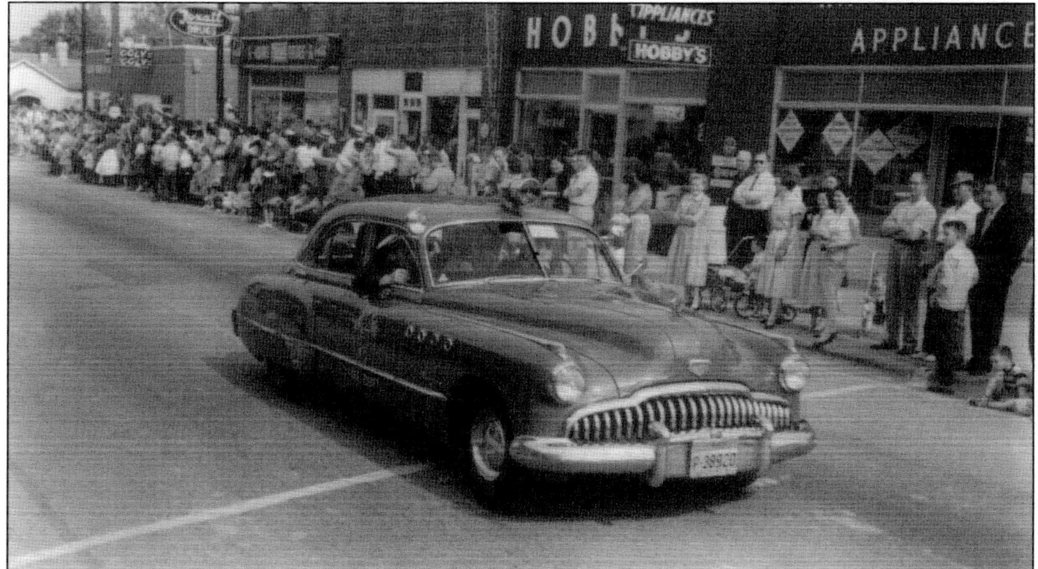

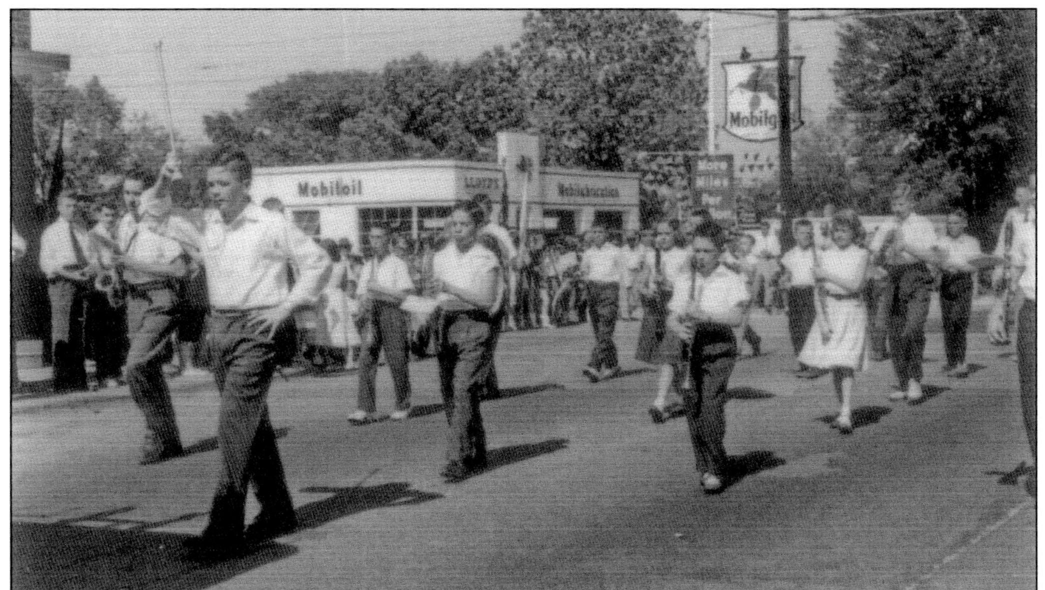

Fireman's Day Parade, 1950s. In 1957, the Cary Fire Department had 24 regular firefighters. They held the fifth annual Fireman's Day in May. The celebration began at 2:30 p.m. with a parade that included North Carolina State University's Air Force ROTC "Marching Airmen," the U.S. Army ROTC Drum and Bugle Corps, and the Army ROTC Pershing Rifles Crack Drill Team, who were all from the state college. From 3:30 p.m. to 5:00 p.m., the fire department entertained children and adults on the high school football field. At 5:30 p.m. was a fish fry, and at 6:30 p.m., a gasoline-powered kiddy automobile was given away. Games and dancing were also featured, with all the activities ending at 11:30 p.m. (Courtesy of Stanley Lorren.)

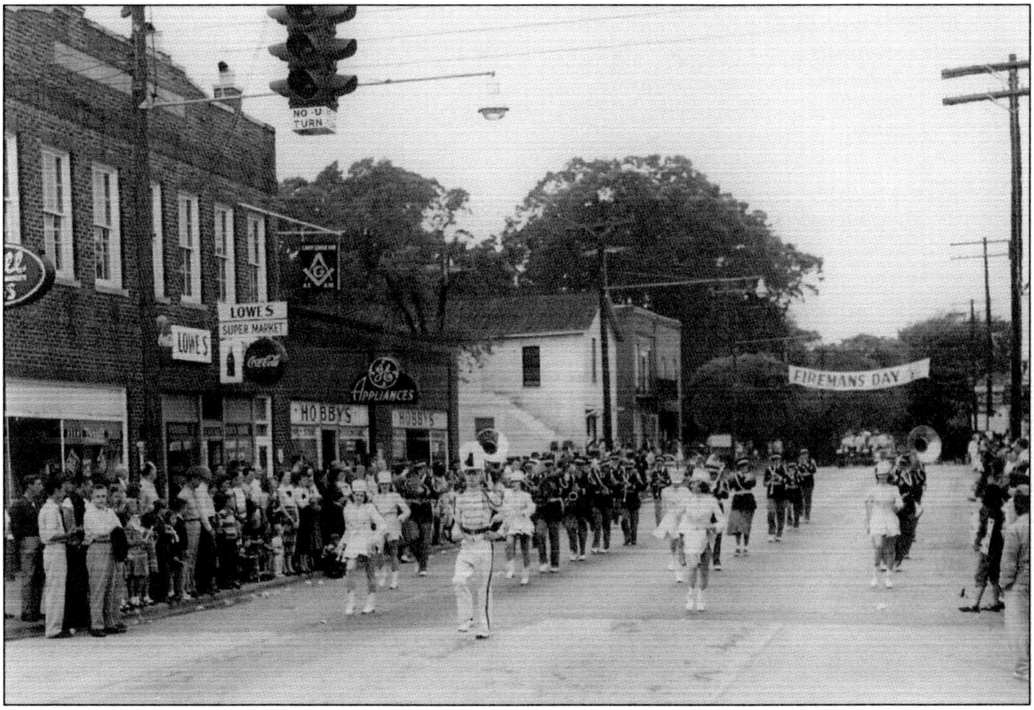

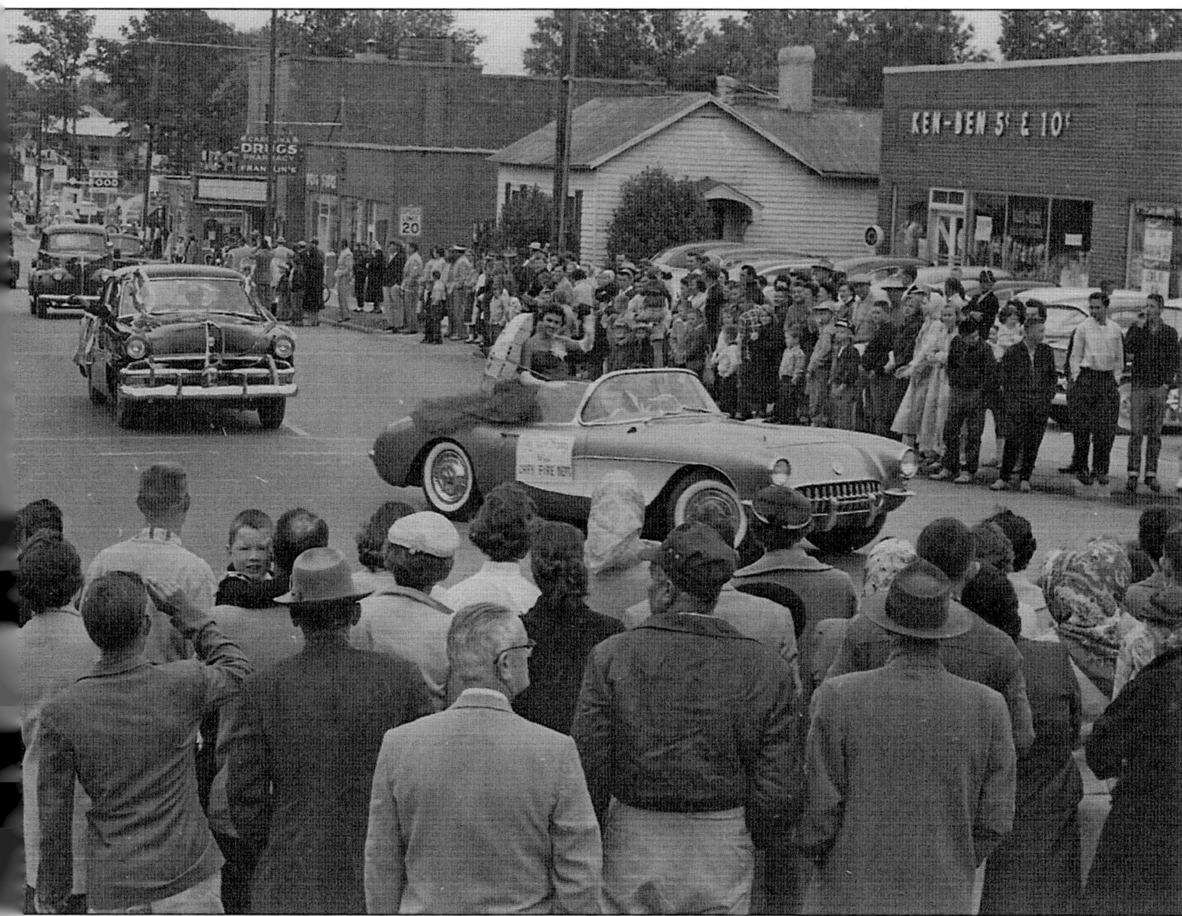

Fireman's Day Celebration. By the end of 1957, a two-way radio system was installed for the fire department. The base station was installed in Station No. 1, with stand-by receivers at the fire chief's house, the town clerk's office, and the ready room at Station No. 2. The radio equipment was also installed in all fire apparatus, the rescue truck, and the chief's car. On May 3, 1958, the sixth annual Fireman's Day took place. The firefighters continued their fund-raising efforts for the new fire station. They auctioned 10 green bricks, with the highest bidder getting his name engraved in one of the first stones in the new building. It was expected to be completed in 1961. (Courtesy of Stanley Lorren.)

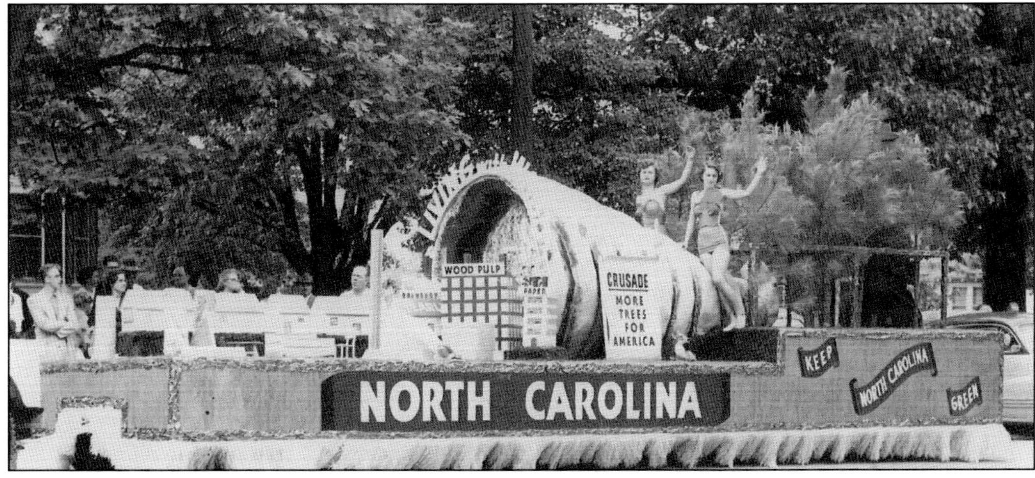

FIREMAN'S DAY FLOATS AND OTHER FUN THINGS. In 1959, Cary held its seventh annual Fireman's Day celebration, which began with the parade at 3:30 p.m. Other events included a traditional fish fry, door prizes, and a square dance in the Winn-Dixie parking lot on Chatham Street. In 1960, the eighth annual Fireman's Day was held on May 7. Just as in 1959, the parade began at 3:30 p.m., supper was served at the high school cafeteria from 5:00 p.m. until 8:00 p.m., games were offered from 6:30 p.m. until 8:00 p.m., and a street dance was held from 8:00 p.m. until midnight. Drawings were held for various prizes, and an open house was held at the emergency shelter set up at the Cary Methodist Church from noon until 4:30 p.m. (Both, courtesy of Stanley Lorren.)

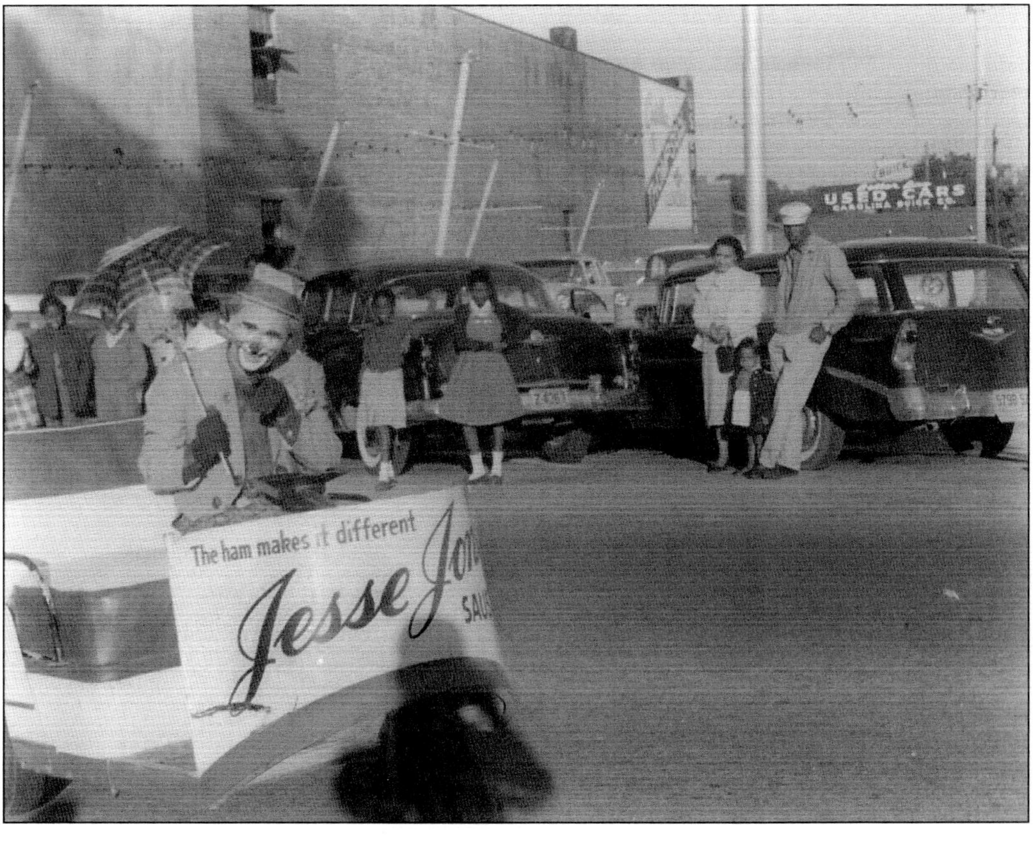

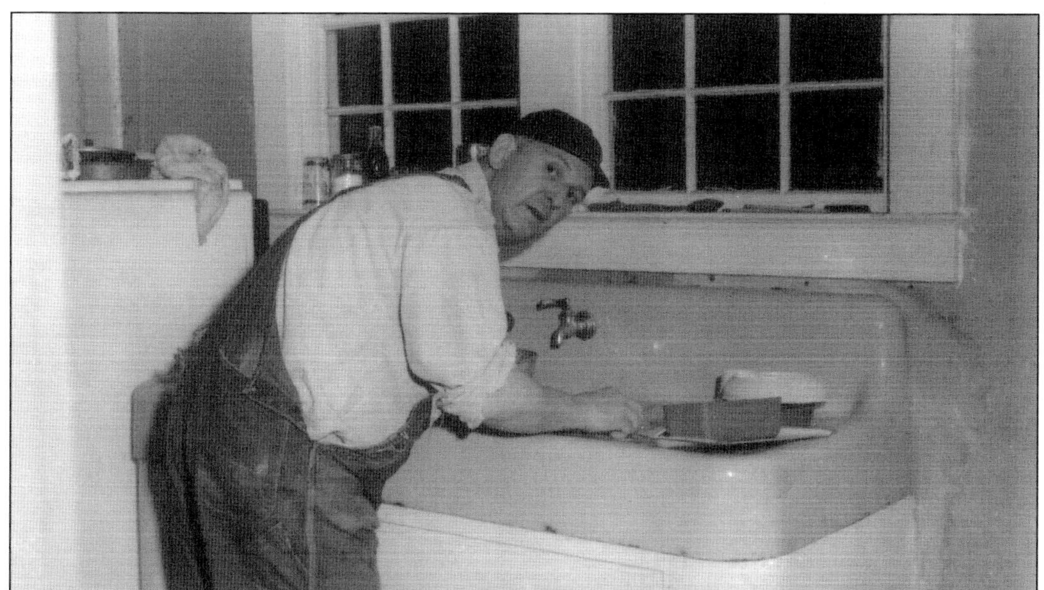

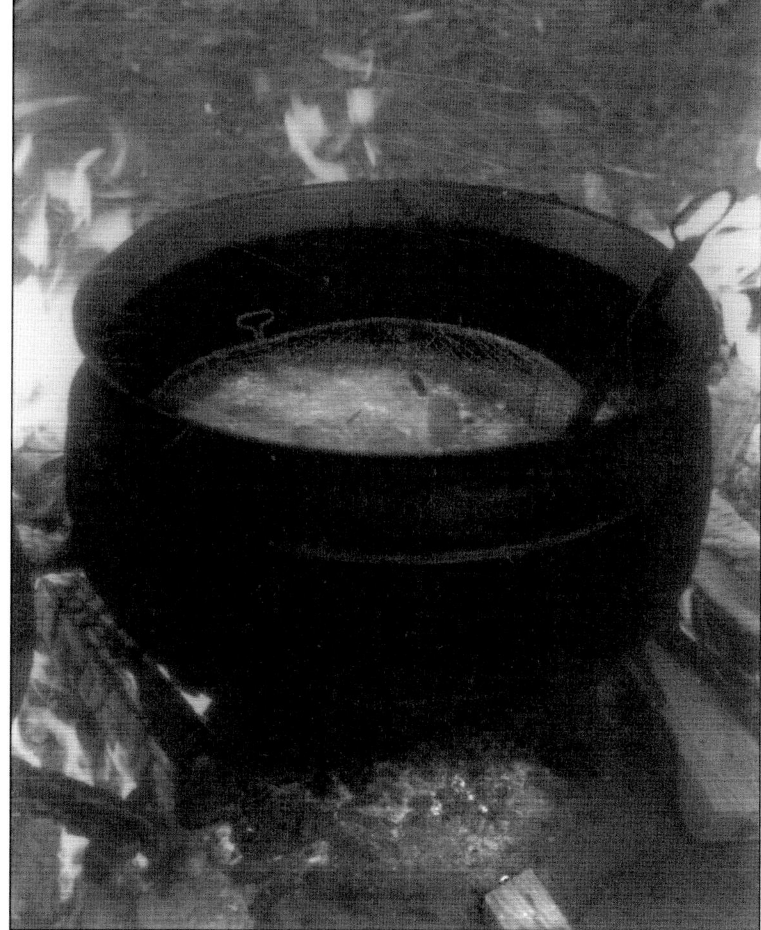

Fish Fries. Charity events were a crucial part of the Cary Fire Department. In 1960, not only did Cary have a town fire department, but it also had a rural one. To distinguish it from the Cary town fire department, it was called Yrac (Cary spelled backwards). The department relied on events like these to raise the funds needed to continue to fight fires in Cary. Bob Pleasants is seen washing up after an event. The fried fish was usually served in the high school cafeteria and was prepared by the firefighters, their wives, and members of the Fire Auxiliary Association. (Both, courtesy of Stanley Lorren.)

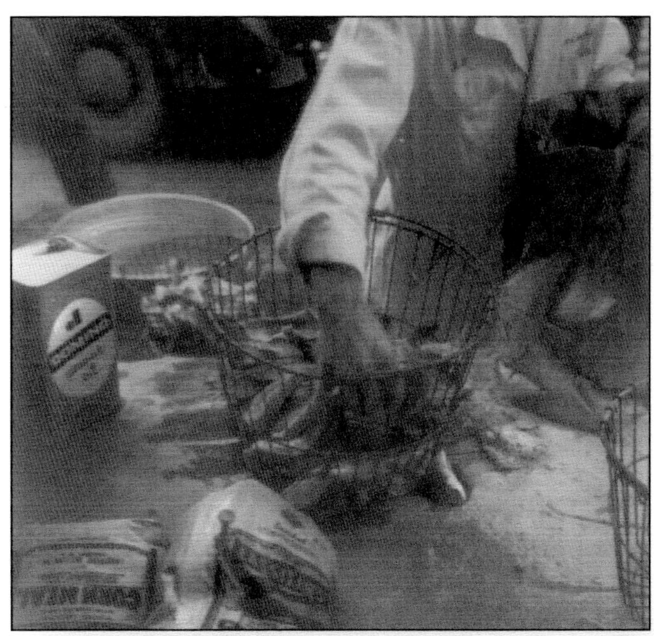

FUND-RAISING FISH FRIES. Lassiter corn meal and Domino sugar were just a couple of ingredients used at the fish fries. The firefighter on the left is Paul Matthews, and the other is identified only as "Bill." (Both, courtesy of Stanley Lorren.)

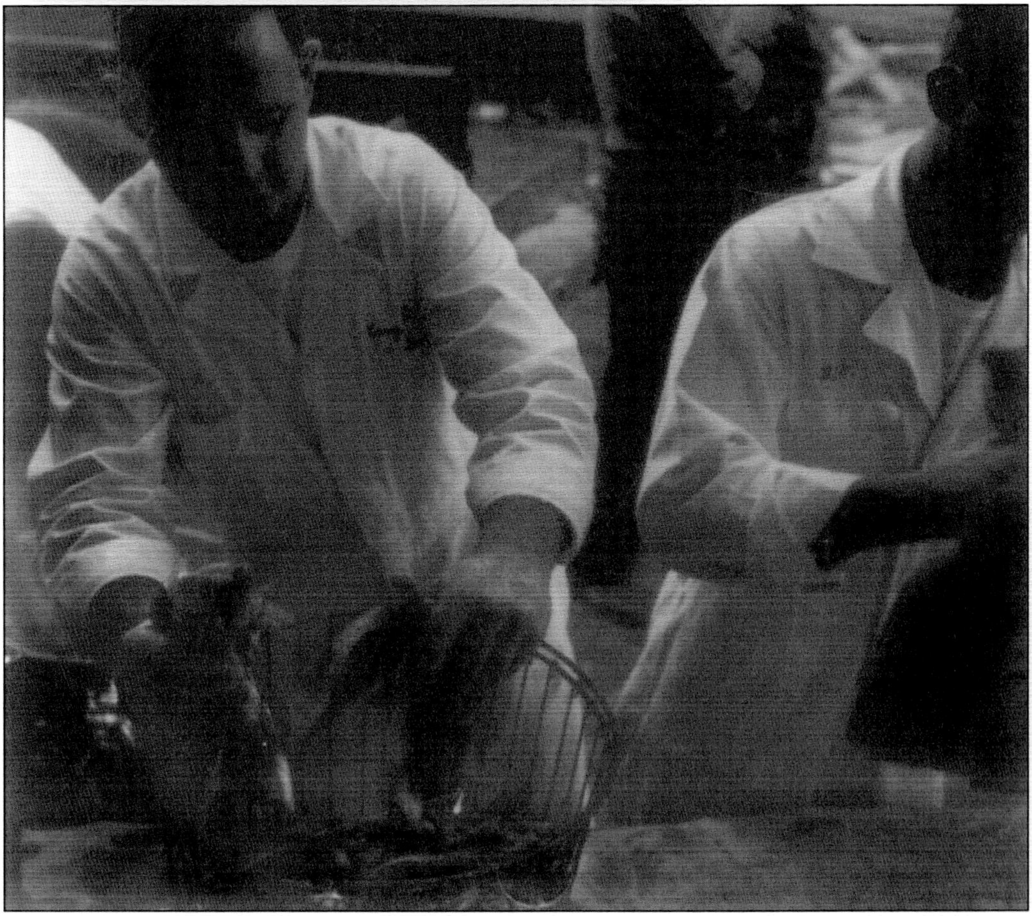

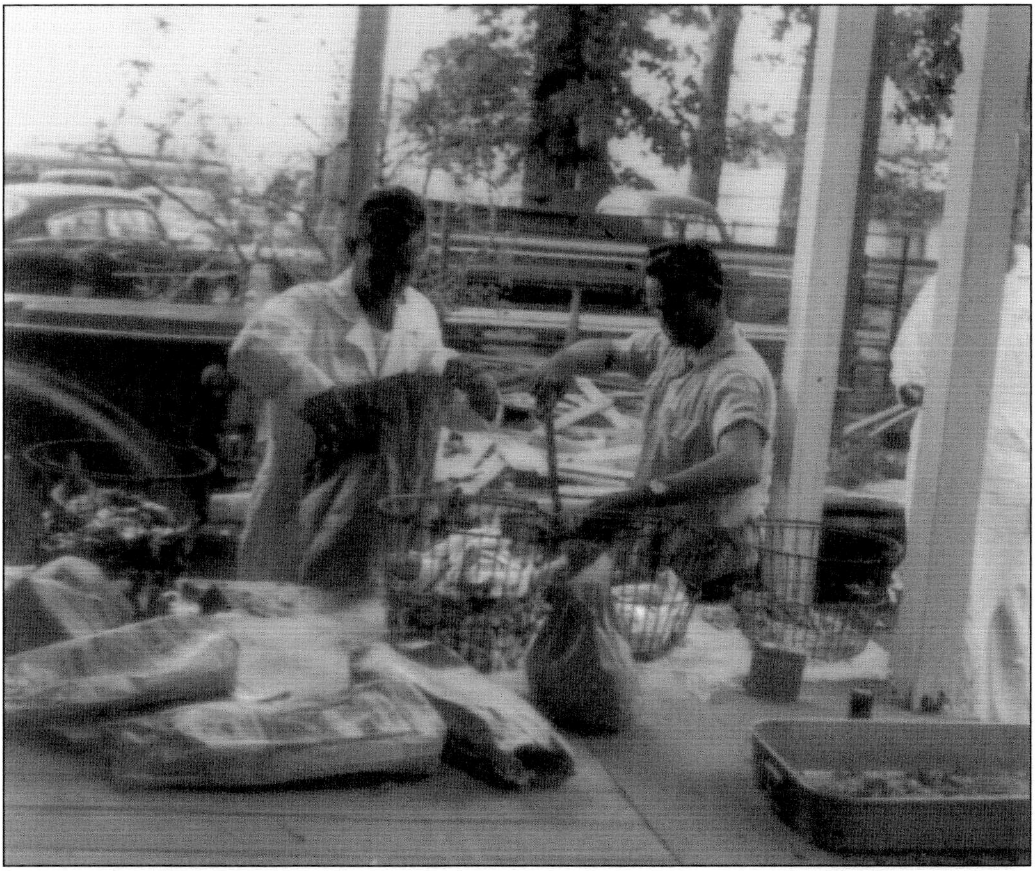

FIREFIGHTERS RAISE FUNDS. In the 1950s, the Cary firefighters found ways to raise money to buy equipment, but they also found ways to give to their community. At Christmastime, they collected toys for the children. (Both, courtesy of Stanley Lorren.)

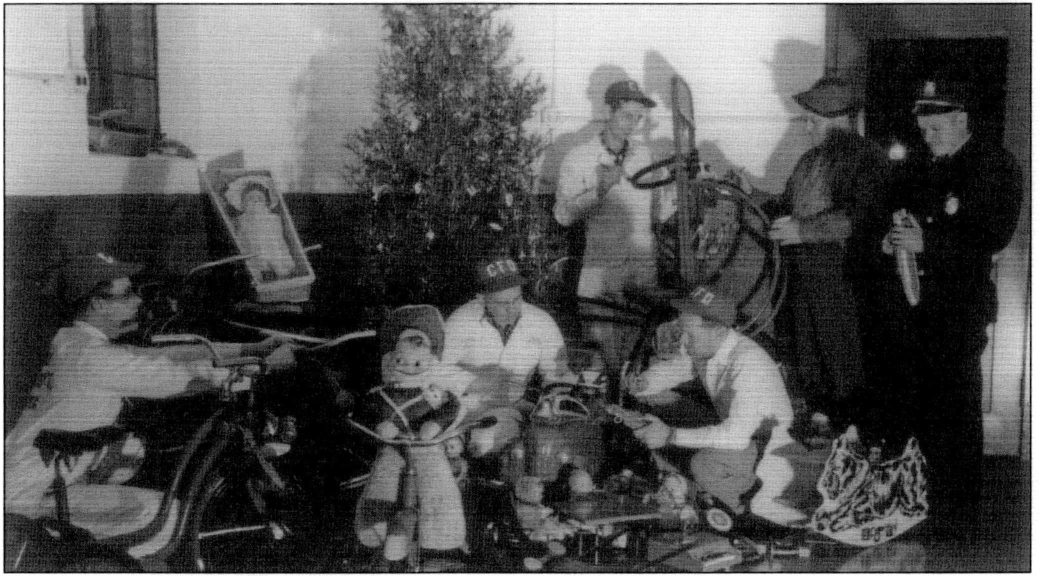

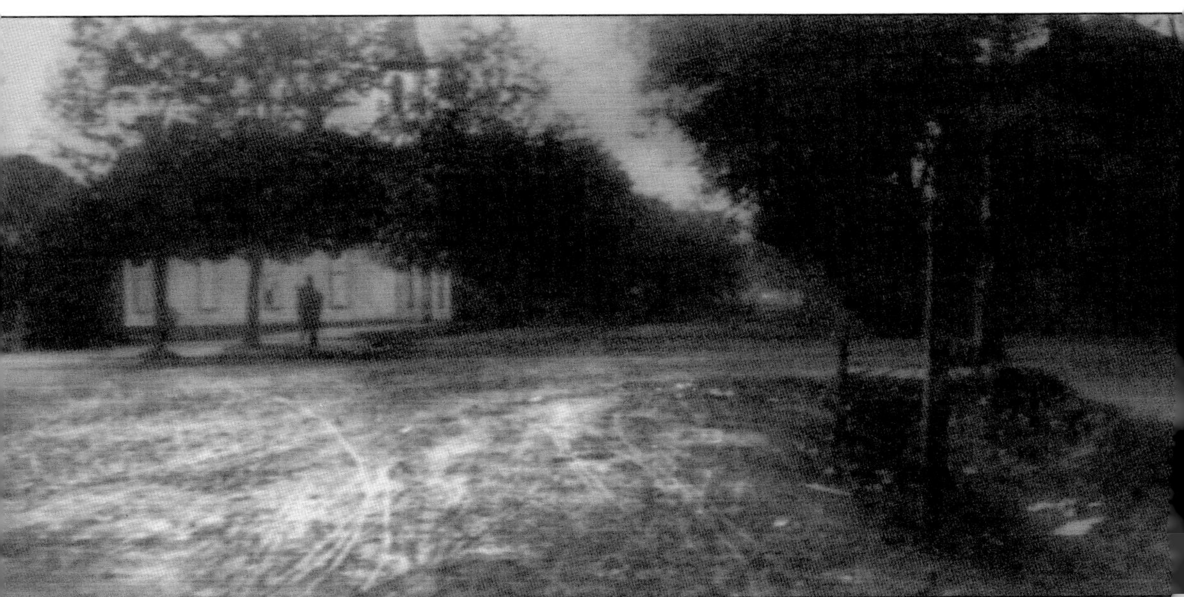

CARY UNITED METHODIST CHURCH AROUND 1913. The church was founded in 1871 and is the oldest church in Cary. Town founder Frank Page donated lumber for its construction. In 1922, the original building was enlarged to include an annex and was covered with brick. (Courtesy of Cary United Methodist Church.)

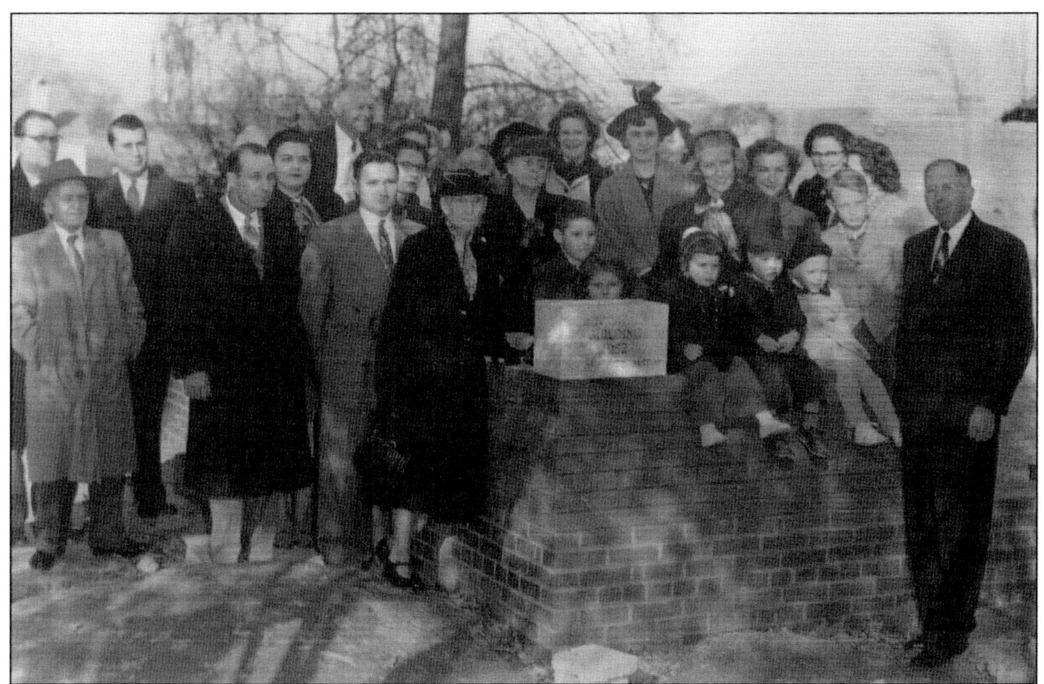

Cary United Methodist Church around 1952. The cornerstone to the new building was laid in 1952. (Courtesy of Robert Warner.)

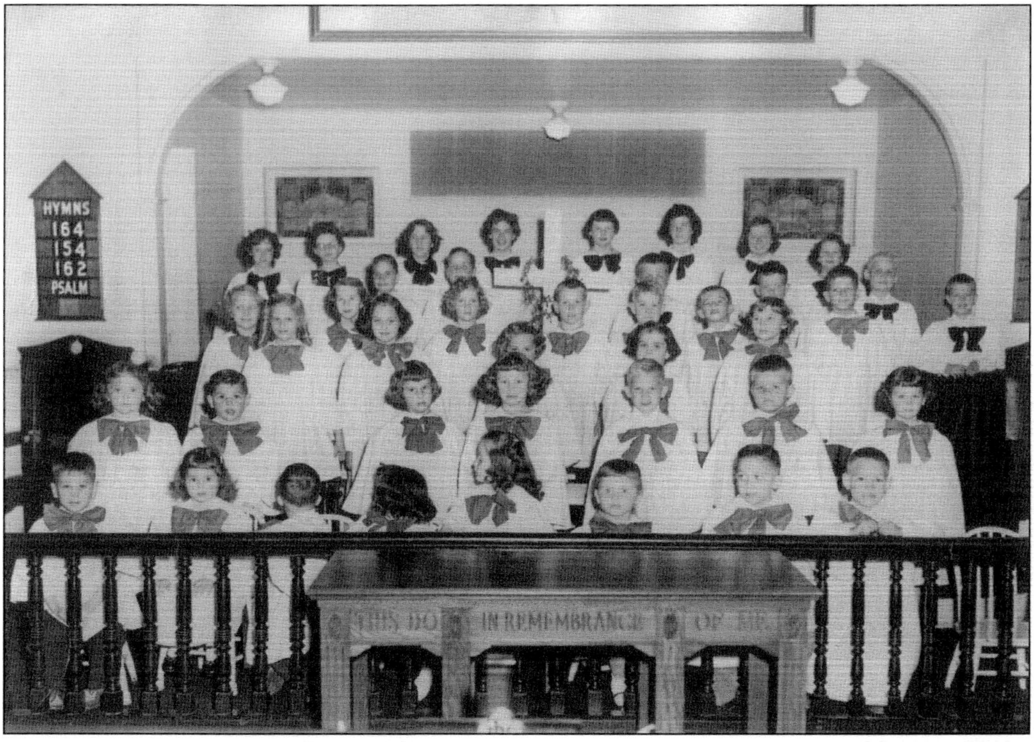

Cary United Methodist Church Choir. This photograph was taken in 1955 at the church. (Courtesy of Cary United Methodist Church.)

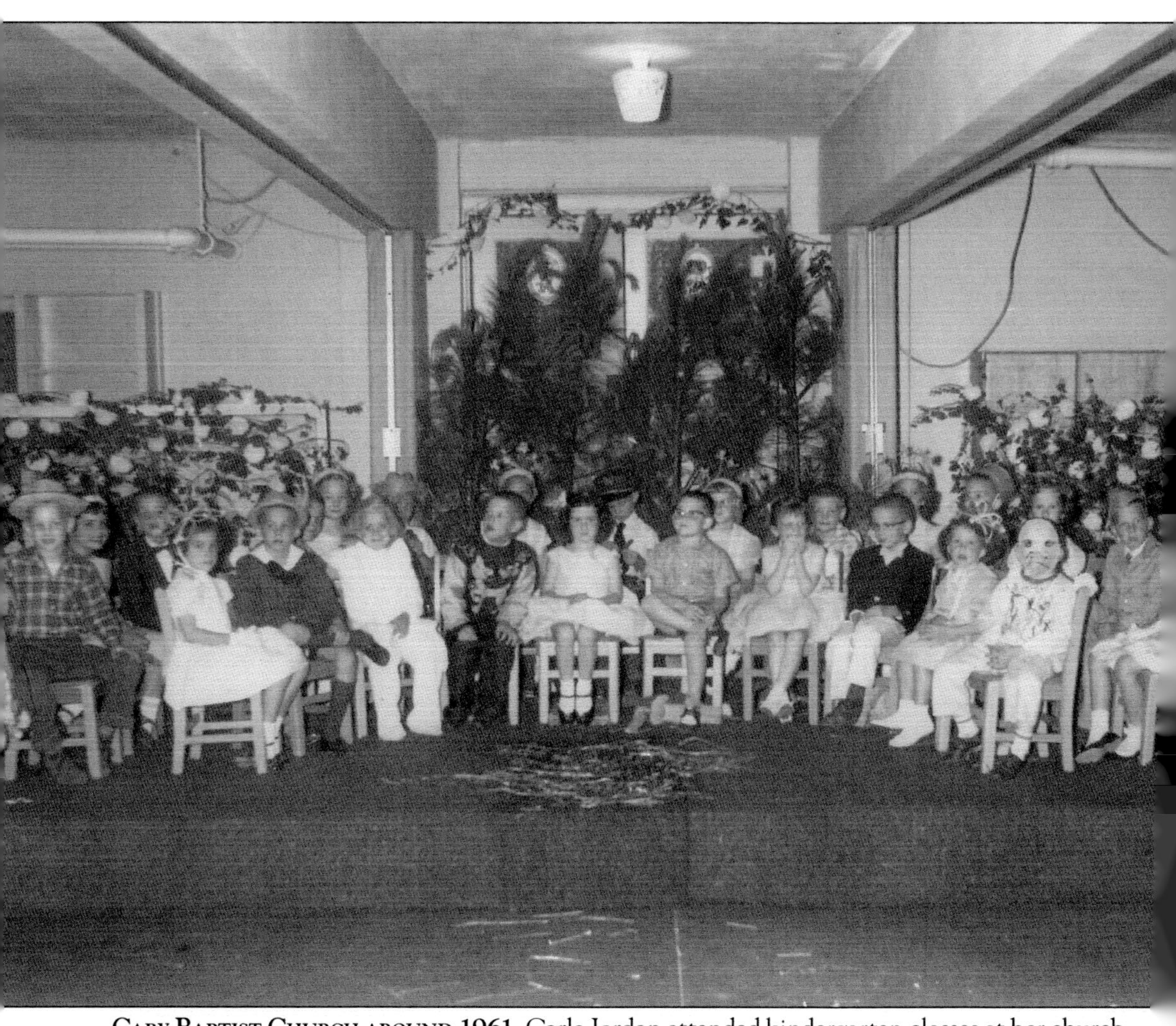

Cary Baptist Church around 1961. Carla Jordan attended kindergarten classes at her church. (Courtesy of C. Y. Jordan.)

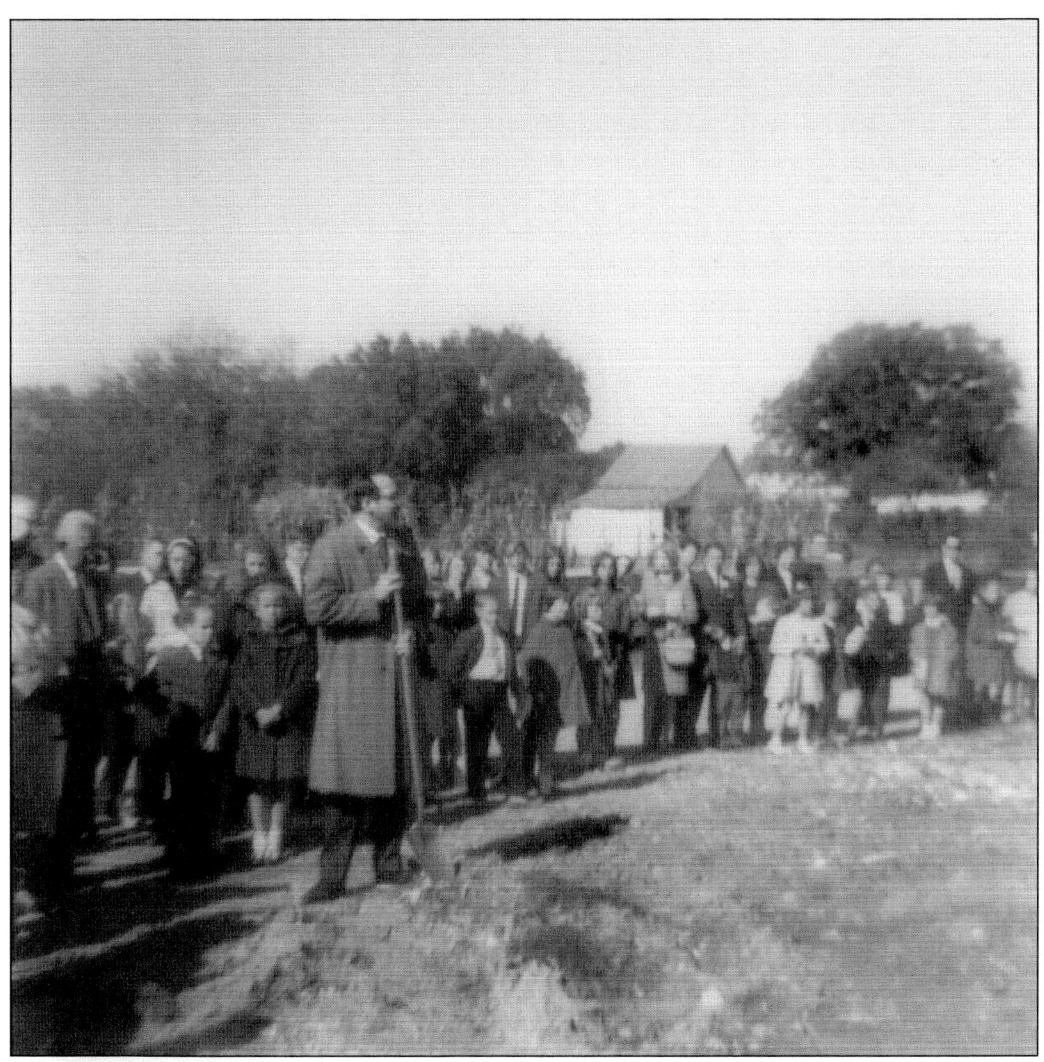

CARY BAPTIST CHURCH AROUND 1966. Minister T. Robert Mullinax digs the first shovel of soil at the ground-breaking ceremony for the new building in 1966. (Courtesy of C. Y. Jordan.)

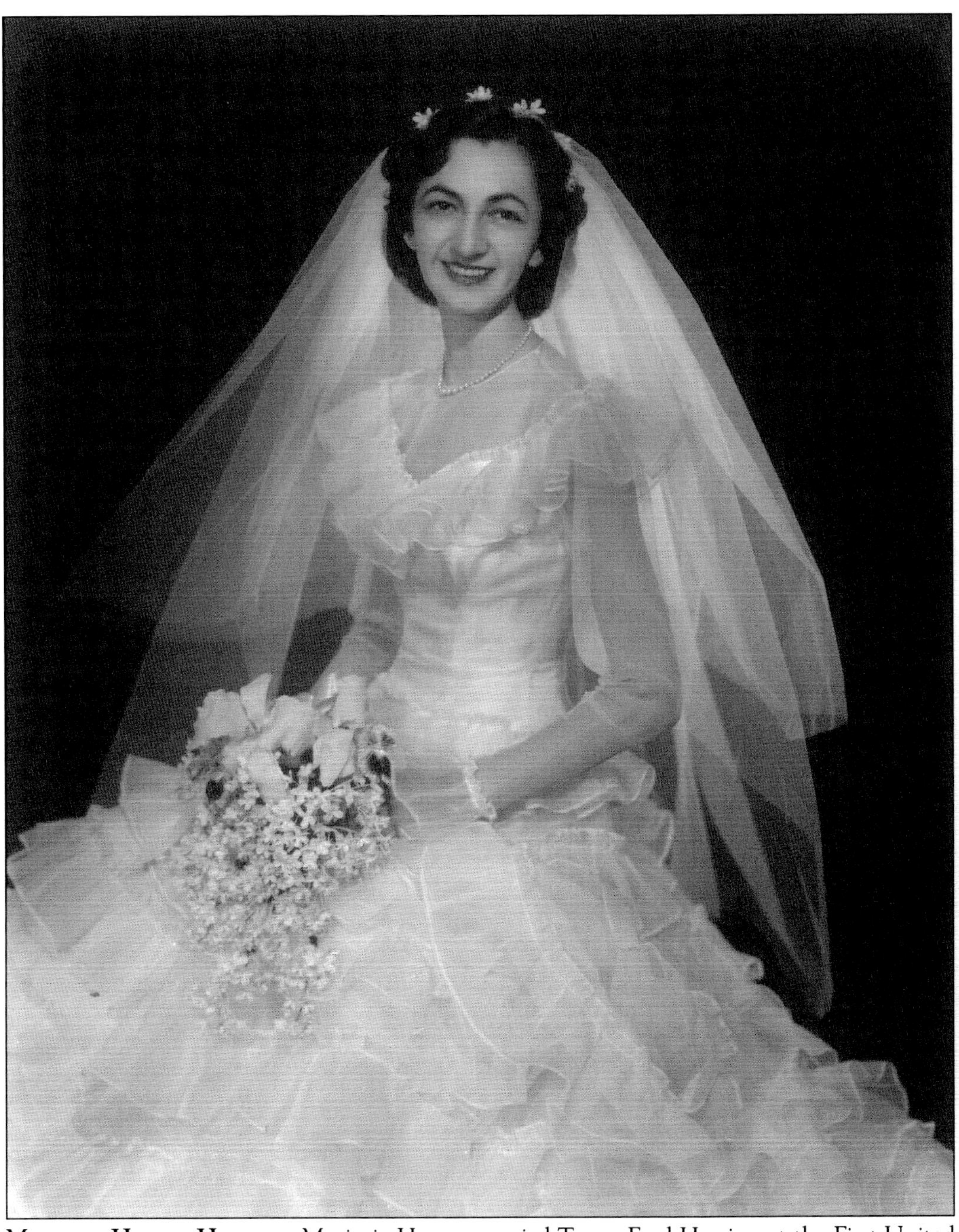

Marjorie Heater-Herring. Marjorie Heater married Texan Fred Herring at the First United Methodist Church on June 30, 1950. Marjorie taught high school in Hoke County and worked in Washington, D.C., for the War Production Board. Her husband, Fred, was an insurance underwriter. (Courtesy of Robert Heater.)

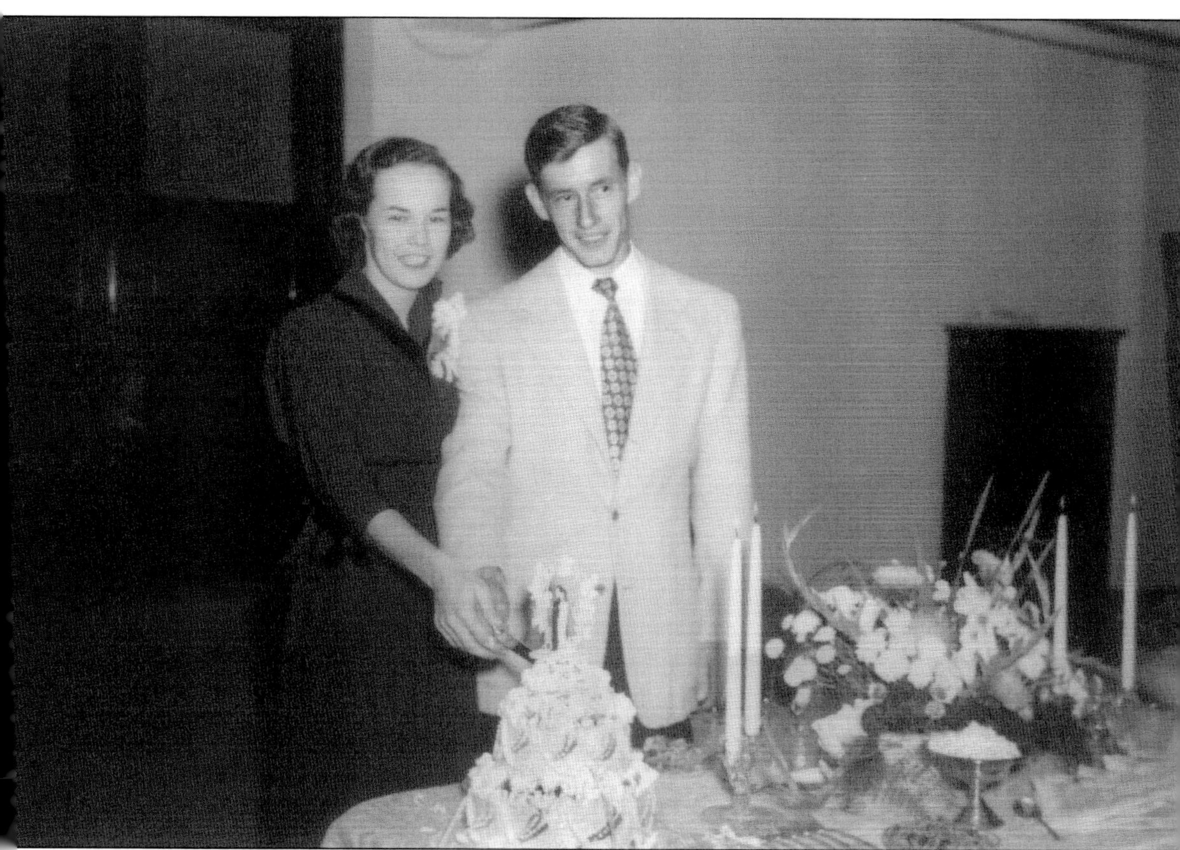

C. Y. JORDAN WEDDING. C. Y. Jordan married Dollie Morris on September 16, 1950, at the Cary Baptist Church. The couple's honeymoon included trips to Nashville, Tennessee, and Virginia. (Courtesy of C. Y. Jordan.)

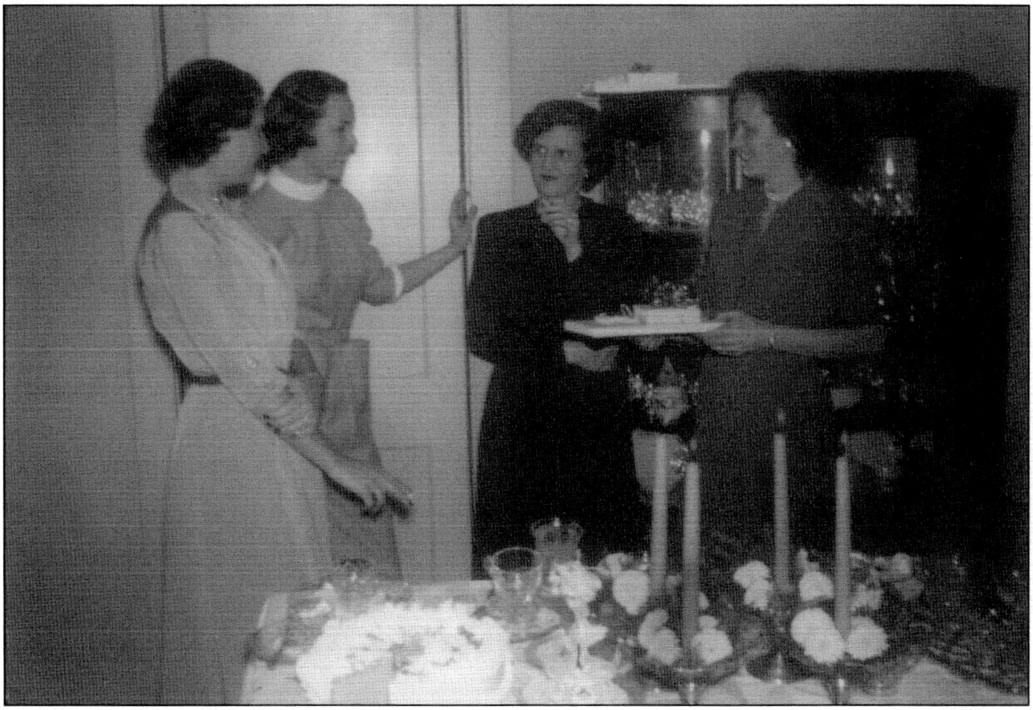

JORDAN AND MATTHEWS REHEARSAL PARTY. The rehearsal party for Marjorie Jordan and Wright Matthews included, from left to right, Betty Jordan Lee, Dollie Morris-Jordan, Hattie Daniels-Jordan, and Katie Morris-Jordan. (Courtesy of C. Y. Jordan.)

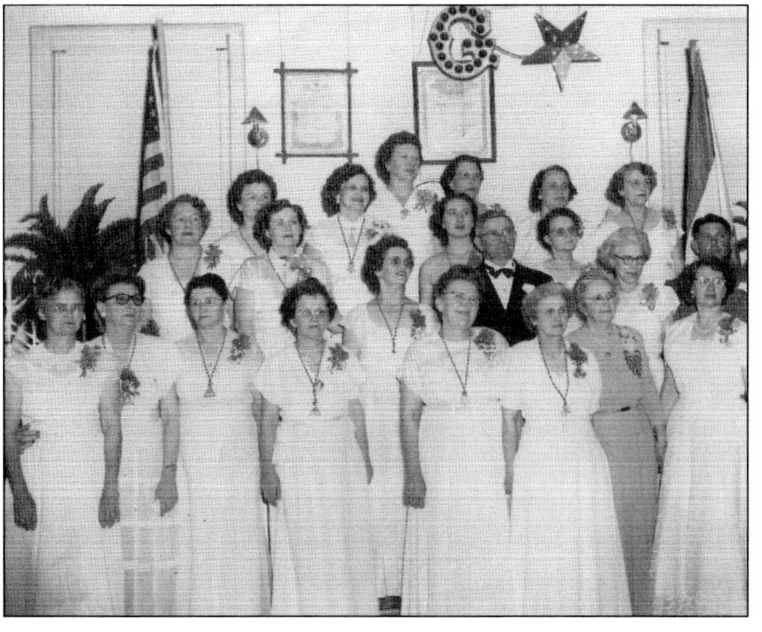

CARY WOMEN'S EASTERN STAR CLUB. This club, considered the female version of the Shriners organization, met above Adams's Drugstore. After the meeting, the women would go down to the drugstore counter and sip Cokes. In the first row at far left is Esther Kell Mitchell, who taught math and geometry in Cary. The woman at left in the third row is Ethel Adams. (Courtesy of Charlie Adams.)